STATUTORY INSTRUME

GW01393208

1995 No. 755 (N.I. 2)

NORTHERN IRELAND

The Children (Northern Ireland) Order 1995

Made ·· *15th March* 1995

Coming into operation on days to be appointed under Article 1(2)

ARRANGEMENT OF ORDER

Article

PART V

CARE AND SUPERVISION

Introductory

General

Care orders

Supervision orders

Education supervision orders

Powers of court

Guardians ad litem

Part IX

Children's homes

Part X

Private arrangements for fostering children

Part XIII

Department's supervisory functions and responsibilities

Part XIV

Parents not married to each other

Part XV

Guardians

Part XVI

Jurisdiction and procedure

Part XVII

Miscellaneous and general

Children accommodated in certain establishments

Search warrants

Effect and duration of orders, etc.

Miscellaneous

SCHEDULES:

At the Court at Buckingham Palace, the 15th day of March 1995

Present,

The Queen's Most Excellent Majesty in Council

Whereas a draft of this Order has been approved by a resolution of each House of Parliament:

Now, therefore, Her Majesty, in exercise of the powers conferred by paragraph 1 of Schedule 1 to the Northern Ireland Act 1974 and of all other powers enabling Her in that behalf, is pleased, by and with the advice of Her Privy Council, to order, and it is hereby ordered, as follows:—

1974 c. 28

PART I

INTRODUCTORY

Title and commencement

1.—(1) This Order may be cited as the Children (Northern Ireland) Order 1995.

(2) This Order shall come into operation on such day or days as the Secretary of State may by order appoint.

(3) An order under paragraph (2) may also appoint a day for the coming into operation of any provision of an order made under section 38(2) of the Northern Ireland Constitution Act 1973 as necessary or expedient in consequence of this Order.

1973 c. 36

Interpretation

2.—(1) The Interpretation Act (Northern Ireland) 1954 shall apply to Article 1 and the following provisions of this Order as it applies to a Measure of the Northern Ireland Assembly.

1954 c. 33 (N.I.)

(2) In this Order—

"Adoption Order" means the Adoption (Northern Ireland) Order 1987;

1987 NI 22

"Article 8 order" has the meaning given in Article 8(2);

"authority", where the reference is to a body, means, except in

Article 165 and subject to paragraphs (3) and (4), a Board;

"authority foster parent" has the meaning given in Article 27(3) (accommodation and maintenance of children looked after by an authority);

"Board" means a Health and Social Services Board;

"care order" has the meaning given in Article 49(1) and also includes any order which by or under any statutory provision has the effect of, or is deemed to be, a care order for the purposes of this Order;

"child", except in Parts X, XI and XII (fostering, child minding and employment) and subject to paragraph 1(1) of Schedule 1, means a person under the age of 18;

"child assessment order" has the meaning given in Article 62(2) (child assessment orders);

"child minder" has the meaning given in Article 119;

"child of the family", in relation to the parties to a marriage, means—

(a) a child of both of those parties;

(b) any other child, not being a child who is placed with those parties as foster parents by an authority or a voluntary organisation, who has been treated by both of those parties as a child of their family;

"children's home" has the meaning given in Part IX;

"compulsory school age" has the meaning assigned to it by Article 46 of the Education and Libraries (Northern Ireland) Order 1986;

1986 NI 3

"contact order" has the meaning given in Article 8(1);

"the court" has the meaning given in Article 164(1) and (2);

"day care" has the same meaning as in Article 19;

"the Department" means the Department of Health and Social Services;

"development" means physical, intellectual, emotional, social or behavioural development;

"disability working allowance" means disability working allowance under Part VII of the Social Security Contributions and Benefits (Northern Ireland) Act 1992;

1992 c. 7

"disabled" means blind, deaf or dumb or suffering from mental disorder of any kind or substantially and permanently handicapped by illness, injury or congenital deformity or such other disability as may be prescribed;

"education supervision order" has the meaning given in Article 49(1);

"emergency protection order" means an order under Article 63;

"family assistance order" means an order under Article 16;

"family credit" means family credit under Part VII of the Social Security Contributions and Benefits (Northern Ireland) Act 1992;

1992 c. 7

"family proceedings" has the meaning given in Article 8(3);

"family proceedings court" has the meaning given in Article 164(4);

"family proceedings rules" means family proceedings rules made under Article 12 of the Family Law (Northern Ireland) Order 1993;

1993 NI 6

"foster a child privately" has the meaning given in Article 106(1);

"guardian of a child" means a guardian (other than a guardian of the fortune or estate of a child) appointed in accordance with the provisions of Article 159 or 160;

"harm" means ill-treatment or the impairment of health or development and the question of whether harm is significant shall be determined in accordance with Article 50(3);

"health" means physical or mental health;

"Health and Social Services trust" means a Health and Social Services trust established under the Health and Personal Social Services (Northern Ireland) Order 1991;

1991 NI 1

"homeless persons" shall be construed in accordance with Part II of the Housing (Northern Ireland) Order 1988;

1988 NI 23

"hospital" has the meaning assigned to it by Article 2(2) of the Health and Personal Social Services (Northern Ireland) Order 1972;

1972 NI 14

"ill-treatment" includes sexual abuse and forms of ill-treatment which are not physical;

"income support" means income support under Part VII of the Social Security Contributions and Benefits (Northern Ireland) Act 1992;

"managers" has the meaning assigned to it by Article 2(2) of the Education and Libraries (Northern Ireland) Order 1986;

1986 NI 3

"medical practitioner" means a fully registered person within the meaning of the Medical Act 1983;

1983 c. 54

"nursing home" has the meaning assigned to it by Article 16 of the Registered Homes (Northern Ireland) Order 1992;

1992 NI 20

"parental responsibility" has the meaning given in Article 6;

"parental responsibility agreement" has the meaning given in Article 7(1)(*b*);

"personal social services" has the meaning assigned to it by Article 2(2) of the Health and Personal Social Services (Northern Ireland) Order 1972;

"police officer" means a member of the Royal Ulster Constabulary or of the Royal Ulster Constabulary Reserve;

PART I

"prescribed", except in Parts II, XII, XV and XVI and Article 176 and in relation to rules of court, means prescribed by regulations made by the Department under this Order;

1986 NI 4

"private hospital" has the meaning assigned to it by Article 90(2) of the Mental Health (Northern Ireland) Order 1986;

"privately fostered child" has the meaning given in Article 106(1);

1950 c. 7 (N.I.)

"probation order" has the meaning assigned to it by section 1 of the Probation Act (Northern Ireland) 1950;

"prohibited steps order" has the meaning given in Article 8(1);

"protected child" means a child who is a protected child for the purposes of Part IV of the Adoption Order;

"public body" means a body established by or under any statutory provision;

"registered children's home" has the meaning given in Article 90(1);

"relative", in relation to a child, means a grandparent, brother, sister, uncle or aunt (whether of the full blood or half blood or by affinity), or step-parent;

"residence order" has the meaning given in Article 8(1);

"residential care home" has the meaning assigned to it by Article 3 of the Registered Homes (Northern Ireland) Order 1992;

"rules of court" includes family proceedings rules, county court rules and magistrates' courts rules (as well as rules of court as defined in section 21(4) of the Interpretation Act (Northern Ireland) 1954);

1986 NI 3

"school" has the meaning assigned to it by Article 2(2) of the Education and Libraries (Northern Ireland) Order 1986;

"service", in relation to any provision made under Part IV, includes any facility;

"special educational needs" has the meaning assigned to it by Article 33(2) of the Education and Libraries (Northern Ireland) Order 1986;

1990 NI 3

"special agency" means a special health and social services agency established under the Health and Personal Social Services (Special Agencies) (Northern Ireland) Order 1990;

"specific issue order" has the meaning given in Article 8(1);

"statutory provision" has the meaning assigned to it by section 1(f) of the Interpretation Act (Northern Ireland) 1954;

"supervision order" has the meaning given in Article 49(1);

"supervised child" and "supervisor", in relation to a supervision order or an education supervision order, mean respectively the child who is (or is to be) under supervision and the person under whose supervision he is (or is to be) by virtue of the order;

"training school" has the meaning assigned to it by section 180(1) of the Children and Young Persons Act (Northern Ireland) 1968;

1968 c. 34 (N.I.)

"upbringing", in relation to any child, includes the care of the child but not his maintenance;

"voluntary home" has the meaning given in Article 74(1);

"voluntary organisation" has the meaning given in Article 74(1).

(3) Where a function is exercisable by a Health and Social Services trust by virtue of an authorisation for the time being in operation under Article 3(1) of the Health and Personal Socal Services (Northern Ireland) Order 1994, references to an authority are, to the extent that that function is exercisable by that trust, references to that trust.

1994 NI 2

(4) References in this Order to the area of an authority in relation to any function are—

(a) where the references are to the area of a Health and Social Services trust, references to the operational area of that trust (as defined in Article 2(2) of the Health and Personal Social Services (Northern Ireland) Order 1972) in relation to that function;

(b) where the references are to the area of a Board, references to so much of the area of the Board as does not fall within the operational area of a Health and Social Services trust in relation to that function.

(5) References in this Order to a child whose father and mother were, or (as the case may be) were not, married to each other at the time of his birth shall be construed in accordance with Article 155.

(6) References in this Order—

(a) to a person with whom a child lives, or is to live, as the result of a residence order; or

(b) to a person in whose favour a residence order is in force,

shall be construed as references to the person named in the order as the person with whom the child is to live.

(7) References in this Order—

(a) to a child who is in the care of an authority shall be construed as references to a child who is in the care of the authority by virtue of a care order;

(b) to a child who is looked after by an authority shall be construed in accordance with Article 25.

(8) References in this Order to accommodation provided by an authority are references to accommodation and maintenance provided as described in Article 27(2).

(9) In determining the "ordinary residence" of a child for any purpose of this Order, there shall be disregarded any period in which he lives in any place—

(a) which is a school or other institution;

(b) in compliance with a residence requirement of a probation order or of a supervision order under this Order or section 74 of the Children and Young Persons Act (Northern Ireland) 1968; or

(c) while he is being provided with accommodation by or on behalf of an authority.

(10) References in this Order to children who are in need shall be construed in accordance with Article 17 (children in need and their families).

PART II

GENERAL

Child's welfare

Child's welfare to be paramount consideration

3.—(1) Where a court determines any question with respect to—

(a) the upbringing of a child; or

(b) the administration of a child's property or the application of any income arising from it,

the child's welfare shall be the court's paramount consideration.

(2) In any proceedings in which any question with respect to the upbringing of a child arises, the court shall have regard to the general principle that any delay in determining the question is likely to prejudice the welfare of the child.

(3) In the circumstances mentioned in paragraph (4), a court shall have regard in particular to—

(a) the ascertainable wishes and feelings of the child concerned (considered in the light of his age and understanding);

(b) his physical, emotional and educational needs;

(c) the likely effect on him of any change in his circumstances;

(d) his age, sex, background and any characteristics of his which the court considers relevant;

(e) any harm which he has suffered or is at risk of suffering;

(f) how capable of meeting his needs is each of his parents and any other person in relation to whom the court considers the question to be relevant;

(g) the range of powers available to the court under this Order in the proceedings in question.

(4) The circumstances are that—

(a) the court is considering whether to make, vary or discharge an Article 8 order, and the making, variation or discharge of the order is opposed by any party to the proceedings; or

(b) the court is considering whether to make, vary or discharge an order under Part V.

(5) Where a court is considering whether or not to make one or more orders under this Order with respect to a child, it shall not make the order or any of the orders unless it considers that doing so would be better for the child than making no order at all.

Reports on child's welfare

4.—(1) A court considering any question with respect to a child under this Order may ask an authority to arrange for a suitably qualified person to report to the court on such matters relating to the welfare of that child as are required to be dealt with in the report.

. (2) The Lord Chancellor may make regulations specifying matters which, unless the court orders otherwise, must be dealt with in any report under this Article.

(3) The report may be made in writing, or orally, as the court requires.

(4) Regardless of any statutory provision or rule of law which would otherwise prevent the court from doing so, the court may take account of—

(a) any statement contained in the report; and

(b) any evidence given in respect of the matters referred to in the report,

in so far as the statement or evidence is, in the opinion of the court, relevant to the question which it is considering.

(5) An authority shall comply with any request for a report under this Article.

Parental responsibility

Parental responsibility for children

5.—(1) Where a child's father and mother were married to each other at the time of his birth, they shall each have parental responsibility for the child.

(2) Where a child's father and mother were not married to each other at the time of his birth—

(a) the mother shall have parental responsibility for the child;

(b) the father shall not have parental responsibility for the child, unless he acquires it in accordance with the provisions of this Order.

(3) The rule of law that a father is the natural guardian of his legitimate child is abolished.

(4) More than one person may have parental responsibility for the same child at the same time.

(5) A person who has parental responsibility for a child at any time shall not cease to have that responsibility solely because some other person subsequently acquires parental responsibility for the child.

(6) Where more than one person has parental responsibility for a child, each of them may act alone and without the other (or others) in meeting that responsibility; but nothing in this Part shall be taken to affect the operation of any statutory provision which requires the consent of more than one person in a matter affecting the child.

(7) The fact that a person has parental responsibility for a child shall not entitle him to act in any way which would be incompatible with any order made with respect to the child under this Order.

(8) A person who has parental responsibility for a child may not surrender or transfer any part of that responsibility to another but may arrange for some or all of it to be met by one or more persons acting on his behalf.

(9) The person with whom any such arrangement is made may himself be a person who already has parental responsibility for the child concerned.

(10) The making of any such arrangement shall not affect any liability of the person making it which may arise from any failure to meet any part of his parental responsibility for the child concerned.

Meaning of "parental responsibility"

6.—(1) In this Order "parental responsibility" means all the rights, duties, powers, responsibilities and authority which by law a parent of a child has in relation to the child and his property.

(2) It also includes the rights, powers and duties which a guardian of the child's fortune or estate (appointed, before the commencement of Part XV (guardians), to act generally) would have had in relation to the child and his property.

(3) The rights referred to in paragraph (2) include, in particular, the right of the guardian to receive or recover in his own name, for the benefit of the child, property of whatever description and wherever situated which the child is entitled to receive or recover.

(4) The fact that a person has, or does not have, parental responsibility for a child shall not affect—

(*a*) any obligation which he may have in relation to the child (such as a statutory duty to maintain the child); or

(*b*) any rights which, in the event of the child's death, he (or any other person) may have in relation to the child's property.

(5) A person who—

(*a*) does not have parental responsibility for a particular child; but

(*b*) has care of the child,

16

may (subject to the provisions of this Order) do what is reasonable in all the circumstances of the case for the purpose of safeguarding or promoting the child's welfare.

Acquisition of parental responsibility

7.—(1) Where a child's father and mother were not married to each other at the time of his birth—

(*a*) the court may, on the application of the father, order that he shall have parental responsibility for the child; or

(*b*) the father and mother may by agreement ("a parental responsibility agreement") provide for the father to have parental responsibility for the child.

(2) No parental responsibility agreement shall have effect for the purposes of this Order unless—

(*a*) it is made in the prescribed form; and

(*b*) it has been recorded in the prescribed manner (if any).

(3) In this Article "prescribed" means prescribed by regulations made by the Department of Finance and Personnel.

(4) Subject to Article 12(4) (residence orders and parental responsibility), an order under paragraph (1)(*a*), or a parental responsibility agreement, may only be brought to an end by an order of the court made on the application—

(*a*) of any person who has parental responsibility for the child; or

(*b*) with leave of the court, of the child himself.

(5) The court may only grant leave under paragraph (4)(*b*) if it is satisfied that the child has sufficient understanding to make the proposed application.

PART III

ORDERS WITH RESPECT TO CHILDREN IN FAMILY PROCEEDINGS

General

Residence, contact and other orders with respect to children

8.—(1) In this Order—

"contact order" means an order requiring the person with whom a child lives, or is to live, to allow the child to visit or stay with the person named in the order, or for that person and the child otherwise to have contact with each other;

"prohibited steps order" means an order that no step which could be taken by a parent in meeting his parental responsibility for a child, and which is of a kind specified in the order, shall be taken by any person without the consent of the court;

"residence order" means an order settling the arrangements to be made as to the person with whom a child is to live; and

"specific issue order" means an order giving directions for the purpose of determining a specific question which has arisen, or which may arise, in connection with any aspect of parental responsibility for a child.

(2) In this Order "Article 8 order" means any of the orders mentioned in paragraph (1) and any order varying or discharging such an order.

(3) For the purposes of this Order "family proceedings" means any proceedings—

(a) under the inherent jurisdiction of the High Court in relation to children; and

(b) under the provisions mentioned in paragraph (4),

but does not include proceedings on an application for leave under Article 173(2) (restriction on use of wardship jurisdiction).

(4) The provisions are—

(a) Part II, this Part, Part V (care and supervision) and Part XV (guardians);

1978 NI 15   (b) the Matrimonial Causes (Northern Ireland) Order 1978;

1980 NI 5   (c) the Domestic Proceedings (Northern Ireland) Order 1980;

(d) Articles 4 and 13 of the Family Law (Miscellaneous Provi-
1984 NI 14   sions) (Northern Ireland) Order 1984;

(e) the Adoption Order;

(f) Part IV of the Matrimonial and Family Proceedings (Nor-
1989 NI 4   thern Ireland) Order 1989;

(g) section 30 of the Human Fertilisation and Embryology Act
1990 c. 37   1990.

Restrictions on making Article 8 orders

9.—(1) No court shall make any Article 8 order, other than a residence order, with respect to a child who is in the care of an authority.

(2) No application may be made by an authority for a residence order or contact order and no court shall make such an order in favour of an authority.

(3) A person who is, or was at any time within the last six months, an authority foster parent of a child may not apply for leave to apply for an Article 8 order with respect to the child unless—

(a) he has the consent of the authority;

(b) he is a relative of the child; or

(c) the child has lived with him for at least three years preceding the application.

(4) The period of three years mentioned in paragraph (3)(*c*) need not be continuous but must have begun not more than five years before the making of the application.

(5) No court shall exercise its powers to make a specific issue order or prohibited steps order—

(*a*) with a view to achieving a result which could be achieved by making a residence or contact order; or

(*b*) in any way which is denied to the High Court (by Article 173(1)) in the exercise of its inherent jurisdiction with respect to children.

(6) No court shall make any Article 8 order which is to have effect for a period which will end after the child has reached the age of 16 unless it is satisfied that the circumstances of the case are exceptional.

(7) No court shall make any Article 8 order, other than one varying or discharging such an order, with respect to a child who has reached the age of 16 unless it is satisfied that the circumstances of the case are exceptional.

Power of court to make Article 8 orders

10.—(1) In any family proceedings in which a question arises with respect to the welfare of any child, the court may make an Article 8 order with respect to the child if—

(*a*) an application for the order has been made by a person who—

(i) is entitled to apply for an Article 8 order with respect to the child; or

(ii) has obtained the leave of the court to make the application; or

(*b*) the court considers that the order should be made even though no such application has been made.

(2) The court may also make an Article 8 order with respect to any child on the application of a person who—

(*a*) is entitled to apply for an Article 8 order with respect to the child; or

(*b*) has obtained the leave of the court to make the application.

(3) This Article is subject to the restrictions imposed by Article 9.

(4) The following persons are entitled to apply to the court for any Article 8 order with respect to a child—

(*a*) any parent or guardian of the child;

(*b*) any person in whose favour a residence order is in force with respect to the child.

(5) The following persons are entitled to apply for a residence or contact order with respect to a child—

(*a*) any party to a marriage (whether or not subsisting) in relation to whom the child is a child of the family;

(*b*) any person with whom the child has lived for a period of at least three years;

(*c*) any person who—

    (i) in any case where a residence order is in force with respect to the child, has the consent of each of the persons in whose favour the order was made;

    (ii) in any case where the child is in the care of an authority, has the consent of that authority; or

    (iii) in any other case, has the consent of each of those (if any) who have parental responsibility for the child.

(6) A person who would not otherwise be entitled (under paragraphs (1) to (5)) to apply for the variation or discharge of an Article 8 order shall be entitled to do so if—

(*a*) the order was made on his application; or

(*b*) in the case of a contact order, he is named in the order.

(7) Any person who falls within a category of person prescribed by rules of court is entitled to apply for any such Article 8 order as may be so prescribed in relation to that category of person.

(8) Where the person applying for leave to make an application for an Article 8 order is the child concerned, the court may only grant leave if it is satisfied that he has sufficient understanding to make the proposed application for the Article 8 order.

(9) Where the person applying for leave to make an application for an Article 8 order is not the child concerned, the court shall, in deciding whether or not to grant leave, have particular regard to—

(*a*) the nature of the proposed application for the Article 8 order;

(*b*) the applicant's connection with the child;

(*c*) any risk there might be of that proposed application disrupting the child's life to such an extent that he would be harmed by it; and

(*d*) where the child is being looked after by an authority—

    (i) the authority's plans for the child's future; and

    (ii) the wishes and feelings of the child's parents.

(10) The period of three years mentioned in paragraph (5)(*b*) need not be continuous but must not have begun more than five years before, or ended more than three months before, the making of the application.

General principles and supplementary provisions

11.—(1) In proceedings in which any question of making an Article 8 order, or any other question with respect to such an order, arises, the court shall (in the light of any rules made by virtue of paragraph (2))—

(a) draw up a timetable with a view to determining the question without delay; and

(b) give such directions as it considers appropriate for the purpose of ensuring, so far as is reasonably practicable, that that timetable is adhered to.

(2) Rules of court may—

(a) specify periods within which specified steps must be taken in relation to proceedings in which such questions arise; and

(b) make other provision with respect to such proceedings for the purpose of ensuring, so far as is reasonably practicable, that such questions are determined without delay.

(3) Where a court has power to make an Article 8 order, it may do so at any time during the course of the proceedings in question even though it is not in a position to dispose finally of those proceedings.

(4) Where a residence order is made in favour of two or more persons who do not themselves all live together, the order may specify the periods during which the child is to live in the different households concerned.

(5) Where—

(a) a residence order has been made with respect to a child; and

(b) as a result of the order the child lives, or is to live, with one of two parents who each have parental responsibility for him,

the residence order shall cease to have effect if the parents live together for a continuous period of more than six months.

(6) A contact order which requires the parent with whom a child lives to allow the child to visit, or otherwise have contact with, his other parent shall cease to have effect if the parents live together for a continuous period of more than six months.

(7) An Article 8 order may—

(a) contain directions about how it is to be carried into effect;

(b) impose conditions which must be complied with by any person—

(i) in whose favour the order is made;

(ii) who is a parent of the child concerned;

(iii) who is not a parent of his but who has parental responsibility for him; or

(iv) with whom the child is living;

and to whom the conditions are expressed to apply;

(c) be made to have effect for a specified period, or contain provisions which are to have effect for a specified period;

(d) make such incidental, supplemental or consequential provision as the court thinks fit.

Residence orders and parental responsibility

12.—(1) Where the court makes a residence order in favour of the father of a child it shall, if the father would not otherwise have parental responsibility for the child, also make an order under Article 7 giving him that responsibility.

(2) Where the court makes a residence order in favour of any person who is not the parent or guardian of the child concerned that person shall have parental responsibility for the child while the residence order remains in force.

(3) Where a person has parental responsibility for a child as a result of paragraph (2), he shall not have the right—

(*a*) to consent, or refuse to consent, to the making of an application with respect to the child under Article 17 of the Adoption Order;

(*b*) to agree, or refuse to agree, to the making of an adoption order, or an order under Article 57 of the Adoption Order, with respect to the child; or

(*c*) to appoint a guardian for the child.

(4) Where paragraph (1) requires the court to make an order under Article 7 in respect of the father of a child, the court shall not bring that order to an end at any time while the residence order concerned remains in force.

Change of child's name or removal from jurisdiction

13.—(1) Where a residence order is in force with respect to a child, no person shall—

(*a*) cause the child to be known by a new surname; or

(*b*) remove him from the United Kingdom;

without either the written consent of every person who has parental responsibility for the child or the leave of the court.

(2) Paragraph (1)(*b*) shall not prevent the removal of a child, for a period of less than one month, by the person in whose favour the residence order is made.

(3) In making a residence order with respect to a child the court may grant the leave required by paragraph (1)(*b*), either generally or for specified purposes.

Enforcement of residence orders

14.—(1) Where—

(*a*) a residence order is in force with respect to a child in favour of any person; and

(*b*) any other person (including one in whose favour the order is also in force) is in breach of the arrangements settled by the order, the person mentioned in sub-paragraph (*a*) may, as soon as a copy of the order has been served on the other person, enforce it under Article 112(3) of the Magistrates' Courts (Northern Ireland) Order 1981 as if it were an order requiring the other person to produce the child to him. 1981 NI 26

(2) Paragraph (1) is without prejudice to any other remedy open to the person in whose favour the residence order is in force.

Financial relief

Orders for financial relief with respect to children

15.—(1) Schedule 1 (which makes provision in relation to financial relief for children) shall have effect.

(2) The powers of a court of summary jurisdiction under Article 86 of the Magistrates' Courts (Northern Ireland) Order 1981 to revoke, suspend, review, vary or discharge an order for the periodical payment of money and the power of the clerk of petty sessions to vary such an order shall not apply in relation to an order made under Schedule 1.

(3) Schedule 1 is without prejudice to the Child Support (Northern Ireland) Order 1991. 1991 NI 23

Family assistance orders

Family assistance orders

16.—(1) Where, in any family proceedings, the court has power to make an order under this Part with respect to any child, it may (whether or not it makes such an order) make an order requiring an authority to make a suitably qualified person available, to advise, assist and (where appropriate) befriend any person named in the order.

(2) The persons who may be named in an order under this Article (a "family assistance order") are—

(*a*) any parent or guardian of the child;

(*b*) any person with whom the child is living or in whose favour a contact order is in force with respect to the child;

(*c*) the child himself.

(3) No court may make a family assistance order unless—

(*a*) it is satisfied that the circumstances of the case are exceptional; and

(*b*) it has obtained the consent of every person to be named in the order other than the child.

(4) A family assistance order may direct—

(*a*) the person named in the order; or

(b) such of the persons named in the order as may be specified in the order,

to take such steps as may be so specified with a view to enabling the suitably qualified person mentioned in paragraph (1) to be kept informed of the address of any person named in the order and to be allowed to visit him.

(5) Unless it specifies a shorter period, a family assistance order shall have effect for a period of six months beginning with the day on which it is made.

(6) Where—

(a) a family assistance order is in force with respect to a child; and

(b) an Article 8 order is also in force with respect to the child,

the suitably qualified person mentioned in paragraph (1) may refer to the court the question whether the Article 8 order should be varied or discharged.

(7) A family assistance order shall not be made so as to require an authority to make a suitably qualified person available under paragraph (1) unless—

(a) the authority agrees; or

(b) the child concerned lives or will live within its area.

PART IV

SUPPORT FOR CHILDREN AND THEIR FAMILIES

Children in need and their families

Interpretation

17. For the purposes of this Part a child shall be taken to be in need if—

(a) he is unlikely to achieve or maintain, or to have the opportunity of achieving or maintaining, a reasonable standard of health or development without the provision for him of services by an authority under this Part;

(b) his health or development is likely to be significantly impaired, or further impaired, without the provision for him of such services; or

(c) he is disabled,

and "family", in relation to such a child, includes any person who has parental responsibility for the child and any other person with whom he has been living.

General duty of authority to provide personal social services for children in need, their families and others

18.—(1) It shall be the general duty of every authority (in addition to the other duties imposed by this Part)—

    (*a*) to safeguard and promote the welfare of children within its area who are in need; and

    (*b*) so far as is consistent with that duty, to promote the upbringing of such children by their families,

by providing a range and level of personal social services appropriate to those children's needs.

(2) For the purpose principally of facilitating its general duty under this Article, every authority shall have the specific powers and duties set out in Schedule 2.

(3) Any service provided by an authority in the exercise of functions conferred on it by this Article may be provided for the family of a particular child in need or for any member of his family, if the service is provided with a view to safeguarding or promoting the child's welfare.

(4) The Department may by order amend any provision of Schedule 2 or add any further duty or power to those mentioned there.

(5) Every authority—

    (*a*) shall facilitate the provision by others (including in particular voluntary organisations) of services which the authority has power to provide by virtue of this Article or Article 19, 21, 27, 35 or 36; and

    (*b*) may make such arrangements as it sees fit for any person to act on its behalf in the provision of any such service.

(6) The services provided by an authority in the exercise of functions conferred on it by this Article may include giving assistance in kind or, in exceptional circumstances, in cash.

(7) Assistance may be unconditional or subject to conditions as to the repayment of the assistance or of its value (in whole or in part).

(8) Before giving any assistance or imposing any conditions, an authority shall have regard to the means of the child concerned and of each of his parents.

(9) No person shall be liable to make any repayment of assistance or of its value at any time when he is in receipt of income support, family credit or disability working allowance.

Day care for pre-school and other children

19.—(1) In this Article—

    "day care" means any form of care or supervised activity provided for children during the day (whether or not it is provided on a regular basis);

"supervised activity" means an activity supervised by a responsible person.

(2) Every authority shall provide such day care for children in need within the authority's area who are—

(*a*) aged five or under; and

(*b*) not yet attending schools,

as is appropriate.

(3) An authority may provide day care for children within the authority's area who satisfy the conditions mentioned in paragraph (2)(*a*) and (*b*) even though they are not in need.

(4) An authority may provide facilities (including training, advice, guidance and counselling) for those—

(*a*) caring for children in day care; or

(*b*) who at any time accompany such children while they are in day care.

(5) Every authority shall provide for children in need within the authority's area who are attending any school such care or supervised activities as is appropriate—

(*a*) outside school hours; and

(*b*) during school holidays.

(6) An authority may provide such care or supervised activities for children within the authority's area who are attending any school even though those children are not in need.

(7) Every authority shall, in carrying out its functions under this Article, have regard to any day care provided for children within the authority's area by a district council or an education and library board or by other persons.

Review of provision for day care, child minding, etc.

20.—(1) Every authority shall review—

(*a*) the provision which it makes under Article 19;

(*b*) the extent to which the services of child minders are available within the authority's area with respect to children under the age of twelve;

(*c*) the provision for day care within the authority's area made for such children by persons required to register under Article 118(1)(*b*).

(2) A review under paragraph (1) shall be conducted—

(*a*) together with the appropriate education and library board and district councils; and

(*b*) at least once in every review period.

(3) In paragraph (2)(*b*) "review period" means the period of one year beginning with the commencement of this Article and each

subsequent period of three years beginning with an anniversary of that commencement.

(4) In conducting any such review, the authority shall have regard to any exempt provision made within the authority's area with respect to children under the age of twelve.

(5) In paragraph (4) "exempt provision" means provision to which the exemption provided by paragraph (1) or (2) of Article 121 applies (schools, hospitals and other establishments exempt from the registration requirements which apply in relation to the provision of day care).

(6) Where an authority has conducted a review under this Article it shall publish the result of the review—

(*a*) as soon as is reasonably practicable;

(*b*) in such form as it considers appropriate; and

(*c*) together with any proposals it may have with respect to the matters reviewed.

(7) Any review under this Article shall have regard to any representations which the authority considers to be relevant.

Provision of accommodation for children: general

21.—(1) Every authority shall provide accommodation for any child in need within its area who appears to the authority to require accommodation as a result of—

(*a*) there being no person who has parental responsibility for him;

(*b*) his being lost or having been abandoned; or

(*c*) the person who has been caring for him being prevented (whether or not permanently, and for whatever reason) from providing him with suitable accommodation or care.

(2) Where an authority provides accommodation under paragraph (1) for a child who is ordinarily resident in the area of another authority, that other authority may take over the provision of accommodation for the child within—

(*a*) three months of being notified in writing that the child is being provided with accommodation; or

(*b*) such other longer period as may be prescribed.

(3) Every authority shall provide accommodation for any child in need within its area who has reached the age of 16 and whose welfare the authority considers is likely to be seriously prejudiced if it does not provide him with accommodation.

(4) An authority may provide accommodation for any child within the authority's area (even though a person who has parental responsibility for him is able to provide him with accommodation) if the authority considers that to do so would safeguard or promote the child's welfare.

27

(5) An authority may provide accommodation for any person who has reached the age of 16 but is under 21 in any home provided under Part VII which takes children who have reached the age of 16 if the authority considers that to do so would safeguard or promote his welfare.

(6) Before providing accommodation under this Article, an authority shall, so far as is reasonably practicable and consistent with the child's welfare—

(a) ascertain the child's wishes regarding the provision of accommodation; and

(b) give due consideration (having regard to his age and understanding) to such wishes of the child as the authority has been able to ascertain.

Powers of person with parental responsibility

22.—(1) An authority may not provide accommodation under Article 21 for any child if any person who—

(a) has parental responsibility for him; and

(b) is willing and able to—

(i) provide accommodation for him; or

(ii) arrange for accommodation to be provided for him,

objects.

(2) Any person who has parental responsibility for a child may at any time remove the child from accommodation provided by or on behalf of the authority under Article 21.

(3) Paragraphs (1) and (2) do not apply while any person—

(a) in whose favour a residence order is in force with respect to the child; or

(b) who has care of the child by virtue of an order made in the exercise of the High Court's inherent jurisdiction with respect to children,

agrees to the child being looked after in accommodation provided by or on behalf of the authority.

(4) Where there is more than one such person as is mentioned in paragraph (3), all of them must agree.

(5) Paragraphs (1) and (2) do not apply where a child who has reached the age of 16 agrees to being provided with accommodation under Article 21.

Provision of accommodation for children in police protection

23.—(1) Every authority shall make provision for the reception and accommodation of children who are removed or kept away from home under Part VI.

(2) Every authority shall receive, and provide accommodation for, children in police protection whom the authority is requested to receive under Article 65(5)(*e*).

(3) Where a child has been removed under Part VI and he is not being provided with accommodation by an authority, any reasonable expenses of accommodating him shall be recoverable from the authority in whose area he is ordinarily resident.

Recoupment of cost of providing services, etc.

24.—(1) Where an authority provides any service under Article 18 or 19, other than advice, guidance or counselling, the authority may recover from a person specified in paragraph (4) such charge for the service as the authority considers reasonable.

(2) Where the authority is satisfied that that person's means are insufficient for it to be reasonably practicable for him to pay the charge, the authority shall not require him to pay more than he can reasonably be expected to pay.

(3) No person shall be liable to pay any charge under paragraph (1) at any time when he is in receipt of income support, family credit or disability working allowance.

(4) The persons are—

    (*a*) where the service is provided for a child under 16, each of his parents;

    (*b*) where it is provided for a child who has reached the age of 16, the child himself; and

    (*c*) where it is provided for a member of the child's family, that member.

(5) Any charge under paragraph (1) may, without prejudice to any other method of recovery, be recovered summarily as a civil debt.

(6) Where an authority provides any accommodation under Article 21(1) or Article 23(1) or (2) for a child who was (before the authority began to look after him) ordinarily resident within the area of another authority, the first authority may recover any reasonable expenses incurred by it in providing the accommodation and maintaining the child from the other authority.

Children looked after by an authority

Interpretation

25.—(1) In this Order any reference to a child who is looked after by an authority is a reference to a child who is—

    (*a*) in the care of the authority; or

    (*b*) provided with accommodation by the authority.

(2) In paragraph (1)(*b*) "accommodation" means accommodation which is provided for a continuous period of more than 24 hours.

(3) Paragraph (1) is subject to Article 2(8).

General duty of authority

26.—(1) Every authority looking after a child shall—

(*a*) safeguard and promote his welfare; and

(*b*) make such use of services available for children cared for by their own parents as appears to the authority reasonable in his case.

(2) Before making any decision with respect to a child whom it is looking after, or proposing to look after, an authority shall, so far as is reasonably practicable, ascertain the wishes and feelings of—

(*a*) the child;

(*b*) his parents;

(*c*) any person who is not a parent of his but who has parental responsibility for him; and

(*d*) any other persons whose wishes and feelings the authority considers to be relevant,

regarding the matter to be decided.

(3) In making any such decision an authority shall give due consideration—

(*a*) having regard to his age and understanding, to such wishes and feelings of the child as the authority has been able to ascertain;

(*b*) to such wishes and feelings of any person mentioned in paragraph (2)(*b*) to (*d*) as the authority has been able to ascertain; and

(*c*) to the child's religious persuasion, racial origin and cultural and linguistic background.

(4) If it appears to an authority that it is necessary, for the purpose of protecting members of the public from serious injury, to exercise its powers with respect to a child whom it is looking after in a manner which may not be consistent with its duties under this Article, the authority may do so.

(5) If the Department considers it necessary, for the purpose of protecting members of the public from serious injury, to give directions to an authority with respect to the exercise of the authority's powers with respect to a child whom it is looking after, the Department may give such directions to the authority.

(6) Where any such directions are given to an authority, it shall comply with them even though doing so is inconsistent with its duties under this Article.

Accommodation and maintenance for children

27.—(1) Every authority looking after a child shall—

(*a*) when he is in the care of the authority, provide accommodation for him; and

(*b*) maintain him in other respects apart from providing accommodation for him.

(2) An authority shall provide accommodation and maintenance for any child whom it is looking after by—

(*a*) placing him (subject to paragraph (5) and any regulations made by the Department) with—

(i) a family;

(ii) a relative of his; or

(iii) any other suitable person,

on such terms as to payment by the authority and otherwise as the authority may determine;

(*b*) maintaining him in a home provided under Part VII;

(*c*) maintaining him in a voluntary home;

(*d*) maintaining him in a registered children's home;

(*e*) maintaining him in a home or institution provided by a government department or a prescribed public body; or

(*f*) making such other arrangements as—

(i) seem appropriate to the authority; and

(ii) comply with any regulations made by the Department.

(3) Any person with whom a child has been placed under paragraph (2)(*a*) is referred to in this Order as an authority foster parent unless he falls within paragraph (4).

(4) A person falls within this paragraph if he is—

(*a*) a parent of the child;

(*b*) a person who is not a parent of the child but who has parental responsibility for him; or

(*c*) where the child is in care and there was a residence order in force with respect to him immediately before the care order was made, a person in whose favour the residence order was made.

(5) Where a child is in the care of an authority, it may only allow him to live with a person who falls within paragraph (4) in accordance with regulations made by the Department.

(6) For the purposes of paragraph (5) a child shall be regarded as living with a person if he stays with that person for a continuous period of more than 24 hours.

(7) Subject to any regulations made by the Department for the purposes of this paragraph, any authority looking after a child shall make arrangements to enable him to live with—

31

(*a*) a person falling within paragraph (4); or

(*b*) a relative, friend or other person connected with him,

unless that would not be reasonably practicable or consistent with his welfare.

(8) Where an authority provides accommodation for a child whom it is looking after, the authority shall, subject to the provisions of this Part and so far as is reasonably practicable and consistent with his welfare, secure that—

(*a*) the accommodation is near his home; and

(*b*) where the authority is also providing accommodation for a sibling of his, they are accommodated together.

(9) Where an authority provides accommodation for a child whom it is looking after and who is disabled, the authority shall, so far as is reasonably practicable, secure that the accommodation is not unsuitable to his particular needs.

Regulations under Article 27

28.—(1) Regulations under Article 27(2)(*a*) may, in particular, make provision—

(*a*) with regard to the welfare of children placed with authority foster parents;

(*b*) as to the arrangements to be made by authorities in connection with the health and education of such children;

(*c*) as to the records to be kept by authorities;

(*d*) for securing that a child is not placed with an authority foster parent unless that person is approved as an authority foster parent;

(*e*) for securing that where possible the authority foster parent with whom a child is to be placed is—

(i) of the same religious persuasion as the child; or

(ii) gives an undertaking that the child will be brought up in that religious persuasion;

(*f*) for securing that children placed with authority foster parents, and the premises in which they are accommodated, will be supervised and inspected by an authority and that the children will be removed from those premises if their welfare appears to require it;

(*g*) as to the circumstances in which an authority may make arrangements for duties imposed on it by the regulations to be discharged on its behalf.

(2) Regulations under Article 27(2)(*f*) may, in particular, make provision as to—

(*a*) the persons to be notified of any proposed arrangements;

(*b*) the opportunities such persons are to have to make representations in relation to the arrangements proposed;

(c) the persons to be notified of any proposed changes in arrangements;

(d) the records to be kept by authorities;

(e) the supervision by authorities of any arrangements made.

(3) Regulations under Article 27(5) may, in particular, impose requirements on an authority as to—

(a) the making of any decision by an authority to allow a child to live with any person falling within Article 27(4) (including requirements as to those who must be consulted before the decision is made, and those who must be notified when it has been made);

(b) the supervision or medical examination of the child concerned;

(c) the removal of the child, in such circumstances as may be prescribed, from the care of the person with whom he has been allowed to live;

(d) the records to be kept by authorities.

Promotion and maintenance of contact between child and family

29.—(1) Where a child is being looked after by an authority, the authority shall, unless it is not reasonably practicable or consistent with his welfare, endeavour to promote contact between the child and—

(a) his parents;

(b) any person who is not a parent of his but who has parental responsibility for him; and

(c) any relative, friend or other person connected with him.

(2) Where a child is being looked after by an authority—

(a) the authority shall take such steps as are reasonably practicable to secure that—

(i) his parents; and

(ii) any person who is not a parent of his but who has parental responsibility for him,

are kept informed of where he is being accommodated; and

(b) every such person shall secure that the authority is kept informed of the address of that person.

(3) Where an authority ("the receiving authority") takes over the provision of accommodation for a child from another authority ("the transferring authority") under Article 21(2)—

(a) the receiving authority shall (where reasonably practicable) inform—

(i) the child's parents; and

(ii) any person who is not a parent of his but who has parental responsibility for him;

33

(b) paragraph (2)(a) shall apply to the transferring authority, as well as the receiving authority, until at least one such person has been informed of the change; and

(c) paragraph (2)(b) shall not require any person to inform the receiving authority of his address until he has been so informed.

(4) Nothing in this Article requires an authority to inform any person of the whereabouts of a child if—

(a) the child is in the care of the authority; and

(b) the authority has reasonable cause to believe that informing the person would prejudice the child's welfare.

(5) Any person who fails without reasonable excuse to comply with paragraph (2)(b) shall be guilty of an offence and liable on summary conviction to a fine not exceeding level 2 on the standard scale.

(6) It shall be a defence in any proceedings under paragraph (5) to prove that the defendant was residing at the same address as another person who was the child's parent or had parental responsibility for the child and had reasonable cause to believe that the other person had informed the appropriate authority that both of them were residing at that address.

Visits to or by children: expenses

30.—(1) Paragraph (2) applies where—

(a) a child is being looked after by an authority; and

(b) the conditions mentioned in paragraph (3) are satisfied.

(2) The authority may—

(a) make payments to—

(i) a parent of the child;

(ii) any person who is not a parent of his but who has parental responsibility for him; or

(iii) any relative, friend or other person connected with him,

in respect of travelling, subsistence or other expenses incurred by that person in visiting the child; or

(b) make payments to the child, or to any person on his behalf, in respect of travelling, subsistence or other expenses incurred by or on behalf of the child in his visiting—

(i) a parent of his;

(ii) any person who is not a parent of his but who has parental responsibility for him; or

(iii) any relative, friend or other person connected with him.

(3) The conditions are that—

(a) it appears to the authority that the visit in question could not otherwise be made without undue financial hardship; and

(b) the circumstances warrant the making of the payments.

Appointment of visitor for child who is not being visited

31.—(1) Where it appears to an authority in relation to any child whom the authority is looking after that—

(a) communication between the child and—

(i) a parent of his, or

(ii) any person who is not a parent of his but who has parental responsibility for him,

has been infrequent; or

(b) he has not visited or been visited by (or lived with) any such person during the preceding twelve months,

and that it would be in the child's best interests for an independent person to be appointed to be his visitor for the purposes of this Article, the authority shall appoint such a visitor.

(2) A person so appointed shall—

(a) have the duty of visiting, advising and befriending the child; and

(b) be entitled to recover from the authority which appointed him any reasonable expenses incurred by him for the purposes of his functions under this Article.

(3) A person's appointment as a visitor in pursuance of this Article shall be terminated if—

(a) he gives notice in writing to the authority which appointed him that he resigns the appointment; or

(b) the authority gives him notice in writing that the authority has terminated it.

(4) The termination of such an appointment shall not prejudice any duty under this Article to make a further appointment.

(5) Where an authority proposes to appoint a visitor for a child under this Article, the appointment shall not be made if—

(a) the child objects to it; and

(b) the authority is satisfied that the child has sufficient understanding to make an informed decision.

(6) Where a visitor has been appointed for a child under this Article, the authority shall terminate the appointment if—

(a) the child objects to its continuing; and

(b) the authority is satisfied that the child has sufficient understanding to make an informed decision.

(7) The Department may make regulations as to the circumstances in which a person appointed as a visitor under this Article is to be regarded as independent of the authority appointing him.

Power to guarantee apprenticeship deeds, etc.

32.—(1) While a child is being looked after by an authority, or is a person qualifying for advice and assistance (within the meaning given by Article 35), the authority may undertake any obligation by way of guarantee under any deed of apprenticeship or articles of clerkship which he enters into.

(2) Where an authority has undertaken any such obligation under any deed or articles it may at any time (whether or not it is still looking after the person concerned) undertake the like obligation under any supplemental deed or articles.

Arrangements to assist children to live abroad

33.—(1) An authority may only arrange for, or assist in arranging for, any child in its care to live outside Northern Ireland with the approval of the court.

(2) An authority may, with the approval of every person who has parental responsibility for the child, arrange for, or assist in arranging for, any other child looked after by the authority to live outside Northern Ireland.

(3) The court shall not give its approval under paragraph (1) unless it is satisfied that—

(*a*) living outside Northern Ireland would be in the child's best interests;

(*b*) suitable arrangements have been, or will be, made for his reception and welfare in the country in which he will live;

(*c*) the child has consented to living in that country; and

(*d*) every person who has parental responsibility for the child has consented to his living in that country.

(4) Where the court is satisfied that the child does not have sufficient understanding to give or withhold his consent, it may disregard paragraph (3)(*c*) and give its approval if the child is to live in the country concerned with a parent, guardian, or other suitable person.

(5) Where a person whose consent is required by paragraph (3)(*d*) fails to give his consent, the court may disregard that provision and give its approval if it is satisfied that that person—

(*a*) cannot be found;

(*b*) is incapable of consenting; or

(*c*) is withholding his consent unreasonably.

(6) Article 58 of the Adoption Order (which requires authority for taking or sending abroad a child for adoption) shall not apply in the case of any child who is to live outside Northern Ireland with the approval of the court given under this Article.

(7) Where a court decides to give its approval under this Article it may order that its decision is not to have effect during the appeal period.

(8) In paragraph (7) "the appeal period" means—

(*a*) where an appeal is made against the decision, the period between the making of the decision and the determination of the appeal; and

(*b*) otherwise, the period during which an appeal may be made against the decision.

Death of children being looked after by an authority

34.—(1) If a child who is being looked after by an authority dies, the authority—

(*a*) shall notify the Department;

(*b*) shall, so far as is reasonably practicable, notify the child's parents and every person who is not a parent of his but who has parental responsibility for him;

(*c*) may, with the consent (so far as it is reasonably practicable to obtain it) of every person who has parental responsibility for the child, arrange for the child's body to be buried or cremated; and

(*d*) may, if the conditions mentioned in paragraph (2) are satisfied, make payments to any person who has parental responsibility for the child, or any relative, friend or other person connected with the child, in respect of travelling, subsistence or other expenses incurred by that person in attending the child's funeral.

(2) The conditions are that—

(*a*) it appears to the authority that the person concerned could not otherwise attend the child's funeral without undue financial hardship; and

(*b*) that the circumstances warrant the making of the payments.

(3) Paragraph (1) does not authorise cremation where it does not accord with the practice of the child's religious persuasion.

(4) Where an authority has exercised its power under paragraph (1)(*c*) with respect to a child who was under 16 when he died, the authority may recover from any parent of the child any expenses incurred by the authority.

(5) Any sums so recoverable shall, without prejudice to any other method of recovery, be recoverable summarily as a civil debt.

(6) Nothing in this Article affects any statutory provision regulating or authorising the burial, cremation or anatomical examination of the body of a deceased person.

Advice and assistance for certain children

Advice and assistance for certain children

35.—(1) Where a child is being looked after by an authority, the

PART IV

authority shall advise, assist and befriend him with a view to promoting his welfare when he ceases to be looked after by the authority.

(2) In this Part "a person qualifying for advice and assistance" means a person within the authority's area who is under 21 and who was at any time after reaching the age of 16 but while still a child—

(a) looked after by an authority;

(b) accommodated by or on behalf of a voluntary organisation;

(c) accommodated in a registered children's home;

(d) accommodated for a consecutive period of at least three months in—

(i) any accommodation provided by an education and library board; or

(ii) any residential care home; or

(iii) any hospital; or

(iv) any nursing home; or

(v) any prescribed accommodation; or

(e) privately fostered;

but who is no longer so looked after, accommodated or fostered.

(3) Paragraph (2)(d) applies even if the period of three months mentioned there began before the child reached the age of 16.

(4) Where—

(a) an authority knows that there is within its area a person qualifying for advice and assistance;

(b) the conditions in paragraph (5) are satisfied; and

(c) that person has asked the authority for help of a kind which the authority can give under this Article,

the authority shall (if he was being looked after by an authority or was accommodated by or on behalf of a voluntary organisation) and may (in any other case) advise and befriend him.

(5) The conditions are that—

(a) it appears to the authority that the person concerned is in need of advice and being befriended;

(b) where that person was not being looked after by the authority, the authority is satisfied that the person by whom he was being looked after does not have the necessary facilities for advising or befriending him.

(6) Where as a result of this Article an authority is under a duty, or is empowered, to advise and befriend a person, the authority may also give him assistance.

Assistance: further provisions

36.—(1) Assistance given under Article 35 may be in kind or, in exceptional circumstances, in cash.

(2) An authority may give assistance to any person who qualifies for advice and assistance by virtue of Article 35(2)(*a*) by—

(*a*) contributing to expenses incurred by him in living near the place where he is, or will be—

(i) employed or seeking employment; or

(ii) receiving education or training; or

(*b*) making a grant to enable him to meet expenses connected with his education or training.

(3) Where an authority is assisting a person under paragraph (2) by making a contribution or grant with respect to a course of education or training, the authority may—

(*a*) continue to do so even though he reaches the age of 21 before completing the course; and

(*b*) disregard any interruption in his attendance on the course if he resumes it as soon as is reasonably practicable.

(4) Paragraphs (7) to (9) of Article 18 shall apply in relation to assistance given under Article 35 as they apply in relation to assistance given under Article 18.

Supplementary

37.—(1) Every authority shall establish a procedure for considering any representations (including any complaint) made to the authority by a person qualifying for advice and assistance about the discharge of the authority's functions under this Part in relation to him.

(2) In carrying out any consideration of representations under paragraph (1), an authority shall comply with any regulations made by the Department for the purposes of this Article.

(3) Where it appears to an authority that a person whom the authority has been advising and befriending under Article 35, as a person qualifying for advice and assistance, proposes to live, or is living, in the area of another authority, the authority shall inform that other authority.

(4) Where a child who is accommodated—

(*a*) by or on behalf of a voluntary organisation or in a registered children's home; or

(*b*) as mentioned in Article 35(2)(*d*),

ceases to be so accommodated, after reaching the age of 16, the person providing the accommodation shall inform the authority within whose area the child proposes to live.

Contributions towards maintenance of children looked after by an authority

Interpretation

38. In Articles 39 to 43—

39

"contribution notice" has the meaning given in Article 40(1);

"contribution order" has the meaning given in Article 41(2);

"contributor" has the meaning given in Article 39(1).

Liability to contribute

39.—(1) Where an authority is looking after a child (other than in the cases mentioned in paragraph (7)), the authority shall consider whether it should recover contributions towards the child's maintenance from any person liable to contribute (a "contributor").

(2) An authority may only recover contributions from a contributor if the authority considers it reasonable to do so.

(3) The persons liable to contribute are—

(*a*) where the child is under 16, each of his parents;

(*b*) where he has reached the age of 16, the child himself.

(4) A person shall not be liable to contribute during any period when he is in receipt of income support, family credit or disability working allowance.

(5) A person shall not be liable to contribute towards the maintenance of a child in the care of an authority in respect of any period during which the child is allowed by the authority (under Article 27(5)) to live with a parent of his.

(6) A contributor shall not be obliged to make any contribution towards a child's maintenance except as agreed or determined in accordance with Articles 40 to 43.

(7) The cases referred to in paragraph (1) are where the child is looked after by an authority under—

(*a*) Article 23;

(*b*) an interim care order.

Agreed contributions

40.—(1) Contributions towards a child's maintenance may only be recovered if the authority has served a notice (a "contribution notice") on the contributor specifying—

(*a*) the weekly sum which the authority considers that he should contribute; and

(*b*) arrangements for payment.

(2) The contribution notice must be in writing and dated.

(3) Arrangements for payment shall, in particular, include—

(*a*) the date on which liability to contribute begins (which must not be earlier than the date of the notice);

(*b*) the date on which liability under the notice will end (if the child has not before that date ceased to be looked after by the authority); and

40

(c) the date on which the first payment is to be made.

(4) The authority may specify in a contribution notice a weekly sum which is a standard contribution determined by the authority for all children looked after by it.

(5) The authority shall not specify in a contribution notice a weekly sum greater than that which the authority considers—

(a) it would normally be prepared to pay if it had placed a similar child with authority foster parents; and

(b) it is reasonably practicable for the contributor to pay (having regard to his means).

(6) An authority may at any time withdraw a contribution notice (without prejudice to the authority's power to serve another).

(7) Where the authority and the contributor agree—

(a) the sum which the contributor is to contribute; and

(b) arrangements for payment,

(whether as specified in the contribution notice or otherwise) and the contributor notifies the authority in writing that he so agrees, the authority may recover summarily as a civil debt any contribution which is overdue and unpaid.

(8) A contributor may, by serving a notice in writing on the authority, withdraw his agreement in relation to any period of liability falling after the date of service of the notice.

(9) Paragraph (7) is without prejudice to any other method of recovery.

Contribution orders

41.—(1) Where a contributor has been served with a contribution notice and has—

(a) failed to reach any agreement with the authority as mentioned in Article 40(7) within the period of one month beginning with the day on which the contribution notice was served; or

(b) served a notice under Article 40(8) withdrawing his agreement,

the authority may apply to the court for an order under this Article.

(2) On such an application the court may make an order (a "contribution order") requiring the contributor to contribute a weekly sum towards the child's maintenance in accordance with arrangements for payment specified by the court.

(3) A contribution order—

(a) shall not specify a weekly sum greater than that specified in the contribution notice; and

(b) shall be made with due regard to the contributor's means.

41

(4) A contribution order shall not—

(*a*) take effect before the date specified in the contribution notice; or

(*b*) have effect while the contributor is not liable to contribute (by virtue of Article 39); or

(*c*) remain in force after the child has ceased to be looked after by the authority which obtained the order.

(5) An authority shall not apply to the court under paragraph (1) in relation to a contribution notice which the authority has withdrawn.

(6) Where—

(*a*) a contribution order is in force;

(*b*) the authority serves another contribution notice; and

(*c*) the contributor and the authority reach an agreement under Article 40(7) in respect of that other contribution notice,

the effect of the agreement shall be to discharge the order from the date on which it is agreed that the agreement shall take effect.

(7) Where an agreement is reached under paragraph (6) the authority shall notify the court—

(*a*) of the agreement; and

(*b*) of the date on which it took effect.

(8) A contribution order may be varied or revoked on the application of the contributor or the authority.

(9) In proceedings for the variation of a contribution order, the authority shall specify—

(*a*) the weekly sum which, having regard to Article 40, the authority proposes that the contributor should contribute under the order as varied; and

(*b*) the proposed arrangements for payment.

(10) Where a contribution order is varied, the order—

(*a*) shall not specify a weekly sum greater than that specified by the authority in the proceedings for variation; and

(*b*) shall be made with due regard to the contributor's means.

(11) An appeal shall lie in accordance with rules of court from any order made under this Article.

Enforcement of contribution orders, etc.

42.—(1) A contribution order shall be an order to which Article 98(11) of the Magistrates' Courts (Northern Ireland) Order 1981 applies.

1981 NI 26

(2) Where a contributor has agreed, or has been ordered, to make contributions to an authority, any other authority within whose area the contributor is for the time being living may—

(a) at the request of the authority which served the contribution notice; and

(b) subject to agreement as to any sum to be deducted in respect of services rendered,

collect from the contributor any contributions due on behalf of the authority which served the notice.

(3) The power to collect sums under paragraph (2) includes power to—

(a) receive and give a discharge from any contributions due; and

(b) (if necessary) enforce payment of any contributions,

even though those contributions may have fallen due at a time when the contributor was living elsewhere.

(4) Any contribution collected under paragraph (2) shall be paid (subject to any agreed deduction) to the authority which served the contribution notice.

(5) In any proceedings under this Article, a document which purports to be—

(a) a copy of an order made by a court under Article 41; and

(b) certified as a true copy by the clerk of the court,

shall be evidence of the order.

(6) In any proceedings under this Article, a certificate which—

(a) purports to be signed by an authorised officer of the authority which obtained the contribution order; and

(b) states that any sum due to the authority under the order is overdue and unpaid,

shall be evidence that the sum is overdue and unpaid.

Regulations

43. The Department may make regulations—

(a) as to the considerations which an authority must take into account in deciding—

(i) whether it is reasonable to recover contributions; and

(ii) what the arrangements for payment should be;

(b) as to the procedures which an authority must follow in reaching agreements with—

(i) contributors (under Articles 40 and 41); and

(ii) any other authority (under Article 42).

Miscellaneous

Secure accommodation

44.—(1) In this Article "secure accommodation" means accommodation provided for the purpose of restricting liberty.

(2) Subject to paragraphs (3) to (10), a child who is being looked after by an authority may not be placed, and, if placed, may not be kept, in secure accommodation unless it appears—

(a) that—

    (i) he has a history of absconding and is likely to abscond from any other description of accommodation; and

    (ii) if he absconds, he is likely to suffer significant harm; or

(b) that if he is kept in any other description of accommodation he is likely to injure himself or other persons.

(3) The Department may by regulations—

(a) specify a maximum period—

    (i) beyond which a child may not be kept in secure accommodation without the authority of the court; and

    (ii) for which the court may authorise a child to be kept in secure accommodation;

(b) empower the court to authorise a child to be kept in secure accommodation for such further period as the regulations may specify; and

(c) provide that an application to the court under this Article shall be made only by an authority.

(4) A court hearing an application under this Article shall determine whether any relevant criteria for keeping a child in secure accommodation are satisfied in his case.

(5) If a court determines that any such criteria are satisfied, it shall make an order authorising the child to be kept in secure accommodation and specifying the maximum period for which he may be so kept.

(6) On any adjournment of the hearing of an application under this Article, a court may make an interim order permitting the child to be kept during the period of the adjournment in secure accommodation.

(7) No court shall exercise the powers conferred by this Article in respect of a child who is not legally represented in that court unless, having been informed of his right to apply for legal aid and having had the opportunity to do so, he refused or failed to apply.

(8) The Department may by regulations provide that—

(a) this Article shall or shall not apply to any description of children specified in the regulations;

(b) this Article shall have effect in relation to children of a description specified in the regulations subject to such modifications as may be so specified;

(c) such other provisions as may be so specified shall have effect for the purpose of determining whether a child of a description specified in the regulations may be placed or kept in secure accommodation.

(9) The giving of an authorisation under this Article shall not prejudice any power of any court to give directions relating to the child to whom the authorisation relates.

(10) This Article is subject to Article 22(2) (power of person with parental responsibility to remove child from accommodation provided by or on behalf of an authority).

Reviews and representations

45.—(1) The Department may make regulations requiring the case of each child who is being looked after by an authority to be reviewed in accordance with the provisions of the regulations.

(2) The regulations may, in particular, make provision—

(*a*) as to the manner in which each case is to be reviewed;

(*b*) as to the considerations to which the authority is to have regard in reviewing each case;

(*c*) as to the time when each case is first to be reviewed and the frequency of subsequent reviews;

(*d*) requiring the authority, before conducting any review, to seek the views of—

(i) the child;

(ii) his parents;

(iii) any person who is not a parent of his but who has parental responsibility for him; and

(iv) any other person whose views the authority considers to be relevant,

including, in particular, the views of those persons in relation to any particular matter which is to be considered in the course of the review;

(*e*) requiring the authority to consider, in the case of a child who is in the care of the authority, whether an application should be made to discharge the care order;

(*f*) requiring the authority to consider, in the case of a child in accommodation provided by the authority, whether the accommodation accords with the requirements of this Part;

(*g*) requiring the authority to inform the child, so far as is reasonably practicable, of any steps he may take under this Order;

(*h*) requiring the authority to make arrangements, including arrangements with such other bodies providing services as it considers appropriate, to implement any decision which it proposes to make in the course, or as a result, of the review;

(*i*) requiring the authority to notify details of the result of the review and of any decision taken by the authority in consequence of the review to—

    (i) the child;

    (ii) his parents;

    (iii) any person who is not a parent of his but who has parental responsibility for him; and

    (iv) any other person who the authority considers ought to be notified;

(*j*) requiring the authority to monitor the arrangements which it has made with a view to ensuring that they comply with the regulations.

(3) Every authority shall establish a procedure for considering any representations (including any complaint) made to it by—

(*a*) any child who is being looked after by the authority or who is not being looked after by the authority but is in need;

(*b*) a parent of his;

(*c*) any person who is not a parent of his but who has parental responsibility for him;

(*d*) any authority foster parent;

(*e*) such other person as the authority considers has a sufficient interest in the child's welfare to warrant his representations being considered by the authority,

about the discharge of any of the authority's functions under this Part in relation to the child.

(4) The procedure shall ensure that at least one person who is not a member or officer of the authority takes part in—

(*a*) the consideration of representations under this Article; and

(*b*) any discussions which are held by the authority about the action (if any) to be taken in relation to the child in the light of those representations;

and the authority may pay him such fee and reasonable expenses as the Department considers appropriate.

(5) In carrying out any consideration of representations under this Article an authority shall comply with any regulations made by the Department for the purpose of regulating the procedure to be followed.

(6) The Department may make regulations requiring an authority to monitor the arrangements that it has made with a view to ensuring that they comply with any regulations made for the purposes of paragraph (5).

(7) Where any representation has been considered under the procedure established by an authority under this Article, the authority shall—

(*a*) have due regard to the findings of those considering the representation; and

(*b*) take such steps as are reasonably practicable to notify (in writing)—

  (i) the person making the representation;

  (ii) the child (if the authority considers that he has sufficient understanding); and

  (iii) such other persons (if any) as appear to the authority to be likely to be affected,

of the authority's decision in the matter and the authority's reasons for taking that decision and of any action which the authority has taken, or proposes to take.

(8) Every authority shall give such publicity to its procedure for considering representations under this Article as the authority considers appropriate.

Co-operation between authorities and other bodies

46.—(1) Where it appears to an authority that any body mentioned in paragraph (3) could, by taking any specified action, help in the exercise of any of the authority's functions under this Part, the authority may request the help of that body, specifying the action.

(2) A body whose help is so requested shall comply with the request if it is compatible with that body's own statutory or other duties and obligations and does not unduly prejudice the discharge of any of its functions.

(3) The bodies are—

  (*a*) any Board;

  (*b*) any education and library board;

  (*c*) any Health and Social Services trust or special agency;

  (*d*) any district council;

  (*e*) the Northern Ireland Housing Executive; and

  (*f*) such other persons as the Department may direct for the purposes of this Article.

(4) Where an authority complies with a request under paragraph (2) in relation to a child or other person who is ordinarily resident within the area of another authority, the first authority may recover any reasonable expenses incurred by it in respect of that child or person from the other authority.

(5) Every authority shall assist any education and library board with the provision of services for any child within the authority's area who has special educational needs.

Consultation with education and library boards

47.—(1) Where—

  (*a*) a child is being looked after by an authority; and

  (*b*) the authority proposes to provide accommodation for him in an establishment at which education is provided for children

PART IV

who are accommodated there,

the authority shall, so far as is reasonably practicable, consult the appropriate education and library board before doing so.

(2) Where any such proposal is carried out, the authority shall, as soon as is reasonably practicable, inform the appropriate education and library board of the arrangements that have been made for the child's accommodation.

(3) Where the child ceases to be accommodated as mentioned in paragraph (1)(b), the authority shall inform the appropriate education and library board.

(4) In this Article "the appropriate education and library board" means—

(a) the education and library board within whose area the establishment is; or

1986 NI 3

(b) in the case of a child who has special educational needs a statement of which is maintained under the Education and Libraries (Northern Ireland) Order 1986, the education and library board which maintains the statement.

Miscellaneous

48.—(1) Nothing in this Part shall affect any duty imposed on an authority by or under any other statutory provision.

(2) Any question arising under Article 21(2), 23(3), 24(6) or 46(4) as to the ordinary residence of a child shall be determined by agreement between the authorities concerned or, in default of agreement, by the Department.

PART V

CARE AND SUPERVISION

Introductory

Interpretation

49.—(1) In this Order—

"care order" means (subject to Article 2(2))—

(a) an order under Article 50(1)(a); and

(b) an interim care order under Article 57;

"supervision order" means—

(a) an order under Article 50(1)(b); and

(b) an interim supervision order under Article 57;

"education supervision order" means an order under Article 55(1).

(2) In this Part "authorised person" means—

(*a*) the National Society for the Prevention of Cruelty to Children and any of its officers; and

(*b*) any person authorised by order of the Department to bring proceedings under Article 50 and any officer of a body which is so authorised.

General

Care orders and supervision orders

50.—(1) On the application of any authority or authorised person, the court may make an order—

(*a*) placing the child with respect to whom the application is made in the care of a designated authority; or

(*b*) putting him under the supervision of a designated authority.

(2) A court may only make a care or a supervision order if it is satisfied—

(*a*) that the child concerned is suffering, or is likely to suffer, significant harm; and

(*b*) that the harm, or likelihood of harm, is attributable to—

(i) the care given to the child, or likely to be given to him if the order were not made, not being what it would be reasonable to expect a parent to give to him; or

(ii) the child's being beyond parental control.

(3) Where the question of whether harm suffered by a child is significant turns on the child's health or development, his health or development shall be compared with that which could reasonably be expected of a similar child.

(4) No care order or supervision order may be made with respect to a child who has reached the age of 17 (or 16, in the case of a child who is married).

(5) An application under this Article may be made on its own or in any other family proceedings.

(6) The court may—

(*a*) on an application for a care order, make a supervision order;

(*b*) on an application for a supervision order, make a care order.

(7) Where an authorised person proposes to make an application under this Article he shall—

(*a*) if it is reasonably practicable to do so; and

(*b*) before making the application,

consult the authority appearing to him to be the authority in whose area the child concerned is ordinarily resident.

(8) An application made by an authorised person shall not be

entertained by the court if, at the time when it is made, the child concerned is—

    (*a*) the subject of an earlier application for a care or a supervision order, which has not been disposed of; or

    (*b*) subject to—

        (i) a care or a supervision order; or

        (ii) a probation order or an order under section 74(1)(*b*) or (*c*) of the Children and Young Persons Act (Northern Ireland) 1968 (power of court to make fit person order or supervision order on finding of guilt).

(9) The authority designated in a care order must be—

    (*a*) the authority within whose area the child is ordinarily resident; or

    (*b*) where the child does not reside in the area of an authority, the authority within whose area any circumstances arose in consequence of which the order is being made.

Timetable for proceedings

51.—(1) A court hearing an application for an order under this Part shall (in the light of any rules made by virtue of paragraph (2))—

    (*a*) draw up a timetable with a view to disposing of the application without delay; and

    (*b*) give such directions as it considers appropriate for the purpose of ensuring, so far as is reasonably practicable, that that timetable is adhered to.

(2) Rules of court may—

    (*a*) specify periods within which specified steps must be taken in relation to such proceedings; and

    (*b*) make other provision with respect to such proceedings for the purpose of ensuring, so far as is reasonably practicable, that they are disposed of without delay.

Care orders

Effect of care order

52.—(1) Where a care order is made with respect to a child the authority designated by the order shall receive him into its care and keep him in its care while the order remains in force.

(2) Where—

    (*a*) a care order has been made with respect to a child on the application of an authorised person; but

    (*b*) the authority designated by the order was not informed that that person proposed to make the application, the child may be kept in the care of that person until received into the care of the authority.

(3) While a care order is in force with respect to a child, the authority designated by the order shall—

(*a*) have parental responsibility for the child; and

(*b*) have the power (subject to paragraphs (4) to (9)) to determine the extent to which a parent or guardian of the child may meet his parental responsibility for the child.

(4) The authority shall not exercise the power in paragraph (3)(*b*) unless it is satisfied that it is necessary to do so in order to safeguard or promote the child's welfare.

(5) Nothing in paragraph (3)(*b*) shall prevent a parent or guardian of the child who has care of him from doing what is reasonable in all the circumstances of the case for the purpose of safeguarding or promoting his welfare.

(6) While a care order is in force with respect to a child, the authority designated by the order shall not—

(*a*) cause the child to be brought up in any religious persuasion other than that in which he would have been brought up if the order had not been made; or

(*b*) have the right—

(i) to consent or refuse to consent to the making of an application with respect to the child under Article 17 of the Adoption Order;

(ii) to agree or refuse to agree to the making of an adoption order, or an order under Article 57 of that Order, with respect to the child; or

(iii) to appoint a guardian for the child.

(7) While a care order is in force with respect to a child, no person may—

(*a*) cause the child to be known by a new surname; or

(*b*) remove him from the United Kingdom,

without either the written consent of every person who has parental responsibility for the child or the leave of the court.

(8) Paragraph (7)(*b*) does not—

(*a*) prevent the removal of such a child, for a period of less than one month, by, or with the written consent of, the authority in whose care he is; or

(*b*) apply to arrangements for such a child to live outside Northern Ireland (which are governed by Article 33).

(9) The power in paragraph (3)(*b*) is subject (in addition to being subject to the provisions of this Article) to any right, duty, power, responsibility or authority which a parent or guardian of the child has in relation to the child and his property by virtue of any other

statutory provision.

Parental contact etc. with children in care

53.—(1) Where a child is in the care of an authority, the authority shall (subject to the provisions of this Article) allow the child reasonable contact with—

 (*a*) his parents;

 (*b*) any guardian of his;

 (*c*) where there was a residence order in force with respect to the child immediately before the care order was made, the person in whose favour the residence order was made; and

 (*d*) where, immediately before the care order was made, a person had care of the child by virtue of an order made in the exercise of the High Court's inherent jurisdiction with respect to children, that person.

(2) On an application made by the authority or the child, the court may make such order as it considers appropriate with respect to the contact which is to be allowed between the child and any named person.

(3) On an application made by—

 (*a*) any person mentioned in sub-paragraphs (*a*) to (*d*) of paragraph (1); or

 (*b*) any person who has obtained the leave of the court to make the application,

the court may make such order as it considers appropriate with respect to the contact which is to be allowed between the child and that person.

(4) On an application made by the authority or the child, the court may make an order authorising the authority to refuse to allow contact between the child and any person who is mentioned in sub-paragraphs (*a*) to (*d*) of paragraph (1) and named in the order.

(5) When making a care order with respect to a child, or in any family proceedings in connection with a child who is in the care of an authority, the court may make an order under this Article, even though no application for such an order has been made with respect to the child, if the court considers that the order should be made.

(6) An authority may refuse to allow the contact that would otherwise be required by virtue of paragraph (1) or an order under this Article if—

 (*a*) the authority is satisfied that it is necessary to do so in order to safeguard or promote the child's welfare; and

 (*b*) the refusal—

  (i) is decided upon as a matter of urgency; and

  (ii) does not last for more than seven days.

(7) An order under this Article may impose such conditions as the court considers appropriate.

(8) The Department may by regulations make provision as to—

(a) the steps to be taken by an authority which has exercised its powers under paragraph (6);

(b) the circumstances in which, and conditions subject to which, the terms of any order under this Article may be departed from by agreement between the authority and the person in relation to whom the order is made;

(c) notification by an authority of any variation or suspension of arrangements made (otherwise than under an order under this Article) with a view to affording any person contact with a child to whom this Article applies.

(9) The court may vary or discharge any order made under this Article on the application of the authority, the child concerned or the person named in the order.

(10) An order under this Article may be made either at the same time as the care order itself or later.

(11) Before making a care order with respect to any child the court shall—

(a) consider the arrangements which the authority has made, or proposes to make, for affording any person contact with a child to whom this Article applies; and

(b) invite the parties to the proceedings to comment on those arrangements.

Supervision orders

Supervision orders

54.—(1) While a supervision order is in force the supervisor shall—

(a) advise, assist and befriend the supervised child;

(b) take such steps as are reasonably necessary to give effect to the order; and

(c) where—

(i) the order is not wholly complied with; or

(ii) the supervisor considers that the order may no longer be necessary,

consider whether or not to apply to the court for its variation or discharge.

(2) Schedule 3 (which makes further provision with respect to supervision orders) shall have effect.

Education supervision orders

55.—(1) On the application of any education and library board, the court may make an order putting the child with respect to whom the application is made under the supervision of a designated education and library board ("an education supervision order").

(2) A court may only make an education supervision order if it is satisfied that the child concerned is of compulsory school age and is not being properly educated.

(3) For the purposes of this Article, a child is being properly educated only if he is receiving efficient full-time education suitable to his age, ability and aptitude and to any special educational needs he may have.

(4) Where a child is—

(*a*) the subject of a school attendance order which is in force under Part I of Schedule 13 to the Education and Libraries (Northern Ireland) Order 1986 and which has not been complied with; or

1986 NI 3

(*b*) a registered pupil at a school which he is not attending regularly within the meaning of Part II of that Schedule,

then, unless it is proved that he is being properly educated, it shall be assumed that he is not.

(5) An education supervision order may not be made with respect to a child who is in the care of an authority.

(6) The education and library board designated in an education supervision order must be—

(*a*) the education and library board within whose area the child concerned is living or will live; or

(*b*) where—

(i) the child is a registered pupil at a school; and

(ii) the education and library board mentioned in sub-paragraph (*a*) and the education and library board within whose area the school is situated agree,

the latter board.

(7) Where an education and library board proposes to make an application for an education supervision order it shall, before making the application, consult—

(*a*) in the case of a child who is being provided with accommodation by, or on behalf of, an authority, that authority; and

(*b*) in any other case, the authority within whose area the child concerned lives, or will live.

(8) Schedule 4 (which makes further provision with respect to

education supervision orders) shall have effect.

Powers of court

Investigation into child's circumstances

56.—(1) Where, in any family proceedings in which a question arises with respect to the welfare of any child, it appears to the court that it may be appropriate for a care or a supervision order to be made with respect to him, the court may direct the appropriate authority to undertake an investigation of the child's circumstances.

(2) Where the court gives a direction under this Article the authority concerned shall, when undertaking the investigation, consider whether it should—

(a) apply for a care or a supervision order with respect to the child;

(b) provide services or assistance for the child or his family; or

(c) take any other action with respect to the child.

(3) Where an authority undertakes an investigation under this Article, and decides not to apply for a care or a supervision order with respect to the child concerned, the authority shall inform the court of—

(a) its reasons for so deciding;

(b) any service or assistance which the authority has provided, or intends to provide, for the child and his family; and

(c) any other action which the authority has taken, or proposes to take, with respect to the child.

(4) The information shall be given to the court before the end of the period of eight weeks beginning with the date of the direction, unless the court otherwise directs.

(5) The authority named in a direction under paragraph (1) must be—

(a) the authority in whose area the child is ordinarily resident; or

(b) where the child is not ordinarily resident in the area of an authority, the authority within whose area any circumstances arose in consequence of which the direction is being given.

(6) If, on the conclusion of any investigation or review under this Article, the authority decides not to apply for a care or a supervision order with respect to the child—

(a) the authority shall consider whether it would be appropriate to review the case at a later date; and

(b) if the authority decides that it would be, the authority shall determine the date on which that review is to begin.

Interim orders

57.—(1) Where—

(a) in any proceedings on an application for a care or a supervision order, the proceedings are adjourned; or

(b) the court gives a direction under Article 56(1),

the court may make an interim care order or an interim supervision order with respect to the child concerned.

(2) A court shall not make an interim care order or interim supervision order under this Article unless it is satisfied that there are reasonable grounds for believing that the circumstances with respect to the child are as mentioned in Article 50(2).

(3) Where, in any proceedings on an application for a care or a supervision order, a court makes a residence order with respect to the child concerned, it shall also make an interim supervision order with respect to him unless it is satisfied that his welfare will be satisfactorily safeguarded without an interim supervision order being made.

(4) An interim order made under this Article shall have effect for such period as may be specified in the order, but shall in any event cease to have effect on whichever of the following first occurs—

(a) the expiry of the period of eight weeks beginning with the date on which the order is made;

(b) if the order is the second or subsequent such order made with respect to the same child in the same proceedings, the expiry of the relevant period;

(c) in a case which falls within paragraph (1)(a), the disposal of the application;

(d) in a case which falls within paragraph (1)(b), the disposal of an application for a care or a supervision order made by the authority with respect to the child;

(e) in a case which falls within paragraph (1)(b) and in which—

(i) the court has given a direction under Article 56(4), but

(ii) no application for a care or a supervision order has been made with respect to the child,

the expiry of the period fixed by that direction.

(5) In paragraph (4)(b) "the relevant period" means—

(a) the period of four weeks beginning with the date on which the order in question is made; or

(b) the period of eight weeks beginning with the date on which the first order was made if that period ends later than the period mentioned in sub-paragraph (a).

(6) Where the court makes an interim care order or interim supervision order, it may give such directions (if any) as it considers

appropriate with regard to the medical or psychiatric examination or other assessment of the child; but if the child is of sufficient understanding to make an informed decision he may refuse to submit to the examination or other assessment.

(7) A direction under paragraph (6) may be to the effect that there is to be—

(*a*) no such examination or assessment; or

(*b*) no such examination or assessment unless the court directs otherwise.

(8) A direction under paragraph (6) may be—

(*a*) given when the interim order is made or at any time while it is in force; and

(*b*) varied at any time on the application of any person falling within any class of person prescribed by rules of court for the purposes of this paragraph.

(9) Paragraphs 4 and 5 of Schedule 3 shall not apply in relation to an interim supervision order.

(10) Where a court makes an order under this Article it shall, in determining the period for which the order is to be in force, consider whether any party who was, or might have been, opposed to the making of the order was in a position to argue his case against the order in full.

Discharge and variation, etc., of care orders and supervision orders

58.—(1) A care order may be discharged by the court on the application of—

(*a*) any person who has parental responsibility for the child;

(*b*) the child himself; or

(*c*) the authority designated by the order.

(2) A supervision order may be varied or discharged by the court on the application of—

(*a*) any person who has parental responsibility for the child;

(*b*) the child himself; or

(*c*) the supervisor.

(3) On the application of a person who is not entitled to apply for the order to be discharged, but who is a person with whom the child is living, a supervision order may be varied by the court in so far as it imposes a requirement which affects that person.

(4) Where a care order is in force with respect to a child the court may, on the application of any person entitled to apply for the order to be discharged, substitute a supervision order for the care order.

(5) When a court is considering whether to substitute one order for another under paragraph (4) any provision of this Order which would otherwise require Article 50(2) to be satisfied at the time when the proposed order is substituted or made shall be disregarded.

Orders pending appeals in cases about care or supervision orders

59.—(1) Where—

  (*a*) a court dismisses an application for a care order; and

  (*b*) at the time when the court dismisses the application, the child concerned is the subject of an interim care order,

the court may make a care order with respect to the child to have effect subject to such directions (if any) as the court may see fit to include in the order.

(2) Where—

  (*a*) a court dismisses an application for a care order, or an application for a supervision order; and

  (*b*) at the time when the court dismisses the application, the child concerned is the subject of an interim supervision order,

the court may make a supervision order with respect to the child to have effect subject to such directions (if any) as the court may see fit to include in the order.

(3) Where a court grants an application to discharge a care or a supervision order, it may order that—

  (*a*) its decision is not to have effect; or

  (*b*) the care order, or supervision order, is to continue to have effect but subject to such directions as the court sees fit to include in the order.

(4) An order made under this Article shall only have effect for such period, not exceeding the appeal period, as may be specified in the order.

(5) Where—

  (*a*) an appeal is made against any decision of a court under this Article; or

  (*b*) any application is made to the appellate court in connection with a proposed appeal against that decision,

the appellate court may extend the period for which the order in question is to have effect, but not so as to extend it beyond the end of the appeal period.

(6) In this Article "the appeal period" means—

  (*a*) where an appeal is made against the decision in question, the period between the making of that decision and the determination of the appeal; and

  (*b*) otherwise, the period during which an appeal may be made against the decision.

Guardians ad litem

Representation of child and of his interests in certain proceedings

60.—(1) For the purpose of any specified proceedings, the court shall appoint a guardian ad litem for the child concerned unless satisfied that it is not necessary to do so in order to safeguard his interests.

(2) The guardian ad litem shall—
- (*a*) be appointed in accordance with rules of court; and
- (*b*) be under a duty to safeguard the interests of the child in the manner prescribed by such rules.

(3) Where—
- (*a*) the child concerned is not represented by a solicitor; and
- (*b*) any of the conditions mentioned in paragraph (4) is satisfied,

the court may appoint a solicitor to represent him.

(4) The conditions are that—
- (*a*) no guardian ad litem has been appointed for the child;
- (*b*) the child has sufficient understanding to instruct a solicitor and wishes to do so;
- (*c*) it appears to the court that it would be in the child's best interests for him to be represented by a solicitor.

(5) Any solicitor appointed under this Article shall be appointed, and shall represent the child, in accordance with rules of court.

(6) In this Article "specified proceedings" means any proceedings—
- (*a*) on an application for a care or a supervision order;
- (*b*) in which the court has given a direction under Article 56(1) and has made, or is considering whether to make, an interim care order;
- (*c*) on an application for the discharge of a care order or the variation or discharge of a supervision order;
- (*d*) on an application under Article 58(4);
- (*e*) in which the court is considering whether to make a residence order with respect to a child who is the subject of a care order;
- (*f*) with respect to contact between a child who is the subject of a care order and any other person;
- (*g*) under Part VI;
- (*h*) on an appeal against—
  - (i) the making of, or refusal to make, a care order, supervision order or any order under Article 53;
  - (ii) the making of, or refusal to make, a residence order with respect to a child who is the subject of a care order; or

(iii) the variation or discharge, or refusal of an application to vary or discharge, an order of a kind mentioned in head (i) or (ii);

(iv) the refusal of an application under Article 58(4); or

(v) the making of, or refusal to make, an order under Part VI; or

(*i*) which are specified, for the purposes of this Article, by rules of court.

(7) The Department may by regulations provide for the establishment of panels of persons from whom guardians ad litem appointed under this Article must be selected.

(8) Paragraph (7) shall not be taken to prejudice the power of the Lord Chancellor to confer or impose duties on the Official Solicitor under section 75(2) of the Judicature (Northern Ireland) Act 1978.

1978 c. 23

(9) The regulations may, in particular, make provision—

(*a*) for the constitution, administration and procedures of panels and for the appointment of panel managers;

(*b*) for the defrayment of expenses and for the payment of fees and allowances;

(*c*) as to the qualifications for appointment as a guardian ad litem;

(*d*) as to the training to be given to guardians ad litem or to persons with a view to their appointment as guardians ad litem; and

(*e*) for monitoring the work of guardians ad litem.

(10) Rules of court may make provision as to—

(*a*) the assistance which any guardian ad litem may be required by the court to give to it;

(*b*) the consideration to be given by any guardian ad litem, where an order of a specified kind has been made in the proceedings in question, as to whether to apply for the variation or discharge of the order;

(*c*) the participation of guardians ad litem in reviews, of a kind specified in the rules, which are conducted by the court.

(11) Regardless of any statutory provision or rule of law which would otherwise prevent it from doing so, the court may take account of—

(*a*) any statement contained in a report made by a guardian ad litem who is appointed under this Article for the purpose of the proceedings in question; and

(*b*) any evidence given in respect of the matters referred to in the report,

in so far as the statement or evidence is, in the opinion of the court, relevant to the question which the court is considering.

(12) The Department may, with the approval of the Department of Finance and Personnel, make such grants as the Department considers appropriate with respect to expenditure incurred under regulations made under paragraph (7).

Right of guardian ad litem to have access to records

61.—(1) Where a person has been appointed as a guardian ad litem under this Order he shall have the right at all reasonable times to examine and take copies of—

(a) any records of, or held by, an authority or an authorised person which were compiled in connection with the making, or proposed making, by any person of any application under this Order with respect to the child concerned;

(b) any records of, or held by, an authority which were compiled in connection with any relevant functions, so far as those records relate to that child; or

(c) any records of, or held by, an authorised person which were compiled in connection with the activities of that person, so far as those records relate to that child.

(2) In paragraph (1) "relevant functions" means personal social services functions (including functions exercisable on behalf of the Department by virtue of directions under Article 17(1) of the Health and Personal Social Services (Northern Ireland) Order 1972). 1972 NI 14

(3) Where a guardian ad litem takes a copy of any record which he is entitled to examine under this Article, that copy or any part of it shall be admissible as evidence of any matter referred to in any—

(a) report which he makes to the court in the proceedings in question; or

(b) evidence which he gives in those proceedings.

(4) Paragraph (3) has effect regardless of any statutory provision or rule of law which would otherwise prevent the record in question being admissible in evidence.

PART VI

PROTECTION OF CHILDREN

Child assessment orders

62.—(1) On the application of an authority or an authorised person for an order to be made under this Article with respect to a child, the court may make the order if, but only if, it is satisfied that—

(a) the applicant has reasonable cause to suspect that the child is suffering, or is likely to suffer, significant harm;

(b) an assessment of the state of the child's health or development, or of the way in which he has been treated, is required to enable the applicant to determine whether or not the child is suffering, or is likely to suffer, significant harm; and

(c) it is unlikely that such an assessment will be made, or be satisfactory, in the absence of an order under this Article.

(2) In this Order "child assessment order" means an order under this Article.

(3) A court may treat an application under this Article as an application for an emergency protection order.

(4) No court shall make a child assessment order if it is satisfied—

(a) that there are grounds for making an emergency protection order with respect to the child; and

(b) that it ought to make such an order rather than a child assessment order.

(5) A child assessment order shall—

(a) specify the date by which the assessment is to begin; and

(b) have effect for such period, not exceeding seven days beginning with that date, as may be specified in the order.

(6) Where a child assessment order is in force with respect to a child it shall be the duty of any person who is in a position to produce the child—

(a) to produce him to such person as may be named in the order; and

(b) to comply with such directions relating to the assessment of the child as the court thinks fit to specify in the order.

(7) A child assessment order authorises any person carrying out the assessment, or any part of the assessment, to do so in accordance with the terms of the order.

(8) Regardless of paragraph (7), if the child is of sufficient understanding to make an informed decision he may refuse to submit to a medical or psychiatric examination or other assessment.

(9) The child may only be kept away from home—

(a) in accordance with directions specified in the order;

(b) if it is necessary for the purposes of the assessment; and

(c) for such period or periods as may be specified in the order.

(10) Where the child is to be kept away from home, the order shall contain such directions as the court thinks fit with regard to the contact that he must be allowed to have with other persons while away from home.

(11) Any person making an application for a child assessment order shall take such steps as are reasonably practicable to ensure that notice of the application is given to—

(a) the child's parents;

(b) any person who is not a parent of his but who has parental responsibility for him;

(c) any other person caring for the child;

(d) any person in whose favour a contact order is in force with respect to the child;

(e) any person who is allowed to have contact with the child by virtue of an order under Article 53; and

(f) the child,

before the hearing of the application.

(12) Rules of court may make provision as to the circumstances in which—

(a) any of the persons mentioned in paragraph (11); or

(b) such other person as may be specified in the rules,

may apply to the court for a child assessment order to be varied or discharged.

(13) In this Article "authorised person" means a person who is an authorised person for the purposes of Part V.

Orders for emergency protection of children

63.—(1) Where any person ("the applicant") applies to the court for an order to be made under this Article with respect to a child, the court may make the order if, but only if, it is satisfied that—

(a) there is reasonable cause to believe that the child is likely to suffer significant harm if—

(i) he is not removed to accommodation provided by or on behalf of the applicant; or

(ii) he does not remain in the place in which he is then being accommodated; or

(b) in the case of an application made by an authority—

(i) inquiries are being made with respect to the child under Article 66(1)(b); and

(ii) those inquiries are being frustrated by access to the child being unreasonably refused to a person authorised to seek access and the applicant has reasonable cause to believe that access to the child is required as a matter of urgency; or

(c) in the case of an application made by an authorised person—

(i) the applicant has reasonable cause to suspect that a child is suffering, or is likely to suffer, significant harm;

(ii) the applicant is making inquiries with respect to the child's welfare; and

(iii) those inquiries are being frustrated by access to the child being unreasonably refused to a person authorised to seek access and the applicant has reasonable cause to believe that access to the child is required as a matter of urgency.

(2) In this Article—

(a) "authorised person" means a person who is an authorised person for the purposes of Part V; and

(b) "person authorised to seek access" means—

(i) in the case of an application by an authority, an officer of the authority or a person authorised by the authority to act on its behalf in connection with the inquiries; or

(ii) in the case of an application by an authorised person, that person.

(3) Any person—

(a) seeking access to a child in connection with inquiries of a kind mentioned in paragraph (1); and

(b) purporting to be a person authorised to do so,

shall, on being asked to do so, produce some duly authenticated document as evidence that he is such a person.

(4) While an order under this Article (an "emergency protection order") is in force it—

(a) operates as a direction to any person who is in a position to do so to comply with any request to produce the child to the applicant;

(b) authorises—

(i) the removal of the child at any time to accommodation provided by or on behalf of the applicant and his being kept there; or

(ii) the prevention of the child's removal from any hospital, or other place, in which he was being accommodated immediately before the making of the order; and

(c) gives the applicant parental responsibility for the child.

(5) Where an emergency protection order is in force with respect to a child, the applicant—

(a) shall only exercise the power given by virtue of paragraph (4)(b) in order to safeguard the welfare of the child;

(b) shall take, and shall only take, such action in meeting his parental responsibility for the child as is reasonably required to safeguard or promote the welfare of the child (having regard in particular to the duration of the order); and

(c) shall comply with the requirements of any regulations made by the Department for the purposes of this paragraph.

(6) Where the court makes an emergency protection order, it may give such directions (if any) as it considers appropriate with respect to—

(a) the contact which is, or is not, to be allowed between the child and any named person;

(b) the medical or psychiatric examination or other assessment

64

of the child.

(7) Where any direction is given under paragraph (6)(*b*), the child may, if he is of sufficient understanding to make an informed decision, refuse to submit to the examination or other assessment.

(8) A direction under paragraph (6)(*a*) may impose conditions and one under paragraph (6)(*b*) may be to the effect that there is to be—

(*a*) no such examination or assessment; or

(*b*) no such examination or assessment unless the court directs otherwise.

(9) A direction under paragraph (6) may be—

(*a*) given when the emergency protection order is made or at any time while it is in force; and

(*b*) varied at any time on the application of any person falling within any class of person prescribed by rules of court for the purposes of this paragraph.

(10) Where an emergency protection order is in force with respect to a child and—

(*a*) the applicant has exercised the power given by paragraph (4)(*b*)(i) but it appears to him that it is safe for the child to be returned; or

(*b*) the applicant has exercised the power given by paragraph (4)(*b*)(ii) but it appears to him that it is safe for the child to be allowed to be removed from the place in question,

he shall return the child or (as the case may be) allow him to be removed.

(11) Where he is required by paragraph (10) to return the child the applicant shall—

(*a*) return him to the care of the person from whose care he was removed; or

(*b*) if that is not reasonably practicable, return him to the care of—

(i) a parent of his;

(ii) any person who is not a parent of his but who has parental responsibility for him; or

(iii) such other person as the applicant (with the agreement of the court) considers appropriate.

(12) Where the applicant has been required by paragraph (10) to return the child, or to allow him to be removed, he may again exercise his powers with respect to the child (at any time while the emergency protection order remains in force) if it appears to him that a change in the circumstances of the case makes it necessary for him to do so.

(13) Where an emergency protection order has been made with respect to a child, the applicant shall, subject to any direction given

under paragraph (6), allow the child reasonable contact with—

(a) his parents;

(b) any person who is not a parent of his but who has parental responsibility for him;

(c) any person with whom he was living immediately before the making of the order;

(d) any person in whose favour a contact order is in force with respect to him;

(e) any person who is allowed to have contact with the child by virtue of an order under Article 53; and

(f) any person acting on behalf of any of those persons.

(14) Wherever it is reasonably practicable to do so, an emergency protection order shall name the child; and where it does not name him it shall describe him as clearly as possible.

(15) A person shall be guilty of an offence if he intentionally obstructs any person exercising the power under paragraph (4)(b) to remove, or prevent the removal of, a child.

(16) A person guilty of an offence under paragraph (15) shall be liable on summary conviction to a fine not exceeding level 3 on the standard scale.

Duration of emergency protection orders and other supplementary provisions

64.—(1) An emergency protection order shall have effect for such period, not exceeding eight days, as may be specified in the order.

(2) Where an emergency protection order is made with respect to a child who is being kept in police protection under Article 65, the period of eight days mentioned in paragraph (1) shall begin with the first day on which he was taken into police protection under that Article.

(3) Any person who—

(a) has parental responsibility for a child as the result of an emergency protection order; and

(b) is entitled to apply for a care order with respect to the child,

may apply to the court for the period during which the emergency protection order is to have effect to be extended.

(4) On an application under paragraph (3) the court may extend the period during which the order is to have effect by such period, not exceeding seven days, as it thinks fit, but may do so only if it has reasonable cause to believe that the child concerned is likely to suffer significant harm if the order is not extended.

(5) An emergency protection order may only be extended once.

(6) Regardless of any statutory provision or rule of law which would otherwise prevent it from doing so, a court hearing an applica-

tion for, or with respect to, an emergency protection order may take account of—

(a) any statement contained in any report made to the court in the course of, or in connection with, the hearing; or

(b) any evidence given during the hearing,

which is, in the opinion of the court, relevant to the application.

(7) Any of the following may apply to the court for an emergency protection order to be discharged—

(a) the child;

(b) a parent of his;

(c) any person who is not a parent of his but who has parental responsibility for him; or

(d) any person with whom he was living immediately before the making of the order.

(8) No application for the discharge of an emergency protection order shall be heard by the court before the expiry of the period of 72 hours beginning with the making of the order.

(9) No appeal may be made against—

(a) the making of, or refusal to make, an emergency protection order;

(b) the extension of, or refusal to extend, the period during which such an order is to have effect;

(c) the discharge of, or refusal to discharge, such an order; or

(d) the giving of, or refusal to give, any direction in connection with such an order.

(10) Paragraph (7) does not apply—

(a) where the person who would otherwise be entitled to apply for the emergency protection order to be discharged—

(i) was given notice (in accordance with rules of court) of the hearing at which the order was made; and

(ii) was present at that hearing; or

(b) to any emergency protection order the effective period of which has been extended under paragraph (4).

(11) A court making an emergency protection order may direct that the applicant may, in exercising any powers which he has by virtue of the order, be accompanied by a medical practitioner, registered nurse or registered health visitor, if he so chooses.

(12) An emergency protection order may, notwithstanding section 7 of the Sunday Observance Act (Ireland) 1695, be served and executed on a Sunday.

1695 c. 17 (I)

Removal and accommodation of children by police in cases of emergency

65.—(1) Where a constable has reasonable cause to believe that a child would otherwise be likely to suffer significant harm, he may—

(a) remove the child to suitable accommodation and keep him there; or

(b) take such steps as are reasonable to ensure that the child's removal from any hospital, or other place, in which he is then being accommodated is prevented.

(2) For the purposes of this Order, a child with respect to whom a constable has exercised his powers under this Article is referred to as having been taken into police protection.

(3) As soon as is reasonably practicable after taking a child into police protection, the constable shall secure that the case is inquired into by a designated officer.

(4) In this Article "designated officer" means a police officer designated for the purposes of this Article—

(a) by the Chief Constable; or

(b) by such other police officer as the Chief Constable may direct.

(5) As soon as is reasonably practicable after a child has been taken into police protection, the designated officer shall—

(a) inform the authority within whose area the child was found of the steps that have been, and are proposed to be, taken with respect to the child under this Article and the reasons for taking them;

(b) give details to the authority within whose area the child is ordinarily resident ("the appropriate authority") of the place at which the child is being accommodated;

(c) inform the child (if he appears capable of understanding)—

(i) of the steps that have been taken with respect to him under this Article and of the reasons for taking them; and

(ii) of the further steps that may be taken with respect to him under this Article;

(d) take such steps as are reasonably practicable to discover the wishes and feelings of the child; and

(e) where the child was taken into police protection by being removed to accommodation which is not provided—

(i) by or on behalf of an authority; or

(ii) as a refuge, in compliance with the requirements of Article 70,

secure that he is moved to accommodation which is so provided.

(6) As soon as is reasonably practicable after a child has been taken into police protection, the designated officer shall take such steps as are reasonably practicable to inform—

(a) the child's parents;

(b) every person who is not a parent of his but who has parental responsibility for him; and

(c) any other person with whom the child was living immediately before being taken into police protection,

of the steps that have been taken under this Article with respect to the child, the reasons for taking them and the further steps that may be taken with respect to him under this Article.

(7) On completing any inquiry under paragraph (3), the designated officer shall release the child from police protection unless he considers that there is still reasonable cause for believing that the child would be likely to suffer significant harm if released.

(8) No child may be kept in police protection for more than 72 hours.

(9) While a child is being kept in police protection—

(a) neither the constable referred to in paragraph (1) nor the designated officer shall have parental responsibility for him; but

(b) the designated officer shall do what is reasonable in all the circumstances of the case for the purpose of safeguarding or promoting the child's welfare (having regard in particular to the length of the period during which the child will be so protected).

(10) Where a child has been taken into police protection, the designated officer shall allow—

(a) the child's parents;

(b) any person who is not a parent of the child but who has parental responsibility for him;

(c) any person with whom the child was living immediately before he was taken into police protection;

(d) any person in whose favour a contact order is in force with respect to the child;

(e) any person who is allowed to have contact with the child by virtue of an order under Article 53; and

(f) any person acting on behalf of any of those persons,

to have such contact (if any) with the child as, in the opinion of the designated officer, is both reasonable and in the child's best interests.

(11) Where a child who has been taken into police protection is in accommodation provided by, or on behalf of, the appropriate authority, paragraph (10) shall have effect as if it referred to the authority rather than to the designated officer.

Authority's duty to investigate

66.—(1) Where an authority—

(a) is informed that a child who lives, or is found, in the

authority's area—

(i) is the subject of an emergency protection order; or

(ii) is in police protection; or

(b) has reasonable cause to suspect that a child who lives, or is found, in the authority's area is suffering, or is likely to suffer, significant harm,

the authority shall make, or cause to be made, such inquiries as it considers necessary to enable it to decide whether it should take any action to safeguard or promote the child's welfare.

(2) Where an authority has obtained an emergency protection order with respect to a child, the authority shall make, or cause to be made, such inquiries as it considers necessary to enable it to decide what action it should take to safeguard or promote the child's welfare.

(3) The inquiries shall, in particular, be directed towards establishing—

(a) whether the authority should make any application to the court, or exercise any of the authority's other powers under this Order, with respect to the child; and

(b) whether, in the case of a child—

(i) with respect to whom an emergency protection order has been made; and

(ii) who is not in accommodation provided by or on behalf of the authority,

it would be in the child's best interests (while the emergency protection order remains in force) for him to be in such accommodation.

(4) Where inquiries are being made under paragraph (1) with respect to a child, the authority shall (with a view to enabling it to determine what action, if any, to take with respect to him) take such steps as are reasonably practicable—

(a) to obtain access to him; or

(b) to ensure that access to him is obtained, on the authority's behalf, by a person authorised by the authority for the purpose,

unless the authority is satisfied that it already has sufficient information with respect to the child.

(5) Where, as a result of any such inquiries, it appears to the authority that there are matters connected with the child's education which should be investigated, the authority shall consult the relevant education and library board.

(6) Where, in the course of inquiries made under this Article, any officer of the authority or any person authorised by the authority to act on its behalf in connection with those inquiries—

(*a*) is refused access to the child concerned; or

(*b*) is denied information as to the child's whereabouts,

the authority shall apply for an emergency protection order, a child assessment order, a care order or a supervision order with respect to the child unless it is satisfied that his welfare can be satisfactorily safeguarded without the authority's doing so.

(7) If, on the conclusion of any inquiries or review made under this Article, the authority decides not to apply for an emergency protection order, a child assessment order, a care order or a supervision order the authority shall—

(*a*) consider whether it would be appropriate to review the case at a later date; and

(*b*) if the authority decides that it would be, determine the date on which that review is to begin.

(8) Where, as a result of complying with this Article, an authority concludes that it should take action to safeguard or promote the child's welfare the authority shall take that action (so far as it is both within the power of the authority and reasonably practicable for it to do so).

(9) Where an authority is conducting inquiries under this Article, it shall be the duty of anyone to whom this paragraph applies to assist the authority with those inquiries (in particular by providing relevant information and advice) if called upon by the authority to do so.

(10) Paragraph (9) does not oblige anyone to assist an authority where to do so would be unreasonable in all the circumstances of the case.

(11) Paragraph (9) applies to—

(*a*) any Board;

(*b*) any education and library board;

(*c*) any Health and Social Services trust;

(*d*) the Northern Ireland Housing Executive;

(*e*) any special agency; and

(*f*) such other persons as the Department may direct for the purposes of this Article.

(12) Where an authority is making inquiries under this Article with respect to a child who appears to the authority to be ordinarily resident within the area of another authority, the authority shall consult that other authority, which may undertake the necessary inquiries in its place.

Powers to assist in discovery of children who may be in need of emergency protection

67.—(1) Where it appears to a court making an emergency protection order that adequate information as to the child's whereabouts—

(a) is not available to the applicant for the order; but

(b) is available to another person,

it may include in the order a provision requiring that other person to disclose, if asked to do so by the applicant, any information that he may have as to the child's whereabouts.

(2) No person shall be excused from complying with such a requirement on the ground that complying might incriminate him or his spouse of an offence; but a statement or admission made in complying shall not be admissible in evidence against either of them in proceedings for any offence other than perjury.

(3) An emergency protection order may authorise the applicant to enter premises specified by the order and search for the child with respect to whom the order is made.

(4) Where the court is satisfied that there is reasonable cause to believe that there may be another child on those premises with respect to whom an emergency protection order ought to be made, it may make an order authorising the applicant to search for that other child on those premises.

(5) Where—

(a) an order has been made under paragraph (4);

(b) the child concerned has been found on the premises; and

(c) the applicant is satisfied that the grounds for making an emergency protection order exist with respect to him,

the order shall have effect as if it were an emergency protection order.

(6) Where an order has been made under paragraph (4), the applicant shall notify the court of its effect.

(7) A person shall be guilty of an offence if he intentionally obstructs any person exercising the power of entry and search under paragraph (3) or (4).

(8) A person guilty of an offence under paragraph (7) shall be liable on summary conviction to a fine not exceeding level 3 on the standard scale.

(9) Where, on an application made by any person for a warrant under this Article, it appears to the court—

(a) that a person attempting to exercise powers under an emergency protection order has been prevented from doing so by being refused entry to the premises concerned or access to the child concerned; or

(b) that any such person is likely to be so prevented from exercising any such powers,

it may issue a warrant authorising any constable to assist the person mentioned in sub-paragraph (a) or (b) in the exercise of those powers, using reasonable force if necessary.

(10) Every warrant issued under this Article shall be addressed to, and executed by, a constable who shall be accompanied by the person applying for the warrant if—

(*a*) that person so desires; and

(*b*) the court by whom the warrant is issued does not direct otherwise.

(11) A court granting an application for a warrant under this Article may direct that the constable may, in executing the warrant, be accompanied by a medical practitioner, registered nurse or registered health visitor if he so chooses.

(12) An application for a warrant under this Article shall be made in the manner and form prescribed by rules of court.

(13) Wherever it is reasonably practicable to do so, an order under paragraph (4), an application for a warrant under this Article and any such warrant shall name the child; and where it does not name him it shall describe him as clearly as possible.

Abduction of children in care, etc.

68.—(1) A person shall be guilty of an offence if, knowingly and without lawful authority or reasonable excuse, he—

(*a*) takes a child to whom this Article applies away from the responsible person;

(*b*) keeps such a child away from the responsible person; or

(*c*) induces, assists or incites such a child to run away or stay away from the responsible person.

(2) This Article applies in relation to a child who is—

(*a*) in care;

(*b*) the subject of an emergency protection order; or

(*c*) in police protection,

and in this Article "the responsible person" means any person who for the time being has care of him by virtue of the care order, the emergency protection order, or Article 65, as the case may be.

(3) A person guilty of an offence under this Article shall be liable on summary conviction to imprisonment for a term not exceeding six months, or to a fine not exceeding level 5 on the standard scale, or to both.

Recovery of abducted children, etc.

69.—(1) Where it appears to the court that there is reason to believe that a child to whom this Article applies—

(*a*) has been unlawfully taken away or is being unlawfully kept away from the responsible person;

(*b*) has run away or is staying away from the responsible person; or

(*c*) is missing,

the court may make an order under this Article ("a recovery order").

(2) This Article applies to the same children to whom Article 68 applies and in this Article "the responsible person" has the same meaning as in that Article.

(3) A recovery order—

(a) operates as a direction to any person who is in a position to do so to produce the child on request to any authorised person;

(b) authorises the removal of the child by any authorised person;

(c) requires any person who has information as to the child's whereabouts to disclose that information, if asked to do so, to a constable or an officer of the court;

(d) authorises a constable to enter any premises specified in the order and search for the child, using reasonable force if necessary.

(4) The court may make a recovery order only on the application of—

(a) any person who has parental responsibility for the child by virtue of a care order or emergency protection order; or

(b) where the child is in police protection, the designated officer.

(5) A recovery order shall name the child and—

(a) any person who has parental responsibility for the child by virtue of a care order or emergency protection order; or

(b) where the child is in police protection, the designated officer.

(6) Premises may only be specified under paragraph (3)(d) if it appears to the court that there are reasonable grounds for believing the child to be on them.

(7) In this Article—

"authorised person" means—

(a) any person specified by the court;

(b) any constable;

(c) any person who is authorised—

(i) after the recovery order is made; and

(ii) by a person who has parental responsibility for the child by virtue of a care order or an emergency protection order,

to exercise any power under a recovery order; and

"designated officer" means the police officer designated for the purposes of Article 65.

(8) Where a person is authorised as mentioned in paragraph (c) of the definition of "authorised person" in paragraph (7)—

(a) the authorisation shall identify the recovery order; and

(b) any person claiming to be so authorised shall, if asked to do so, produce some duly authenticated document showing that he is so authorised.

(9) A person shall be guilty of an offence if he intentionally obstructs an authorised person exercising the power under paragraph (3)(*b*) to remove a child.

(10) A person guilty of an offence under this Article shall be liable on summary conviction to a fine not exceeding level 3 on the standard scale.

(11) No person shall be excused from complying with any request made under paragraph (3)(*c*) on the ground that complying with it might incriminate him or his spouse of an offence; but a statement or admission made in complying shall not be admissible in evidence against either of them in proceedings for an offence other than perjury.

(12) Where a child is made the subject of a recovery order whilst being looked after by an authority, any reasonable expenses incurred by an authorised person in giving effect to the order shall be recoverable from the authority.

Refuges for children at risk

70.—(1) Where it is proposed to use a voluntary home or a registered children's home to provide a refuge for children who appear to be at risk of harm, the Department may issue a certificate under this Article with respect to that home.

(2) Where an authority or voluntary organisation arranges for a foster parent to provide such a refuge, the Department may issue a certificate under this Article with respect to that foster parent.

(3) In paragraph (2) "foster parent" means a person who is, or who from time to time is, an authority foster parent or a foster parent with whom children are placed by a voluntary organisation.

(4) The Department may by regulations—

    (*a*) make provision as to the manner in which certificates may be issued;

    (*b*) impose requirements which must be complied with while any certificate is in force; and

    (*c*) provide for the withdrawal of certificates in prescribed circumstances.

(5) Where a certificate is in force with respect to a home, none of the provisions mentioned in paragraph (7) shall apply in relation to any person providing a refuge for any child in that home.

(6) Where a certificate is in force with respect to a foster parent, none of the provisions mentioned in paragraph (7) shall apply in relation to the provision by him of a refuge for any child in accordance with arrangements made by the authority or voluntary organisation.

(7) The provisions are—

(*a*) Article 68;

(*b*) sections 140(6) and 144(3) of the Children and Young Persons Act (Northern Ireland) 1968 (escapes from training schools, etc.);

(*c*) section 71 of the Social Work (Scotland) Act 1968 (harbouring children who have absconded from residential establishments etc.), so far as it applies in relation to anything done in Northern Ireland;

(*d*) section 32(3) of the Children and Young Persons Act 1969 (compelling, persuading, inciting or assisting any person to be absent from detention, etc.), so far as it applies in relation to anything done in Northern Ireland;

(*e*) Article 4 of the Child Abduction (Northern Ireland) Order 1985 (abduction of children by persons other than parents, etc.).

Rules of court and regulations

71.—(1) Without prejudice to Article 165 (rules of court) or any other power to make such rules, rules of court may be made with respect to the procedure to be followed in connection with proceedings under this Part.

(2) The rules may, in particular, make provision—

(*a*) as to the form in which any application is to be made or direction is to be given;

(*b*) prescribing the persons who are to be notified of—

(i) the making, or extension, of an emergency protection order; or

(ii) the making of an application under Article 64(3) or (7); and

(*c*) as to the content of any such notification and the manner in which, and person by whom, it is to be given.

(3) The Department may by regulations provide that, where—

(*a*) an emergency protection order has been made with respect to a child;

(*b*) the applicant for the order was not the authority within whose area the child is ordinarily resident; and

(*c*) that authority is of the opinion that it would be in the child's best interests for the applicant's responsibilities under the order to be transferred to it,

that authority shall (subject to its having complied with any requirements imposed by the regulations) be treated, for the purposes of this Order, as though it and not the original applicant had applied for, and been granted, the order.

(4) Regulations made under paragraph (3) may, in particular, make provision as to—

(a) the considerations to which the authority shall have regard in forming an opinion as mentioned in paragraph (3)(c); and

(b) the time at which responsibility under any emergency protection order is to be treated as having been transferred to an authority.

Part VII

HOMES PROVIDED BY AN AUTHORITY

Provision of homes by an authority

72.—(1) Every authority shall, to such extent as it considers appropriate, provide homes—

(a) for the care and accommodation of children looked after by the authority; and

(b) for purposes connected with the welfare of children (whether or not looked after by the authority).

(2) Every authority shall have regard to the need to make different types of provision for different children.

Regulations

73.—(1) The Department may make regulations—

(a) as to the placing of children in homes provided under this Part;

(b) as to the conduct of such homes; and

(c) for securing the welfare of children in such homes.

(2) The regulations may, in particular—

(a) prescribe standards to which the premises used for such homes are to conform;

(b) impose requirements as to the accommodation, staff and equipment to be provided in such homes, and as to the arrangements to be made for protecting the health of children in such homes;

(c) provide for the control and discipline of children in such homes;

(d) impose requirements as to the keeping of records and giving of notices in respect of children in such homes;

(e) impose requirements as to the facilities which are to be provided for giving religious instruction to children in such homes;

(f) authorise the Department to limit the number of children who may be accommodated in any particular home provided under this Part;

(g) provide that, to such extent as may be provided for in the regulations, the Department may in special circumstances direct that any provision of regulations under this Article which is specified in the direction shall not apply in relation to a particular home or the premises used by such a home.

Part VIII

Voluntary homes and voluntary organisations

Introductory

Interpretation

74.—(1) In this Order—

"voluntary home" means, subject to paragraph (2), any home providing care and accommodation for children which is carried on by a voluntary organisation;

"voluntary organisation" means any association carrying on or proposing to carry on any activities otherwise than for the purpose of gain by the association or by individual members.

(2) A home is not a voluntary home if it is—

(a) a registered children's home;

(b) a residential care home;

(c) a hospital (including a private hospital) or nursing home;

(d) a school;

(e) a training school;

(f) used primarily for the accommodation of homeless persons;

(g) used primarily for or in connection with the provision of cultural, recreational, leisure, social or physical activities;

(h) exempted by regulations made by the Department for the purposes of this paragraph.

(3) In this Part—

"home" includes any institution;

"notice" and "notify" mean respectively notice in writing and notify in writing;

"the relevant requirements" means any requirements of this Part and of regulations under Article 89 and any conditions imposed under Article 81.

(4) Any reference in this Part to an authority in relation to a voluntary home is a reference to the authority in whose area the home is, or is to be, situated.

Voluntary organisations

Provision of accommodation for children

75.—(1) A voluntary organisation which provides accommodation for a child shall do so by—

   (*a*) placing him (subject to paragraph (2)) with—

   (i) a family;

   (ii) a relative of his; or

   (iii) any other suitable person,

   on such terms as to payment by the organisation and otherwise as the organisation may determine;

   (*b*) maintaining him in a voluntary home;

   (*c*) maintaining him in a home provided under Part VII;

   (*d*) maintaining him in a registered children's home;

   (*e*) maintaining him in a home provided by the Secretary of State, a government department or a prescribed public body; or

   (*f*) making such other arrangements (subject to paragraph (3)) as seem appropriate to the organisation.

(2) The Department may make regulations as to the placing of children with foster parents by voluntary organisations and the regulations may, in particular, make provision similar to the provision that may be made under Article 27(2)(*a*) (placing of children by an authority).

(3) The Department may make regulations as to the arrangements which may be made under paragraph (1)(*f*) and the regulations may in particular make provision similar to the provision that may be made under Article 27(2)(*f*) (other arrangements made by an authority).

(4) The Department may make regulations requiring any voluntary organisation which is providing accommodation for a child—

   (*a*) to review his case; and

   (*b*) to consider any representations (including any complaint) made to the organisation by any prescribed person,

in accordance with the provisions of the regulations.

(5) Regulations under paragraph (4) may in particular make provision similar to the provision that may be made under Article 45 (reviews where child looked after by an authority).

(6) Regulations under paragraphs (2) to (4) may provide that any person who, without reasonable excuse, contravenes a regulation shall be guilty of an offence and liable on summary conviction to a fine not exceeding level 4 on the standard scale.

Duties of voluntary organisations

76.—(1) Where a child is accommodated by or on behalf of a voluntary organisation, the organisation shall—

(*a*) safeguard and promote his welfare;

(*b*) make such use of the services and facilities available for children cared for by their own parents as appears to the organisation reasonable in his case; and

(*c*) advise, assist and befriend him with a view to promoting his welfare when he ceases to be so accommodated.

(2) Before making any decision with respect to any such child the organisation shall, so far as is reasonably practicable, ascertain the wishes and feelings of—

(*a*) the child;

(*b*) his parents;

(*c*) any person who is not a parent of his but who has parental responsibility for him; and

(*d*) any other person whose wishes and feelings the organisation considers to be relevant,

regarding the matter to be decided.

(3) In making any such decision the organisation shall give due consideration—

(*a*) having regard to the child's age and understanding, to such wishes and feelings of his as the organisation has been able to ascertain;

(*b*) to such other wishes and feelings mentioned in paragraph (2) as the organisation has been able to ascertain; and

(*c*) to the child's religious persuasion, racial origin and cultural and linguistic background.

(4) Every voluntary organisation shall, at such times and in such form as the Department may direct, transmit to the Department such particulars as the Department may require with respect to children accommodated by or on behalf of the voluntary organisation.

Duties of an authority

77.—(1) Every authority shall satisfy itself that any voluntary organisation providing accommodation—

(*a*) within the authority's area for any child; or

(*b*) outside that area for any child on behalf of the authority,

is satisfactorily safeguarding and promoting the welfare of the children so provided with accommodation.

(2) Every authority shall arrange for children who are accommodated within its area by or on behalf of voluntary organisations to be visited in the interests of their welfare.

(3) The Department may make regulations—

(a) requiring every child who is accommodated by or on behalf of a voluntary organisation, to be visited by an officer of the authority—

(i) in prescribed circumstances; and

(ii) on specified occasions or within specified periods; and

(b) imposing requirements which must be met by any authority, or officer of an authority, carrying out functions under this Article.

(4) If an authority is not satisfied that the welfare of any child who is accommodated by or on behalf of a voluntary organisation is being satisfactorily safeguarded or promoted, the authority shall—

(a) unless it considers that it would not be in the best interests of the child, take such steps as are reasonably practicable to secure that the care and accommodation of the child are undertaken by—

(i) a parent of his;

(ii) any person who is not a parent of his but who has parental responsibility for him; or

(iii) a relative of his; and

(b) consider the extent to which (if at all) the authority should exercise any of its functions with respect to the child.

(5) Any person authorised by an authority may for the purpose of enabling the authority to discharge its duties under this Article—

(a) enter at any reasonable time and inspect any premises in which children are being accommodated as mentioned in paragraph (1) or (2);

(b) inspect any children there;

(c) require any person to furnish him with such records of a kind required to be kept by regulations made under Article 89 (in whatever form they are held), or allow him to inspect such records, as he may at any time direct.

(6) Any person exercising the power conferred by paragraph (5) shall, if asked to do so, produce some duly authenticated document showing his authority to do so.

(7) Any person authorised to exercise the power to inspect records conferred by paragraph (5)—

(a) shall be entitled at any reasonable time to have access to, and inspect and check the operation of, any computer and any associated apparatus or material which is or has been in use in connection with the records in question; and

(b) may require—

(i) the person by whom or on whose behalf the computer is or has been so used; or

(ii) any person having charge of, or otherwise concerned with the operation of, the computer, apparatus or material, to afford him such assistance as he may reasonably require.

(8) Any person who intentionally obstructs another in the exercise of any power conferred by paragraph (5) or (7) shall be guilty of an offence and liable on summary conviction to a fine not exceeding level 3 on the standard scale.

Voluntary homes

Persons disqualified from carrying on, or being employed in, voluntary homes

78.—(1) A person who is disqualified (under Article 109) from fostering a child privately shall not carry on, or be otherwise concerned in the management of, or have any financial interest in, a voluntary home unless he has—

(a) disclosed to the authority the fact that he is so disqualified; and

(b) obtained the consent of the authority in writing.

(2) No person shall employ a person who is so disqualified in a voluntary home unless he has—

(a) disclosed to the authority the fact that that person is so disqualified; and

(b) obtained the consent of the authority in writing.

(3) Where an authority refuses to give its consent under this Article, the authority shall inform the applicant by a notice which states—

(a) the reason for the refusal;

(b) the applicant's right to appeal against the refusal to a Registered Homes Tribunal under Article 87; and

(c) the time within which he may do so.

(4) Any person who contravenes paragraph (1) or (2) shall be guilty of an offence and liable on summary conviction to imprisonment for a term not exceeding six months or to a fine not exceeding level 5 on the standard scale or to both.

(5) Where a person contravenes paragraph (2) he shall not be guilty of an offence if he proves that he did not know, and had no reasonable grounds for believing, that the person whom he was employing was disqualified under Article 109.

Voluntary homes not to be carried on unless registered

79.—(1) No voluntary home shall be carried on unless it is registered under this Part.

(2) The register may be kept by means of a computer.

(3) Any person who, without reasonable excuse, carries on a voluntary home in contravention of paragraph (1) shall be guilty of an offence and liable on summary conviction to a fine not exceeding level 5 on the standard scale.

Application for registration

80.—(1) An application for the registration of a voluntary home shall be made—

    (*a*) by the person carrying on, or intending to carry on, the home; and

    (*b*) to the authority in whose area the home is, or is to be, situated.

(2) The application shall be made in the prescribed manner and shall be accompanied by such particulars as may be prescribed.

(3) If the authority is satisfied that a voluntary home with respect to which an application has been made in accordance with this Part complies or (as the case may be) will comply—

    (*a*) with such requirements as may be prescribed, and

    (*b*) with such other requirements (if any) as appear to the authority to be appropriate,

the authority shall grant the application, either unconditionally or subject to conditions imposed under Article 81.

(4) Before deciding whether or not to grant an application the authority shall comply with any prescribed requirements.

(5) Regulations made for the purposes of paragraph (4) may, in particular, make provision as to the inspection of the home in question at prescribed times.

(6) Where an application is granted, the authority shall notify the applicant that the home has been registered under this Part as from such date as may be specified in the notice.

(7) Where an application is granted subject to conditions imposed under Article 81, the authority shall also notify the applicant of those conditions.

(8) If the authority is not satisfied as mentioned in paragraph (3), it shall refuse the application.

Power to impose conditions

81.—(1) The authority may grant an application for registration subject to such conditions relating to the conduct of the home as the authority thinks fit.

(2) The authority may—

    (*a*) vary or cancel any condition for the time being in force with respect to a home by virtue of this Article; or

    (*b*) impose an additional condition,

either on the application of the person carrying on the home or without such an application.

(3) Where the authority varies or cancels or imposes a condition under paragraph (2) with respect to a home, the authority shall notify the person carrying on the home that the condition has been varied or cancelled or imposed as from such date as may be specified in the notice.

(4) If any condition imposed or varied under this Article is not complied with, the person carrying on the home shall, if he has no reasonable excuse, be guilty of an offence and liable on summary conviction to a fine not exceeding level 4 on the standard scale.

Cancellation of registration

82.—(1) The person carrying on a voluntary home may at any time make an application, in such manner and including such particulars as may be prescribed, for the cancellation by the authority of the registration of the home.

(2) If on any annual review under Article 86, or at any other time, it appears to the authority that a voluntary home is being carried on otherwise than in accordance with the relevant requirements, the authority may cancel the registration of the home.

(3) The authority may at any time cancel the registration of a voluntary home on the ground—

(a) that the person carrying on the home has been convicted of an offence under this Part or any regulations made under Article 89; or

(b) that any other person has been convicted of such an offence in relation to the home.

(4) Where the authority cancels the registration of a voluntary home, the authority shall notify the person carrying on the home that the registration has been cancelled as from such date as may be specified in the notice.

Cases where an authority must serve notice of proposal

83.—(1) Where—

(a) a person applies for the registration of a voluntary home; and

(b) the authority proposes to grant his application subject to conditions,

the authority shall give him notice of its proposal and of the conditions subject to which it proposes to grant his application.

(2) The authority need not give notice under paragraph (1) if it proposes to grant the application subject only to conditions which—

(a) the applicant specified in the application; or

(b) the authority and the applicant have subsequently agreed.

(3) The authority shall give an applicant notice of a proposal to refuse his application.

(4) The authority shall give any person carrying on a voluntary home notice of a proposal—

   (*a*) to cancel the registration;

   (*b*) to vary or cancel any condition for the time being in force with respect to the home by virtue of this Part; or

   (*c*) to impose any additional condition.

(5) The authority need not give notice under paragraph (4) if it proposes—

   (*a*) to cancel the registration on the application of the person carrying on the home; or

   (*b*) to vary or cancel or impose a condition as mentioned in paragraph (4) on the application of, or with the agreement of, that person.

(6) A notice under this Article shall give the authority's reasons for its proposal.

Right to make representations

84.—(1) A notice under Article 83 shall state that within 14 days of service of the notice any person on whom it is served may in writing require the authority to give him an opportunity to make representations to it concerning the proposal.

(2) Where a notice has been served under Article 83, the authority shall not determine the matter until—

   (*a*) any person on whom the notice was served has made representations to the authority concerning the matter;

   (*b*) the period during which any such person could have required the authority to give him an opportunity to make representations has elapsed without the authority being required to give such an opportunity; or

   (*c*) the conditions specified in paragraph (3) are satisfied.

(3) The conditions are—

   (*a*) that a person on whom the notice was served has required the authority to give him an opportunity to make representations to the authority concerning the matter;

   (*b*) that the authority has allowed him a reasonable period to make his representations; and

   (*c*) that he has failed to make them within that period.

(4) The representations may be made, at the option of the person making them, either in writing or orally.

(5) If he informs the authority that he desires to make oral representations, the authority shall give him an opportunity of appearing before and of being heard by the authority.

Decision to adopt proposal

85.—(1) If the authority decides to adopt the proposal it shall serve notice of its decision on any person on whom it was required to serve notice of the proposal.

(2) A notice under this Article shall be accompanied by an explanation of the right of appeal conferred by Article 87.

(3) Subject to paragraph (4), the authority's decision shall not take effect—

(*a*) if no appeal is brought, until the end of the period of 28 days referred to in Article 87(3); and

(*b*) if an appeal is brought, until it is determined or abandoned.

(4) Paragraph (3) does not apply to a decision to adopt a proposal to refuse an application for registration.

Annual review of registration

86.—(1) The authority shall, at the end of the period of twelve months beginning with the date of registration of a voluntary home, and annually thereafter, review its registration for the purpose of determining whether the registration should continue in force or be cancelled under Article 82(2).

(2) If on any such annual review the authority is satisfied that the home is being carried on in accordance with the relevant requirements, the authority shall determine that the registration should continue in force.

(3) The authority shall give to the person carrying on the home notice of the determination under paragraph (2).

Appeals

87.—(1) An appeal against a decision of an authority under this Part shall lie to a Registered Homes Tribunal.

(2) An appeal shall be brought by notice given to the authority.

(3) No appeal shall be brought by a person more than 28 days after service on him of notice of the decision.

(4) On an appeal the Tribunal may confirm the authority's decision or direct that it shall not have effect.

(5) A Tribunal may also on an appeal—

(*a*) vary any condition in force by virtue of Article 81 with respect to the home to which the appeal relates;

(*b*) direct that any such condition shall cease to have effect; or

(*c*) direct that any such condition as the Tribunal thinks fit shall have effect with respect to the home.

(6) An authority shall comply with any direction given by a Tribunal under this Article.

Prohibition on further applications

88.—(1) Where an application for the registration of a home is refused, no further application may be made within the period of six months beginning with the date when the applicant is notified of the refusal.

(2) Paragraph (1) shall have effect, where an appeal against the refusal of an application is determined or abandoned, as if the reference to the date when the applicant is notified of the refusal were a reference to the date on which the appeal is determined or abandoned.

(3) Where the registration of a home is cancelled, no application for the registration of the home shall be made within the period of six months beginning with the date of cancellation.

(4) Paragraph (3) shall have effect, where an appeal against the cancellation of the registration of a home is determined or abandoned, as if the reference to the date of cancellation were a reference to the date on which the appeal is determined or abandoned.

Regulations

Regulations

89.—(1) The Department may make regulations—

(*a*) as to the placing of children in voluntary homes;

(*b*) as to the conduct of such homes; and

(*c*) for securing the welfare of the children in such homes.

(2) The regulations may in particular—

(*a*) prescribe standards to which the premises used for such homes are to conform;

(*b*) impose requirements as to the accommodation, staff and equipment to be provided in such homes;

(*c*) impose requirements as to the arrangements to be made for protecting the health of children in such homes;

(*d*) provide for the control and discipline of children in such homes;

(*e*) require the furnishing to an authority of information as to the facilities provided for—

(i) the parents of children in such homes;

(ii) persons who are not parents of such children but who have parental responsibility for them; and

(iii) other persons connected with such children,

to visit and communicate with the children;

(*f*) prohibit the use of accommodation for the purpose of restricting the liberty of children in such homes;

(g) impose requirements as to the keeping of records and giving of notices with respect to children in such homes;

(h) impose requirements as to the facilities which are to be provided for giving religious instruction to children in such homes;

(i) make provision as to the carrying out of annual reviews under Article 86;

(j) authorise an authority to limit the number of children who may be accommodated in any particular voluntary home;

(k) require notice to be given to an authority of any change of the person carrying on or in charge of a voluntary home or of the premises used by such a home;

(l) provide that, to such extent as may be provided for in the regulations, the Department may in special circumstances direct that any provision of regulations under this Article which is specified in the direction shall not apply in relation to a particular home or the premises used by such a home.

(3) The regulations may provide that a contravention of any specified provision of the regulations, without reasonable excuse, shall be an offence against the regulations.

(4) Any person guilty of such an offence shall be liable on summary conviction to a fine not exceeding level 4 on the standard scale.

PART IX

CHILDREN'S HOMES

Introductory

Interpretation

90.—(1) In this Order—

"children's home" means, subject to Article 91, a home which provides (or usually provides or is intended to provide) care and accommodation for children;

"registered children's home" means a children's home registered under this Part.

(2) In this Part—

"home" includes any institution;

"notice" and "notify" mean respectively notice in writing and notify in writing;

"the relevant requirements" means any requirements of this Part and of regulations under Article 105, and any conditions imposed under Article 97.

(3) Any reference in this Part to an authority in relation to a children's home means the authority in whose area the home is, or is to be, situated.

"Children's home" further defined

91.—(1) A child is not cared for and accommodated in a children's home when he is cared for and accommodated by—

(*a*) a parent of his;

(*b*) a person who is not a parent of his but who has parental responsibility for him;

(*c*) any relative of his; or

(*d*) a person who fosters him (within the meaning of Article 119) and not more than two other children.

(2) A home is not a children's home if it is—

(*a*) a home provided under Part VII or a voluntary home;

(*b*) a residential care home;

(*c*) a hospital (including a private hospital) or nursing home;

(*d*) a school;

(*e*) a training school;

(*f*) used primarily for the accommodation of homeless persons;

(*g*) used primarily for or in connection with the provision of cultural, recreational, leisure, social or physical activities;

(*h*) exempted by regulations made by the Department for the purposes of this paragraph,

or if it does not fall within sub-paragraphs (*a*) to (*h*) but is provided by the Secretary of State, a government department or a prescribed public body.

(3) A child shall not be treated as cared for and accommodated in a children's home when—

(*a*) any person mentioned in paragraph (1)(*a*) or (*b*) is living at the home; or

(*b*) the person caring for him is doing so in his personal capacity and not in the course of carrying out his duties in relation to the home.

(4) Schedule 5 shall have effect for the purpose of setting out the circumstances in which a person may foster more than three children without being treated as carrying on a children's home.

General

Duties of person carrying on children's home

92.—(1) Where a child is accommodated in a children's home, the person carrying on the home shall—

(*a*) safeguard and promote the child's welfare;

(*b*) make such use of the services and facilities available for children cared for by their own parents as appears to that person reasonable in the case of the child; and

(c) advise, assist and befriend him with a view to promoting his welfare when he ceases to be so accommodated.

(2) Before making any decision with respect to any such child the person carrying on the home shall, so far as is reasonably practicable, ascertain the wishes and feelings of—

(a) the child;

(b) his parents;

(c) any other person who is not a parent of his but who has parental responsibility for him; and

(d) any person whose wishes and feelings the person carrying on the home considers to be relevant,

regarding the matter to be decided.

(3) In making any such decision the person carrying on the home shall give due consideration—

(a) having regard to the child's age and understanding, to such wishes and feelings of his as he has been able to ascertain;

(b) to such other wishes and feelings mentioned in paragraph (2) as he has been able to ascertain; and

(c) to the child's religious persuasion, racial origin and cultural and linguistic background.

(4) Every person carrying on a children's home shall, at such times and in such form as the Department may direct, transmit to the Department such particulars as the Department may require with respect to the children accommodated in the home.

Duties of an authority

93.—(1) Every authority shall satisfy itself that any person carrying on a children's home which provides accommodation—

(a) within the authority's area for any child; or

(b) outside that area for any child on behalf of the authority,

is satisfactorily safeguarding and promoting the welfare of the children so provided with accommodation.

(2) Every authority shall arrange for children who are accommodated within its area in a children's home to be visited in the interests of their welfare.

(3) The Department may make regulations—

(a) requiring every child who is accommodated in a children's home within an authority's area to be visited by an officer of the authority—

(i) in prescribed circumstances; and

(ii) on specified occasions or within specified periods; and

(b) imposing requirements which must be met by any authority, or officer of an authority, carrying out functions under this Article.

(4) If an authority is not satisfied that the welfare of any child who is accommodated in a children's home is being satisfactorily safeguarded or promoted, the authority shall—

    (*a*) unless it considers that it would not be in the best interests of the child, take such steps as are reasonably practicable to secure that the care and accommodation of the child are undertaken by—

        (i) a parent of his;

        (ii) any person who is not a parent of his but who has parental responsibility for him; or

        (iii) a relative of his; and

    (*b*) consider the extent to which (if at all) the authority should exercise any of its functions with respect to the child.

(5) Any person authorised by an authority may, for the purpose of enabling the authority to discharge its duties under this Article—

    (*a*) enter at any reasonable time and inspect any children's home;

    (*b*) inspect any children there;

    (*c*) require any person to furnish him with such records of a kind required to be kept by regulations made under Article 105 (in whatever form they are held), or allow him to inspect such records, as he may at any time direct.

(6) Any person exercising the power conferred by paragraph (5) shall, if asked to do so, produce some duly authenticated document showing his authority to do so.

(7) Any person authorised to exercise the power to inspect records conferred by paragraph (5)—

    (*a*) shall be entitled at any reasonable time to have access to, and inspect and check the operation of, any computer and any associated apparatus or material which is or has been in use in connection with the records in question; and

    (*b*) may require—

        (i) the person by whom or on whose behalf the computer is or has been so used; or

        (ii) any person having charge of, or otherwise concerned with the operation of, the computer, apparatus or material,

    to afford him such assistance as he may reasonably require.

(8) Any person who intentionally obstructs another in the exercise of any power conferred by paragraph (5) or (7) shall be guilty of an offence and liable on summary conviction to a fine not exceeding level 3 on the standard scale.

Persons disqualified from carrying on, or being employed in,
children's homes

94.—(1) A person who is disqualified (under Article 109) from

91

fostering a child privately shall not carry on, or be otherwise concerned in the management of, or have any financial interest in, a children's home unless he has—

(a) disclosed to the authority the fact that he is so disqualified; and

(b) obtained the consent of the authority in writing.

(2) No person shall employ a person who is so disqualified in a children's home unless he has—

(a) disclosed to the authority the fact that that person is so disqualified; and

(b) obtained the consent of the authority in writing.

(3) Where an authority refuses to give its consent under this Article, the authority shall inform the applicant by a notice which states—

(a) the reason for the refusal;

(b) the applicant's right to appeal against the refusal to a Registered Homes Tribunal under Article 103; and

(c) the time within which he may do so.

(4) Any person who contravenes paragraph (1) or (2) shall be guilty of an offence and liable on summary conviction to imprisonment for a term not exceeding six months or to a fine not exceeding level 5 on the standard scale or to both.

(5) Where a person contravenes paragraph (2) he shall not be guilty of an offence if he proves that he did not know, and had no reasonable grounds for believing, that the person whom he was employing was disqualified under Article 109.

Registration

Children not to be cared for and accommodated in unregistered children's homes

95.—(1) No child shall be cared for and provided with accommodation in a children's home unless the home is registered under this Part.

(2) The register may be kept by means of a computer.

(3) Where any child is at any time cared for and accommodated in a children's home which is not a registered children's home, the person carrying on the home shall, unless he has a reasonable excuse, be guilty of an offence and liable on summary conviction to a fine not exceeding level 5 on the standard scale.

Application for registration

96.—(1) An application for the registration of a children's home shall be made—

(*a*) by the person carrying on, or intending to carry on, the home; and

(*b*) to the authority in whose area the home is, or is to be, situated.

(2) The application shall be made in the prescribed manner and shall be accompanied by—

(*a*) such particulars as may be prescribed; and

(*b*) such reasonable fee as the Department may determine.

(3) If the authority is satisfied that a children's home with respect to which an application has been made in accordance with this Part complies or (as the case may be) will comply—

(*a*) with such requirements as may be prescribed, and

(*b*) with such other requirements (if any) as appear to the authority to be appropriate,

the authority shall grant the application, either unconditionally or subject to conditions imposed under Article 97.

(4) Before deciding whether or not to grant an application the authority shall comply with any prescribed requirements.

(5) Regulations made for the purposes of paragraph (4) may, in particular, make provision as to the inspection of the home in question at prescribed times.

(6) Where an application is granted, the authority shall notify the applicant that the home has been registered under this Part as from such date as may be specified in the notice.

(7) Where an application is granted subject to conditions imposed under Article 97, the authority shall also notify the applicant of those conditions.

(8) If the authority is not satisfied as mentioned in paragraph (3), it shall refuse the application.

Power to impose conditions

97.—(1) The authority may grant an application for registration subject to such conditions relating to the conduct of the home as the authority thinks fit.

(2) The authority may—

(*a*) vary or cancel any condition for the time being in force with respect to a home by virtue of this Article; or

(*b*) impose an additional condition,

either on the application of the person carrying on the home or without such an application.

(3) Where the authority varies or cancels or imposes a condition under paragraph (2) with respect to a home, the authority shall notify the person carrying on the home that the condition has been varied

or cancelled or imposed as from such date as may be specified in the notice.

(4) If any condition imposed or varied under this Article is not complied with, the person carrying on the home shall, if he has no reasonable excuse, be guilty of an offence and liable on summary conviction to a fine not exceeding level 4 on the standard scale.

Cancellation of registration

98.—(1) The person carrying on a registered children's home may at any time make an application, in such manner and including such particulars as may be prescribed, for the cancellation by the authority of the registration of the home.

(2) If on any annual review under Article 102, or at any other time, it appears to the authority that a registered children's home is being carried on otherwise than in accordance with the relevant requirements, the authority may cancel the registration of the home.

(3) The authority may at any time cancel the registration of a children's home on the ground—

(a) that the person carrying on the home has been convicted of an offence under this Part or any regulations made under Article 105; or

(b) that any other person has been convicted of such an offence in relation to the home.

(4) Where the authority cancels the registration of a children's home, the authority shall notify the person carrying on the home that the registration has been cancelled as from such date as may be specified in the notice.

Cases where an authority must serve notice of proposal

99.—(1) Where—

(a) a person applies for the registration of a children's home; and

(b) the authority proposes to grant his application subject to conditions,

the authority shall give him notice of its proposal and of the conditions subject to which it proposes to grant his application.

(2) The authority need not give notice under paragraph (1) if it proposes to grant the application subject only to conditions which—

(a) the applicant specified in the application; or

(b) the authority and the applicant have subsequently agreed.

(3) The authority shall give an applicant notice of a proposal to refuse his application.

(4) The authority shall give any person carrying on a registered children's home notice of a proposal—

    (*a*) to cancel the registration;

    (*b*) to vary or cancel any condition for the time being in force with respect to the home by virtue of this Part; or

    (*c*) to impose any additional condition.

(5) The authority need not give notice under paragraph (4) if it proposes—

    (*a*) to cancel the registration on the application of the person carrying on the home; or

    (*b*) to vary or cancel or impose a condition as mentioned in paragraph (4) on the application of, or with the agreement of, that person.

(6) A notice under this Article shall give the authority's reasons for its proposal.

Right to make representations

100.—(1) A notice under Article 99 shall state that within 14 days of service of the notice any person on whom it is served may in writing require the authority to give him an opportunity to make representations to it concerning the proposal.

(2) Where a notice has been served under Article 99, the authority shall not determine the matter until—

    (*a*) any person on whom the notice was served has made representations to the authority concerning the matter;

    (*b*) the period during which any such person could have required the authority to give him an opportunity to make representations has elapsed without the authority being required to give such an opportunity; or

    (*c*) the conditions specified in paragraph (3) are satisfied.

(3) The conditions are—

    (*a*) that a person on whom the notice was served has required the authority to give him an opportunity to make representations to the authority concerning the matter;

    (*b*) that the authority has allowed him a reasonable period to make his representations; and

    (*c*) that he has failed to make them within that period.

(4) The representations may be made, at the option of the person making them, either in writing or orally.

(5) If he informs the authority that he desires to make oral representations, the authority shall give him an opportunity of appearing before and of being heard by the authority.

Decision to adopt proposal

101.—(1) If the authority decides to adopt the proposal, it shall serve notice of its decision on any person on whom the authority was required to serve notice of the proposal.

(2) A notice under this Article shall be accompanied by an explanation of the right of appeal conferred by Article 103.

(3) Subject to paragraph (4), the authority's decision shall not take effect—

　　(*a*) if no appeal is brought, until the end of the period of 28 days referred to in Article 103(3); and

　　(*b*) if an appeal is brought, until it is determined or abandoned.

(4) Paragraph (3) does not apply to a decision to adopt a proposal to refuse an application for registration.

Annual review of registration

102.—(1) The authority shall, at the end of the period of twelve months beginning with the date of registration of a children's home, and annually thereafter, review its registration for the purpose of determining whether the registration should continue in force or be cancelled under Article 98(2).

(2) If on any such annual review the authority is satisfied that the home is being carried on in accordance with the relevant requirements, the authority shall determine that, subject to paragraph (3), the registration should continue in force.

(3) The authority shall give to the person carrying on the home notice of the determination under paragraph (2) and the notice shall require him to pay to the authority with respect to the review such reasonable fee as the Department may determine.

(4) It shall be a condition of the home's continued registration that the fee is so paid before the expiry of the period of 28 days beginning with the date on which the notice is received by the person carrying on the home.

Appeals

103.—(1) An appeal against a decision of an authority under this Part shall lie to a Registered Homes Tribunal.

(2) An appeal shall be brought by notice given to the authority.

(3) No appeal shall be brought by a person more than 28 days after service on him of notice of the decision.

(4) On an appeal the Tribunal may confirm the authority's decision or direct that it shall not have effect.

(5) A Tribunal may also on an appeal—

(a) vary any condition in force by virtue of Article 97 with respect to the home to which the appeal relates;

(b) direct that any such condition shall cease to have effect; or

(c) direct that any such condition as the Tribunal thinks fit shall have effect with respect to the home.

(6) An authority shall comply with any direction given by a Tribunal under this Article.

Prohibition on further applications

104.—(1) Where an application for the registration of a home is refused, no further application may be made within the period of six months beginning with the date when the applicant is notified of the refusal.

(2) Paragraph (1) shall have effect, where an appeal against the refusal of an application is determined or abandoned, as if the reference to the date when the applicant is notified of the refusal were a reference to the date on which the appeal is determined or abandoned.

(3) Where the registration of a home is cancelled, no application for the registration of the home shall be made within the period of six months beginning with the date of cancellation.

(4) Paragraph (3) shall have effect, where an appeal against the cancellation of the registration of a home is determined or abandoned, as if the reference to the date of cancellation were a reference to the date on which the appeal is determined or abandoned.

Regulations

Regulations

105.—(1) The Department may make regulations—

(a) as to the placing of children in registered children's homes;

(b) as to the conduct of such homes; and

(c) for securing the welfare of the children in such homes.

(2) The regulations may in particular—

(a) prescribe standards to which the premises used for such homes are to conform;

(b) impose requirements as to the accommodation, staff and equipment to be provided in such homes;

(c) impose requirements as to the arrangements to be made for protecting the health of children in such homes;

(d) provide for the control and discipline of children in such homes;

(e) require the furnishing to an authority of information as to the facilities provided for—

    (i) the parents of children in such homes;

    (ii) persons who are not parents of such children but who have parental responsibility for them; and

    (iii) other persons connected with such children,

    to visit and communicate with the children;

(f) prohibit the use of accommodation for the purpose of restricting the liberty of children in such homes;

(g) impose requirements as to the keeping of records and giving of notices with respect to children in such homes;

(h) impose requirements as to the facilities which are to be provided for giving religious instruction to children in such homes;

(i) make provision as to the carrying out of annual reviews under Article 102;

(j) authorise an authority to limit the number of children who may be accommodated in any particular registered children's home;

(k) require notice to be given to an authority of any change of the person carrying on or in charge of a registered children's home or of the premises used by such a home;

(l) make provision similar to that made by regulations under Article 45;

(m) provide that, to such extent as may be provided for in the regulations, the Department may in special circumstances direct that any provision of regulations under this Article which is specified in the direction shall not apply in relation to a particular home or the premises used by such a home.

(3) The regulations may provide that a contravention of any specified provision of the regulations, without reasonable excuse, shall be an offence against the regulations.

(4) Any person guilty of such an offence shall be liable on summary conviction to a fine not exceeding level 4 on the standard scale.

PART X

PRIVATE ARRANGEMENTS FOR FOSTERING CHILDREN

Interpretation

106.—(1) In this Order—

"foster a child privately" means look after the child in circumstances in which he is a privately fostered child;

"privately fostered child" means a child who is cared for, and provided with accommodation by, someone other than—

    (a) a parent of his;

(*b*) a person who is not a parent of his but who has parental responsibility for him; or

(*c*) a relative of his.

(2) Paragraph (1) is subject to—

(*a*) the provisions of Articles 90, 91 and 95 (children's homes); and

(*b*) the exceptions made by Article 107 (privately fostered children further defined).

(3) In this Part "child" means a person who is under the age of 16 or, if he is disabled, under the age of 18.

Privately fostered children further defined

107.—(1) A child is not a privately fostered child if the person caring for and accommodating him—

(*a*) has done so for a period of less than 28 days; and

(*b*) does not intend to do so for any longer period.

(2) A child is not a privately fostered child while he is being looked after by an authority.

(3) A child is not a privately fostered child while he is in the care of any person—

(*a*) in premises in which any—

(i) parent of his;

(ii) person who is not a parent of his but who has parental responsibility for him; or

(iii) person who is a relative of his and who has assumed responsibility for his care,

is for the time being living;

(*b*) in any children's home;

(*c*) in accommodation provided by or on behalf of any voluntary organisation;

(*d*) in any school in which he is receiving full-time education;

(*e*) in any residential care home;

(*f*) in any hospital (including a private hospital) or nursing home; or

(*g*) in any home or institution not specified in sub-paragraphs (*b*) to (*f*) but provided by the Secretary of State, a government department or a prescribed public body,

but sub-paragraphs (*b*) to (*g*) do not apply where the person caring for the child is doing so in his personal capacity and not in the course of carrying out his duties in relation to the establishment mentioned in the sub-paragraph in question.

(4) A child is not a privately fostered child while he is living with

PART X

any person in compliance with a probation order which includes a residence requirement.

(5) A child is not a privately fostered child while—

(a) he is committed to the care of a fit person under section 74 of the Children and Young Persons Act (Northern Ireland) 1968; or

1968 c. 34 (N.I.)

(b) he is living with any person in compliance with a supervision order under that section which includes a residence requirement.

(6) A child is not a privately fostered child while he is liable to be detained, or subject to guardianship, under the Mental Health (Northern Ireland) Order 1986.

1986 NI 4

(7) A child is not a privately fostered child while—

(a) he is placed in the care of a person who proposes to adopt him under arrangements made by an adoption agency within the meaning of—

(i) Article 3 of the Adoption Order; or

1976 c. 36

(ii) section 1 of the Adoption Act 1976; or

1978 c. 28

(iii) section 1 of the Adoption (Scotland) Act 1978;

(b) he is a protected child.

Welfare of privately fostered children

108.—(1) Every authority shall—

(a) satisfy itself that the welfare of children who are privately fostered within the authority's area is being satisfactorily safeguarded and promoted; and

(b) secure that such advice is given to those caring for them as appears to the authority to be needed.

(2) The Department may make regulations—

(a) requiring every child who is privately fostered within an authority's area to be visited by an officer of the authority—

(i) in prescribed circumstances; and

(ii) on specified occasions or within specified periods; and

(b) imposing requirements which are to be met by any authority, or officer of an authority, in carrying out functions under this Article.

(3) Where any person who is authorised by an authority to visit privately fostered children has reasonable cause to believe that—

(a) any privately fostered child is being accommodated in premises within the authority's area; or

(b) it is proposed to accommodate any such child in any such premises,

he may at any reasonable time inspect those premises and any children there.

(4) Any person exercising the power under paragraph (3) shall, if so required, produce some duly authenticated document showing his authority to do so.

(5) If an authority is not satisfied that the welfare of any child who is privately fostered within the authority's area is being satisfactorily safeguarded or promoted the authority shall—

(a) unless it considers that it would not be in the best interests of the child, take such steps as are reasonably practicable to secure that the care and accommodation of the child is undertaken by—

(i) a parent of his;

(ii) any person who is not a parent of his but who has parental responsibility for him; or

(iii) a relative of his; and

(b) consider the extent to which (if at all) it should exercise any of its functions under this Order with respect to the child.

Persons disqualified from being private foster parents

109.—(1) Unless he has disclosed the fact to the appropriate authority and obtained its written consent, a person shall not foster a child privately if he is disqualified from doing so by regulations made by the Department for the purposes of this Article.

(2) The regulations may, in particular, provide for a person to be so disqualified where—

(a) an order of a kind specified in the regulations has been made at any time with respect to him;

(b) an order of a kind so specified has been made at any time with respect to any child who has been in his care;

(c) a requirement of a kind so specified has been imposed at any time with respect to any such child under any statutory provision;

(d) he has been convicted of any offence of a kind so specified, or has been placed on probation or discharged absolutely or conditionally for any such offence;

(e) he has at any time been disqualified from child minding or providing day care for children under the age of twelve;

(f) a prohibition has been imposed on him at any time under Article 110 or under any other specified statutory provision.

(3) Unless he has disclosed the fact to the appropriate authority and obtained its written consent, a person shall not foster a child privately if—

(a) he lives in the same household as a person who is himself prevented from fostering a child by paragraph (1); or

(b) he lives in a household at which any such person is employed.

(4) Where an authority refuses to give its consent under this Article, it shall inform the applicant by a written notice which states—

(a) the reason for the refusal;

(b) the applicant's right under Article 113 to appeal against the refusal; and

(c) the time within which he may do so.

(5) In this Article—

"the appropriate authority" means the authority within whose area it is proposed to foster the child in question;

"statutory provision" includes any statutory provision having effect, at any time, in any part of the United Kingdom.

Power to prohibit private fostering

110.—(1) This Article applies where a person—

(a) proposes to foster a child privately; or

(b) is fostering a child privately.

(2) Where the authority for the area within which the child is proposed to be, or is being, fostered is of the opinion that—

(a) he is not a suitable person to foster a child;

(b) the premises in which the child will be, or is being, accommodated are not suitable; or

(c) it would be prejudicial to the welfare of the child for him to be, or continue to be, accommodated by that person in those premises,

the authority may impose a prohibition on that person.

(3) A prohibition imposed on any person under paragraph (2) may prohibit him from fostering privately—

(a) any child in any premises within the authority's area;

(b) any child in premises specified in the prohibition; or

(c) a child identified in the prohibition, in premises specified in the prohibition.

(4) An authority which has imposed a prohibition on any person under paragraph (2) may, if it thinks fit, cancel the prohibition—

(a) of its own motion; or

(b) on an application made by that person,

if it is satisfied that the prohibition is no longer justified.

(5) Where an authority imposes a requirement on any person under Article 111, it may also impose a prohibition on him under paragraph (2).

(6) Any prohibition imposed by virtue of paragraph (5) shall not have effect unless—

(a) the time specified for compliance with the requirement has expired; and

(*b*) the requirement has not been complied with.

(7) A prohibition imposed under this Article shall be imposed by notice in writing addressed to the person on whom it is imposed and informing him of—

(*a*) the reason for imposing the prohibition;

(*b*) his right under Article 113 to appeal against the prohibition; and

(*c*) the time within which he may do so.

Power to impose requirements

111.—(1) Where a person is fostering any child privately, or proposes to foster any child privately, the appropriate authority may impose on him requirements as to—

(*a*) the number, age and sex of the children who may be privately fostered by him;

(*b*) the standard of the accommodation and equipment to be provided for them;

(*c*) the arrangements to be made with respect to their health and safety; and

(*d*) particular arrangements which must be made with respect to the provision of care for them,

and he shall comply with any such requirement before the end of such period as the authority may specify unless, in the case of a proposal, the proposal is not carried out.

(2) A requirement may be limited to a particular child.

(3) A requirement (other than one imposed under paragraph (1)(*a*)) may be limited by the authority so as to apply only when the number of children fostered by the person exceeds a specified number.

(4) A requirement shall be imposed by notice in writing addressed to the person on whom it is imposed and informing him of—

(*a*) the reason for imposing the requirement;

(*b*) his right under Article 113 to appeal against it; and

(*c*) the time within which he may do so.

(5) An authority may vary any requirement, impose any additional requirement or remove any requirement.

(6) In this Article—

"the appropriate authority" means—

(*a*) the authority within whose area the child is being fostered; or

(*b*) in the case of a proposal to foster a child, the authority within whose area it is proposed that he will be fostered; and

"requirement", in relation to any person, means a requirement imposed on him under this Article.

Regulations requiring notification of fostering, etc.

112.—(1) The Department may by regulations make provision as to—

(*a*) the circumstances in which notification is required to be given in connection with children who are, have been or are proposed to be, fostered privately; and

(*b*) the manner and form in which such notification is to be given.

(2) The regulations may, in particular—

(*a*) require any person who is, or proposes to be, involved (whether or not directly) in arranging for a child to be fostered privately to notify the appropriate authority;

(*b*) require any person who is—

(i) a parent of a child; or

(ii) a person who is not a parent of his but who has parental responsibility for a child,

and who knows that it is proposed that the child should be fostered privately, to notify the appropriate authority;

(*c*) require any parent of a privately fostered child, or person who is not a parent of such a child but who has parental responsibility for him, to notify the appropriate authority of any change in that parent's, or that person's, address;

(*d*) require any person who proposes to foster a child privately, to notify the appropriate authority of his proposal;

(*e*) require any person who is fostering a child privately, or proposes to do so, to notify the appropriate authority of—

(i) any offence of which he has been convicted;

(ii) any disqualification imposed on him under Article 109; or

(iii) any prohibition imposed on him under Article 110;

(*f*) require any person who is fostering a child privately, to notify the appropriate authority of any change in that person's address;

(*g*) require any person who is fostering a child privately to notify the appropriate authority in writing of any person who begins, or ceases, to be part of his household;

(*h*) require any person who has been fostering a child privately, but has ceased to do so, to notify the appropriate authority (indicating, where the child has died, that that is the reason).

(3) In paragraph (2) "the appropriate authority" has the same meaning as in Article 111.

Appeals

113.—(1) A person aggrieved by—

(*a*) a requirement imposed under Article 111;

(*b*) a refusal to consent under Article 109;

(*c*) a prohibition imposed under Article 110;

(*d*) a refusal to cancel such a prohibition;

(*e*) a refusal to make an exemption under paragraph 4 of Schedule 5;

(*f*) a condition imposed in such an exemption; or

(*g*) a variation or cancellation of such an exemption or condition,

may appeal to the court.

(2) The appeal must be made within 14 days from the date on which the person appealing is notified of the requirement, refusal, prohibition, condition, variation or cancellation.

(3) Where the appeal is against—

(*a*) a requirement imposed under Article 111;

(*b*) a condition of an exemption imposed under paragraph 4 of Schedule 5; or

(*c*) a variation or cancellation of such an exemption or condition,

the requirement, condition, variation or cancellation shall not have effect while the appeal is pending.

(4) Where it allows an appeal against a requirement or prohibition, the court may, instead of cancelling the requirement or prohibition—

(*a*) vary the requirement, or allow more time for compliance with it; or

(*b*) if an absolute prohibition has been imposed, substitute for it a prohibition on using the premises after such time as the court may specify unless such specified requirements as the authority had power to impose under Article 111 are complied with.

(5) Any requirement or prohibition specified or substituted by a court under this Article shall be deemed for the purposes of this Part (other than this Article) to have been imposed by the authority under Article 111 or (as the case may be) Article 110.

(6) Where it allows an appeal against a refusal to make an exemption, a condition imposed in such an exemption or a variation or cancellation of such an exemption or condition, the court may—

(*a*) make an exemption;

(*b*) impose a condition; or

(*c*) vary the exemption or condition.

(7) Any exemption made or varied under paragraph (6), or any condition imposed or varied under that paragraph, shall be deemed for the purposes of Schedule 5 (but not for the purposes of this Article) to have been made, varied or imposed under that Schedule.

(8) Nothing in paragraph (1)(*e*) to (*g*) confers any right of appeal on—

(*a*) a person who is, or would be if exempted under Schedule 5, an authority foster parent; or

(*b*) a person who is, or would be if so exempted, a person with whom a child is placed by a voluntary organisation.

Application of this Part to certain school children during holidays

114.—(1) Where a child who is a pupil at a school lives at the school during school holidays for a period of more than two weeks, this Part shall apply in relation to the child as if—

(*a*) while living at the school, he were a privately fostered child; and

(*b*) Articles 107(3)(*d*) and 111 were omitted.

(2) Paragraph (3) applies to any person who proposes to care for and accommodate one or more children at a school in circumstances in which some or all of them will be treated as privately fostered children by virtue of this Article.

(3) That person shall, not less than two weeks before the first of those children is treated as a privately fostered child by virtue of this Article during the holiday in question, give written notice of his proposal to the authority within whose area the child is ordinarily resident ("the appropriate authority"), stating the estimated number of the children.

(4) An authority may exempt any person from the duty of giving notice under paragraph (3).

(5) Any such exemption may be granted for a special period or indefinitely and may be revoked at any time by notice in writing given to the person exempted.

(6) Where a child who is treated as a privately fostered child by virtue of this Article dies, the person caring for him at the school shall, not later than 48 hours after the death, give written notice of it—

(*a*) to the appropriate authority; and

(*b*) where reasonably practicable, to each parent of the child and to every person who is not a parent of his but who has parental responsibility for him.

(7) Where a child who is treated as a privately fostered child by virtue of this Article ceases for any other reason to be such a child,

the person caring for him at the school shall give written notice of the
fact to the appropriate authority.

Advertisements relating to fostering

115. No advertisement indicating that a person will undertake, or
will arrange for, a child to be privately fostered shall be published,
unless it states that person's name and address.

Avoidance of insurances on lives of privately fostered children

116. A person who fosters a child privately and for reward shall be
deemed for the purposes of the Life Assurance Act 1774 as extended
by the Life Insurance (Ireland) Act 1866 to have no interest in the
life of the child.

1774 c. 48
1866 c. 42

Offences

117.—(1) A person shall be guilty of an offence if—

(a) being required, under any provision made by or under this
Part, to give any notice or information—

  (i) he fails without reasonable excuse to give the notice
within the time specified in that provision; or

  (ii) he fails without reasonable excuse to give the information
within a reasonable time; or

  (iii) he makes, or causes or procures another person to make,
any statement in the notice or information which he
knows to be false or misleading in a material particular;

(b) he refuses to allow a privately fostered child to be visited by
a duly authorised officer of an authority;

(c) he intentionally obstructs another in the exercise of the
power conferred by Article 108(3);

(d) he contravenes Article 109;

(e) he fails without reasonable excuse to comply with any requirement imposed by an authority under this Part;

(f) he accommodates a privately fostered child in any premises
in contravention of a prohibition imposed by an authority
under this Part;

(g) he knowingly causes to be published, or publishes, an advertisement which he knows contravenes Article 115.

(2) Where a person contravenes Article 109(3), he shall not be
guilty of an offence under this Article if he proves that he did not
know, and had no reasonable ground for believing, that any person
to whom Article 109(1) applied was living or employed in the
premises in question.

(3) A person guilty of an offence under paragraph (1)(a) shall be
liable on summary conviction to a fine not exceeding level 5 on the
standard scale.

(4) A person guilty of an offence under paragraph (1)(*b*), (*c*) or (*g*) shall be liable on summary conviction to a fine not exceeding level 3 on the standard scale.

(5) A person guilty of an offence under paragraph (1)(*d*) or (*f*) shall be liable on summary conviction to imprisonment for a term not exceeding six months, or to a fine not exceeding level 5 on the standard scale, or to both.

(6) A person guilty of an offence under paragraph (1)(*e*) shall be liable on summary conviction to a fine not exceeding level 4 on the standard scale.

(7) If any person who is required, under any provision of this Part, to give a notice fails to give the notice within the time specified in that provision, proceedings for the offence may be brought at any time within six months from the date when evidence of the offence came to the knowledge of the authority.

1981 NI 26

(8) Paragraph (7) is not affected by anything in Article 19(1)(*a*) of the Magistrates' Courts (Northern Ireland) Order 1981.

PART XI

CHILD MINDING AND DAY CARE FOR YOUNG CHILDREN

Registration

118.—(1) Every authority shall keep a register of—

(*a*) persons who act as child minders on domestic premises within the authority's area; and

(*b*) persons (other than the authority) who provide day care for children under the age of twelve on premises (other than domestic premises) within that area.

(2) In this Part—

"domestic premises" means any premises which are wholly or mainly used as a private dwelling;

"premises" includes a vehicle.

(3) Any register kept under this Article—

(*a*) shall be open to inspection by members of the public at all reasonable times; and

(*b*) may be kept by means of a computer.

Persons who act as child minders

119.—(1) For the purposes of this Part a person acts as a child minder if—

(*a*) he looks after one or more children under the age of twelve for reward; and

(*b*) the period, or the total of the periods, which he spends so looking after children in any day exceeds two hours.

(2) A person who—

(a) is the parent, or a relative, of a child;

(b) has parental responsibility for a child; or

(c) is a foster parent of a child,

does not act as a child minder for the purposes of this Part in relation to that child when looking after him.

(3) For the purposes of this Article, a person fosters a child if—

(a) he is an authority foster parent in relation to the child;

(b) he is a foster parent with whom the child has been placed by a voluntary organisation; or

(c) he fosters the child privately.

(4) A person who is employed as a nanny for a child does not act as a child minder when looking after that child wholly or mainly in the home of the person who employs the nanny.

(5) A person who is so employed by two different employers does not act as a child minder when looking after any of the children concerned wholly or mainly in the home of either of the employers.

(6) For the purposes of this Part a person acts as a nanny for a child when employed to look after the child by—

(a) a parent of the child;

(b) a person who is not a parent of the child but who has parental responsibility for him; or

(c) a person who is a relative of the child and who has assumed responsibility for his care.

Persons who provide day care for children under the age of twelve

120.—(1) For the purposes of this Part a person does not provide day care for children unless the period, or the total of the periods, during which children are looked after exceeds two hours in any day.

(2) Where a person provides day care for children under the age of twelve on different premises situated within the area of the same authority, that person shall be separately registered with respect to each of those premises.

Exemptions

121.—(1) Articles 118 to 120 shall not apply in relation to any child while he is looked after in any school which he is attending for the purposes of full-time education.

(2) Article 118(1)(b) shall not apply in relation to any child looked after in—

(a) a home provided under Part VII;

(b) a voluntary home or a registered children's home;

(c) a nursing home or a residential care home;

(d) a hospital administered by a Board or Health and Social Services trust;

(e) a home or other institution not falling within sub-paragraphs (a) to (d) but provided by the Secretary of State, a government department or a prescribed public body.

(3) The exemption provided by paragraph (1) or (2) shall apply only where the child concerned is being looked after in accordance with provision for day care made by—

(a) the Board, trust, department or other person carrying on the establishment in question as part of the establishment's activities; or

(b) a person employed to work at that establishment and authorised to make that provision as part of the establishment's activities.

(4) Where day care for children under the age of twelve is provided in particular premises on less than six days in any year, that provision shall be disregarded for the purposes of Articles 118 to 120 if the person making it has notified the authority in writing before the first occasion on which the premises concerned are so used in that year.

(5) In paragraph (4) "year" means the year beginning with the day on which the day care in question is (after the commencement of that paragraph) first provided in the premises concerned and any subsequent year.

(6) Article 118(1)(b) shall not apply in relation to such supervised activity (within the meaning of Article 19) as may be prescribed.

Disqualified persons

122.—(1) A person shall not be registered under Article 118 if—

(a) he is disqualified by regulations made by the Department for the purposes of this Article; and

(b) he has not disclosed that fact to the authority and obtained its written consent.

(2) The regulations may, in particular, provide for a person to be disqualified where—

(a) an order of a prescribed kind has been made at any time with respect to him;

(b) an order of a prescribed kind has been made at any time with respect to any child who has been in his care;

(c) a requirement of a prescribed kind has been imposed at any time with respect to such a child under any statutory provision;

(d) he has at any time been refused registration under this Part or any other prescribed statutory provision or had any such registration cancelled;

(*e*) he has been convicted of any offence of a prescribed kind, or has been placed on probation or discharged absolutely or conditionally for any such offence;

(*f*) he has at any time been disqualified from fostering a child privately;

(*g*) a prohibition has been imposed on him at any time under Article 110 or any other prescribed statutory provision; or

(*h*) his rights and powers with respect to a child have at any time been vested in a prescribed body under a prescribed statutory provision.

(3) A person who lives—

(*a*) in the same household as a person who is himself disqualified by the regulations; or

(*b*) in a household at which any such person is employed,

shall be disqualified unless he has disclosed the fact to the authority and obtained its written consent.

(4) A person who is disqualified shall not provide day care, or be concerned in the management of, or have any financial interest in, any provision of day care unless he has—

(*a*) disclosed the fact to the authority; and

(*b*) obtained its written consent.

(5) No person shall employ, in connection with the provision of day care, a person who is disqualified, unless he has—

(*a*) disclosed to the authority the fact that that person is so disqualified; and

(*b*) obtained its written consent.

(6) In this Article "statutory provision" includes any statutory provision having effect at any time in any part of the United Kingdom.

Application for registration

123.—(1) On receipt of an application for registration under this Part from any person who is acting, or proposes to act, in any way which requires him to be registered under this Part, an authority shall register him if—

(*a*) the application is properly made; and

(*b*) the authority is not otherwise entitled to refuse to register him.

(2) An application for registration under this Part shall be of no effect unless it contains—

(*a*) a statement with respect to the applicant which complies with the requirements of regulations made for the purposes of this Article by the Department; and

(b) a statement with respect to any person assisting or likely to be assisting in looking after children on the premises in question, or living or likely to be living there, which complies with the requirements of such regulations.

(3) Where a person provides, or proposes to provide, day care for children under the age of twelve on different premises situated within the area of the same authority, he shall make a separate application with respect to each of those premises.

Refusal of registration

124.—(1) An authority may refuse to register an applicant for registration under Article 118(1)(*a*) if the authority is satisfied that—

(*a*) the applicant; or

(*b*) any person looking after, or likely to be looking after, any children on any premises on which the applicant is, or is likely to be, child minding,

is not fit to look after children under the age of twelve.

(2) An authority may refuse to register an applicant for registration under Article 118(1)(*a*) if the authority is satisfied that—

(*a*) any person living, or likely to be living, at any premises on which the applicant is, or is likely to be, child minding; or

(*b*) any person employed, or likely to be employed, on those premises,

is not fit to be in the proximity of children under the age of twelve.

(3) An authority may refuse to register an applicant for registration under Article 118(1)(*b*) if the authority is satisfied that any person looking after, or likely to be looking after, any children on the premises to which the application relates is not fit to look after children under the age of twelve.

(4) An authority may refuse to register an applicant for registration under Article 118(1)(*b*) if the authority is satisfied that—

(*a*) any person living, or likely to be living, at the premises to which the application relates; or

(*b*) any person employed, or likely to be employed, on those premises,

is not fit to be in the proximity of children under the age of twelve.

(5) An authority may refuse to register an applicant for registration under this Part if the authority is satisfied—

(*a*) in the case of an application for registration under Article 118(1)(*a*), that any premises on which the applicant is, or is likely to be, child minding; or

(*b*) in the case of an application for registration under Article 118(1)(*b*), that the premises to which the application relates,

are not fit to be used for looking after children under the age of twelve, whether because of their condition or the condition of any equipment used on the premises or for any reason connected with their situation, construction or size.

Requirements to be complied with by child minders

125.—(1) Where an authority registers a person under Article 118(1)(*a*), it shall impose such reasonable requirements on him as it considers appropriate in his case.

(2) In imposing requirements on him, the authority shall—

(*a*) specify the maximum number of children, or the maximum number of children within specified age groups, whom he may look after when acting as a child minder;

(*b*) require him to secure that any premises on which he so looks after any child, and the equipment used in those premises, are adequately maintained and kept safe;

(*c*) require him to keep a record of the name and address of—

(i) any child so looked after by him on any premises within the authority's area;

(ii) any person who assists in looking after any such child; and

(iii) any person living, or likely at any time to be living, at those premises;

(*d*) require him to notify the authority in writing of any change in the persons mentioned in sub-paragraph (*c*)(ii) and (iii).

(3) The Department may by regulations make provision as to—

(*a*) requirements which must be imposed by an authority under this Article in prescribed circumstances;

(*b*) requirements of such descriptions as may be prescribed which must not be imposed by an authority under this Article.

(4) In determining the maximum number of children to be specified under paragraph (2)(*a*), the authority shall take account of the number of other children who may at any time be on any premises on which the person concerned acts, or is likely to act, as a child minder.

(5) Where, in addition to the requirements mentioned in paragraph (2), an authority imposes other requirements, those other requirements must not be incompatible with any of the paragraph (2) requirements.

(6) An authority may at any time—

(*a*) vary any requirement imposed under this Article;

(*b*) impose any additional requirement; or

(*c*) remove any requirement.

Requirements to be complied with by persons providing day care for young children

126.—(1) Where an authority registers a person under Article

118(1)(*b*) it shall impose such reasonable requirements on him as it considers appropriate in his case.

(2) Where a person is registered under Article 118(1)(*b*) with respect to different premises within the area of the same authority, this Article applies separately in relation to each registration.

(3) In imposing requirements on him, the authority shall—

(*a*) specify the maximum number of children, or the maximum number of children within specified age groups, who may be looked after on the premises;

(*b*) require him to secure that the premises, and the equipment used in them, are adequately maintained and kept safe;

(*c*) require him to notify the authority of any change in the facilities which he provides or in the period during which he provides them;

(*d*) specify the number of persons required to assist in looking after children on the premises;

(*e*) require him to keep a record of the name and address of—

(i) any child looked after on the registered premises;

(ii) any person who assists in looking after any such child; and

(iii) any person who lives, or is likely at any time to be living, at those premises;

(*f*) require him to notify the authority in writing of any change in the persons mentioned in sub-paragraph (*e*)(ii) and (iii).

(4) The Department may by regulations make provision as to—

(*a*) requirements which must be imposed by an authority under this Article in prescribed circumstances;

(*b*) requirements of such descriptions as may be prescribed which must not be imposed by an authority under this Article.

(5) In paragraph (3) references to children looked after are to children looked after in accordance with the provision of day care made by the registered person.

(6) In determining the maximum number of children to be specified under paragraph (3)(*a*), the authority shall take account of the number of other children who may at any time be on the premises.

(7) Where, in addition to the requirements mentioned in paragraph (3), an authority imposes other requirements, those other requirements must not be incompatible with any of the paragraph (3) requirements.

(8) An authority may at any time—

(*a*) vary any requirement imposed under this Article;

(*b*) impose any additional requirement; or

(*c*) remove any requirement.

Certificate of registration

127.—(1) Where an authority registers a person under Article 118 it shall issue him with a certificate of registration.

(2) The certificate shall specify—

(*a*) the registered person's name and address;

(*b*) in a case falling within Article 118(1)(*b*), the address or situation of the premises concerned; and

(*c*) any requirements imposed under Article 125 or 126.

(3) Where, due to a change of circumstances, any part of the certificate requires to be amended, the authority shall issue an amended certificate.

(4) Where the authority is satisfied that the certificate has been lost or destroyed, the authority shall issue a copy, on payment by the registered person of such fee as may be determined by the Department.

Cancellation of registration

128.—(1) An authority may cancel the registration of any person under Article 118(1)(*a*) if—

(*a*) it appears to the authority that the circumstances of the case are such that it would be justified in refusing to register that person as a child minder;

(*b*) the care provided by that person when looking after any child as a child minder is, in the opinion of the authority, seriously inadequate having regard to the needs of that child; or

(*c*) that person has contravened any requirement imposed on him under Article 125.

(2) An authority may cancel the registration of any person under Article 118(1)(*b*) with respect to particular premises if—

(*a*) it appears to the authority that the circumstances of the case are such that it would be justified in refusing to register that person with respect to those premises;

(*b*) the day care provided by that person on those premises is, in the opinion of the authority, seriously inadequate having regard to the needs of the children concerned; or

(*c*) that person has contravened any requirement imposed on him under Article 126.

(3) An authority may cancel all registrations of any person under Article 118(1)(*b*) if it appears to the authority that the circumstances of the case are such that it would be justified in refusing to register that person with respect to any premises.

(4) Where a requirement to carry out repairs or make alterations or additions has been imposed on a registered person under Article

125 or 126, his registration shall not be cancelled on the ground that the premises are not fit to be used for looking after children if—

(*a*) the time set for complying with the requirement has not expired; and

(*b*) it is shown that the condition of the premises is due to the repairs not having been carried out or the alterations or additions not having been made.

(5) Any cancellation under this Article must be in writing.

(6) In considering the needs of any child for the purposes of paragraph (1)(*b*) or (2)(*b*), an authority shall, in particular, have regard to the child's religious persuasion, racial origin and cultural and linguistic background.

Protection of children in an emergency

129.—(1) If—

(*a*) an authority applies to the court for an order—

(i) cancelling a registered person's registration;

(ii) varying any requirement imposed on a registered person under Article 125 or 126; or

(iii) removing a requirement or imposing an additional requirement on such a person; and

(*b*) it appears to the court that a child who is being, or may be, looked after by that person, or (as the case may be) in accordance with the provision for day care made by that person, is suffering, or is likely to suffer, significant harm,

the court may make the order.

(2) Any such cancellation, variation, removal or imposition shall take effect immediately the order is made.

(3) An application under paragraph (1) may be made *ex parte* and shall be supported by a written statement of the authority's reasons for making it.

(4) Where an order is made under this Article, the authority shall serve on the registered person, as soon as is reasonably practicable after the making of the order—

(*a*) notice of the order and of its terms; and

(*b*) a copy of the statement of the authority's reasons which supported its application for the order.

(5) Where the court imposes or varies any requirement under paragraph (1), the requirement, or the requirement as varied, shall be treated for all purposes, other than those of Article 131, as if it had been imposed under Article 125 or (as the case may be) 126 by the authority.

Inspection

130.—(1) Any person authorised to do so by an authority may at any reasonable time enter—

(a) any domestic premises within the authority's area on which child minding is at any time carried on; or

(b) any premises within the authority's area on which day care for children under the age of twelve is at any time provided.

(2) Where an authority has reasonable cause to believe that a child is being looked after on any premises within the authority's area in contravention of this Part, any person authorised to do so by the authority may enter those premises at any reasonable time.

(3) Any person entering premises under this Article may inspect—

(a) the premises;

(b) any children being looked after on the premises;

(c) the arrangements made for their welfare; and

(d) any records relating to them which are kept for the purposes of this Part.

(4) Every authority shall secure that the premises mentioned in paragraph (1) are inspected at least once every year.

(5) Where—

(a) a person is registered under Article 118; and

(b) an annual inspection of the premises in question is to be carried out under this Article,

the authority shall serve on that person a notice informing him that the inspection is to be carried out.

(6) Any person inspecting any records under this Article—

(a) shall be entitled at any reasonable time to have access to, and inspect and check the operation of, any computer and any associated apparatus or material which is, or has been, in use in connection with the records in question; and

(b) may require—

(i) the person by whom or on whose behalf the computer is or has been so used; or

(ii) any person having charge of, or otherwise concerned with the operation of, the computer, apparatus or material,

to afford him such reasonable assistance as he may require.

(7) A person exercising any power conferred by this Article shall, if so required, produce some duly authenticated document showing his authority to do so.

Appeals

131.—(1) Not less than 14 days before—

(a) refusing an application for registration under Article 118;

(b) cancelling any such registration;

(c) refusing consent under Article 122;

(d) imposing, removing or varying any requirement under Article 125 or 126; or

(e) refusing to grant any application for the variation or removal of any such requirement,

an authority shall send to the applicant, or (as the case may be) registered person, notice in writing of the authority's intention to take the step in question ("the step").

(2) Every such notice shall—

(a) give the authority's reasons for proposing to take the step; and

(b) inform the person concerned of his rights under this Article.

(3) Where the recipient of such a notice informs the authority in writing of his desire to object to the step being taken, the authority shall afford him an opportunity to do so.

(4) Any objection made under paragraph (3) may be made in person or by a representative.

(5) If the authority, after giving the person concerned an opportunity to object to the step being taken, decides nevertheless to take it the authority shall send him written notice of its decision.

(6) A person aggrieved by the taking of any step mentioned in paragraph (1) may appeal against it to the court.

(7) Where the court imposes or varies any requirement under paragraph (8) or (9) the requirement, or the requirement as varied, shall be treated for all purposes (other than this Article) as if it had been imposed by the authority.

(8) Where the court allows an appeal against the refusal or cancellation of any registration under Article 118 it may impose requirements under Article 125 or (as the case may be) 126.

(9) Where the court allows an appeal against such a requirement it may, instead of cancelling the requirement, vary it.

(10) A step of a kind mentioned in paragraph (1)(b) or (d) shall not take effect until the expiry of the time within which an appeal may be brought under this Article or, where such an appeal is brought, before its determination.

Offences

132.—(1) No person shall provide day care for children under the age of twelve on any premises within the area of an authority unless he is registered by the authority under Article 118(1)(b) with respect to those premises.

(2) If any person contravenes paragraph (1) without reasonable

excuse, he shall be guilty of an offence.

(3) No person shall act as a child minder on domestic premises within the area of an authority unless he is registered by the authority under Article 118(1)(a).

(4) Where it appears to an authority that a person has contravened paragraph (3), the authority may serve a notice ("an enforcement notice") on him.

(5) An enforcement notice shall have effect for a period of one year beginning with the date on which it is served.

(6) If a person with respect to whom an enforcement notice is in force contravenes paragraph (3) without reasonable excuse he shall be guilty of an offence.

(7) Paragraph (6) applies whether or not the subsequent contravention occurs within the area of the authority which served the enforcement notice.

(8) Any person who without reasonable excuse contravenes any requirement imposed on him under Article 125 or 126 shall be guilty of an offence.

(9) If any person—

(a) acts as a child minder on domestic premises at any time when he is disqualified by regulations made under Article 122; or

(b) provides day care for children under the age of twelve on premises (other than domestic premises) at any time when he is so disqualified; or

(c) contravenes paragraph (3), (4) or (5) of Article 122,

he shall be guilty of an offence.

(10) Where a person contravenes paragraph (3) of Article 122 he shall not be guilty of an offence under this Article if he proves that he did not know, and had no reasonable grounds for believing, that the person in question was living or employed in the household.

(11) Where a person contravenes paragraph (5) of Article 122 he shall not be guilty of an offence under this Article if he proves that he did not know, and had no reasonable grounds for believing, that the person whom he was employing was disqualified.

(12) Any person who intentionally obstructs another in the exercise of any power conferred by Article 130 shall be guilty of an offence.

(13) A person guilty of an offence under this Article shall be liable on summary conviction—

(a) in the case of an offence under paragraph (8), to a fine not exceeding level 4 on the standard scale;

(b) in the case of an offence under paragraph (9), to imprisonment for a term not exceeding six months, or to a fine not exceeding level 5 on the standard scale, or to both;

119

(c) in the case of an offence under paragraph (12), to a fine not exceeding level 3 on the standard scale;

(d) in the case of any other offence, to a fine not exceeding level 5 on the standard scale.

PART XII

EMPLOYMENT OF CHILDREN

Introductory

Interpretation

133.—(1) In this Part—

"broadcasting studio" means a studio used in connection with the provision of a programme service;

"child" means a person who is not over school-leaving age;

"performance of a dangerous nature" includes all acrobatic performances and all performances as a contortionist;

"programme service" has the same meaning as in the Broadcasting Act 1990;

1990 c. 42

"school-leaving age" means the upper limit of compulsory school age;

"street trading" includes the hawking of newspapers, matches, flowers and other articles, playing, singing or performing for a profit, shoe-polishing and other similar activities carried on in streets or public places.

(2) For the purposes of this Part a child who assists in a trade or occupation carried on for profit shall be deemed to be employed notwithstanding that he receives no reward for his labour.

Exemptions and saving

134.—(1) The provisions of this Part and of any regulations made under it shall not apply to a child detained in a training school.

(2) The provisions of this Part are in addition to any statutory provision—

(a) relating to the employment of children; or

(b) for giving effect to any international convention regulating employment.

General

General restrictions on the employment of children

135.—(1) No child shall be employed—

(a) so long as he is under the age of 13 years; or

(b) before the close of school hours on any day on which he is required to attend school; or

(c) before seven o'clock in the morning or after seven o'clock in the evening on any day; or

(d) for more than two hours on any day on which he is required to attend school,

except in accordance with any statutory provision (including this Part and regulations made under it).

(2) No child shall be employed in any occupation likely to be injurious to his life, limb, health or education, regard being had to his physical condition.

(3) If any education and library board serves on the employer of any child a copy of a certificate signed by a medical practitioner that any specified occupation is likely to be injurious to the life, limb, health or education of the child, the certificate shall be admissible as evidence in any subsequent proceedings against the employer in respect of the employment of the child.

(4) No child shall engage in or be employed in street trading.

Regulations with respect to the employment of children

136.—(1) The Department may, with the approval of the Department of Education, make regulations with respect to the employment of children and any such regulations may contain provisions—

(a) authorising the employment of children (notwithstanding anything in paragraph (1)(b) of Article 135) for not more than one hour before the commencement of school hours on any day on which they are required to attend school;

(b) specifying the occupations in which children may or may not be employed;

(c) prescribing—

(i) the age below which children are not to be employed;

(ii) the number of hours in each day, or in each week, for which, and the times of day at which, they may be employed;

(iii) the intervals to be allowed to them for meals and rest;

(iv) the holidays or half-holidays to be allowed to them;

(v) any other conditions to be observed in relation to their employment.

(2) Except in so far as is expressly permitted by paragraph (1)(a) and (c)(i), regulations under this Article shall not modify the restrictions contained in Article 135, and any restrictions contained in regulations under this Article shall have effect in addition to the restrictions contained in that Article.

(3) Nothing in Article 135 or in regulations under this Article shall prevent a child from taking part in a performance—

(a) under the authority of a licence granted under this Part; or

121

(b) in a case where by virtue of paragraph (3) of Article 137 no licence under that Article is required for him to take part in the performance.

Performances

Restrictions on taking part in public performances, etc.

137.—(1) A child shall not take part in a performance to which this Article applies unless—

(a) a licence has been granted under Article 138, or

(b) by virtue of paragraph (3), no licence is required.

(2) This Article applies to—

(a) any performance in connection with which a charge is made (whether for admission or otherwise);

(b) any performance in licensed premises within the meaning of the Licensing (Northern Ireland) Order 1990, or in any premises in respect of which a club is registered under the Registration of Clubs (Northern Ireland) Order 1987;

1990 NI 6

1987 NI 14

(c) any broadcast performance;

(d) any performance not falling within sub-paragraph (c) but included in a programme service;

(e) any performance recorded (by whatever means) with a view to its use in a broadcast or a programme service or in a film intended for public exhibition;

and a child shall be treated for the purposes of this Article as taking part in a performance if he takes the place of a performer in any rehearsal or in any preparation for the recording of the performance.

(3) A licence under Article 138 shall not be required for any child to take part in a performance to which this Article applies if—

(a) in the six months preceding the performance he has not taken part in other performances to which this Article applies on more than three days; or

(b) the performance is given under arrangements made by a school or made by a body of persons approved for the purposes of this Article by the Department of Education or by the education and library board in whose area the performance takes place, and no payment in respect of the child's taking part in the performance is made, whether to him or to any other person, except for defraying expenses;

but the Department of Education may, with the approval of the Department, by regulations prescribe conditions to be observed with respect to the hours of work, rest or meals of children taking part in performances as mentioned in sub-paragraph (a).

Granting of licences

138.—(1) The appropriate education and library board may grant a licence for a child to take part in a performance to which Article 137 applies.

(2) The appropriate education and library board referred to in paragraph (1) is—

(*a*) the education and library board in whose area the child resides; or

(*b*) if the child does not reside in Northern Ireland, the education and library board in whose area the applicant or one of the applicants resides or has his place of business; or

(*c*) if the child does not reside in Northern Ireland and the applicant or every applicant neither resides nor has his place of business in Northern Ireland, any education and library board.

(3) Subject to paragraph (4), the education and library board shall not refuse to grant a licence for a child to take part in a performance or series of performances if the board is satisfied—

(*a*) that the child is fit to do so; and

(*b*) that proper provision has been made to secure the child's health and kind treatment; and

(*c*) that, having regard to such provision, if any, as has been or will be made for the child's education, his education will not suffer.

(4) The education and library board shall not grant a licence in respect of a child who is under the age of 14 unless—

(*a*) the licence is for acting and the application for the licence is accompanied by a declaration that the part he is to act cannot be taken except by a child of about his age; or

(*b*) the licence is for dancing in a ballet which does not form part of an entertainment of which anything other than ballet or opera forms part and the application for the licence is accompanied by a declaration that the part he is to dance cannot be taken except by a child of about his age; or

(*c*) the nature of his part in the performance is wholly or mainly musical and either the nature of the performance is also wholly or mainly musical or the performance consists only of opera or ballet.

(5) The power of the education and library board to grant licences under this Article shall be exercisable subject to such restrictions and conditions as the Department of Education may with the approval of the Department prescribe by regulations, and such conditions may include—

(*a*) conditions requiring the approval of an education and library board (and may provide for that approval to be given subject to conditions imposed by the board);

(b) a condition requiring sums earned by the child in respect of whom the licence is granted in taking part in a performance to which the licence relates—

(i) to be paid into the county court and, subject to county court rules, applied or otherwise dealt with for the benefit of that child in such manner as the county court may direct, or

(ii) to be applied or otherwise dealt with in a manner approved by the education and library board.

(6) A licence under this Article shall specify the times, if any, during which the child in respect of whom it is granted may be absent from school for the purposes authorised by the licence; and for the purposes of determining whether, under Article 45 of, and Schedule 13 to, the Education and Libraries (Northern Ireland) Order 1986, a registered pupil of a school has failed to attend regularly at the school, his absence at such times shall be disregarded.

1986 NI 3

(7) An education and library board which grants a licence under this Article authorising a child to take part in a performance in the area of another education and library board shall send that other board such particulars as the Department of Education may with the approval of the Department prescribe by regulations.

Variation and revocation of licences

139.—(1) A licence under Article 138 may be varied on the application of the person holding it by the appropriate education and library board.

(2) The appropriate education and library board may vary or revoke a licence under Article 138 if—

(a) any condition subject to which the licence was granted is not observed; or

(b) the board is not satisfied as to the matters mentioned in paragraph (3) of that Article,

but before varying or revoking the licence, the board shall give to the holder of the licence such notice, if any, of the board's intentions as may be practicable in the circumstances.

(3) The appropriate education and library board referred to in paragraphs (1) and (2) is—

(a) the education and library board which granted the licence; or

(b) any education and library board in whose area the performance or one of the performances to which it relates takes place.

(4) An education and library board which proposes to vary or revoke a licence which was granted by, or relates to a performance in

the area of, another education and library board shall, if practicable, consult that other board.

(5) An education and library board which varies or revokes such a licence shall inform that other board.

Requirement to keep and produce records

140.—(1) The holder of a licence shall keep such records as the Department of Education may, with the approval of the Department, prescribe by regulations.

(2) At any time not later than six months after the performance or last performance to which the licence relates, the holder of the licence shall on request produce the records to an officer of the education and library board which granted, or any education and library board which varied, the licence.

Dangerous performances

Performances endangering life or limb

141. No child shall take part in any performance to which Article 137 applies and in which his life or limbs are endangered.

Training for performances of a dangerous nature

142. No child under the age of twelve shall be trained to take part in performances of a dangerous nature.

Licensing of training children over twelve for performances of a dangerous nature

143.—(1) The appropriate education and library board may grant a licence for a child who is not under the age of twelve to be trained to take part in performances of a dangerous nature and no such child shall be so trained except under and in accordance with the terms of a licence under this Article.

(2) The appropriate education and library board referred to in paragraph (1) is—

 (a) the education and library board in whose area the child resides; or

 (b) the education and library board in whose area the place or any of the places at which the child is to be trained is situate.

(3) The education and library board shall not refuse to grant a licence under this Article if the board is satisfied—

 (a) that the child is fit and willing to be trained; and

 (b) that proper provision has been made to secure his health and kind treatment.

(4) A licence under this Article shall—

(a) specify the place or places at which the child is to be trained;

(b) contain such conditions as the education and library board considers necessary for the child's protection.

(5) The education and library board by which a licence under this Article is granted may vary or revoke the licence—

(a) if any condition subject to which the licence was granted is not observed; or

(b) if it appears to the board that—

(i) the child is no longer fit and willing to be trained; or

(ii) proper provision is no longer being made to secure his health and kind treatment,

but before varying or revoking the licence, the board shall give to the holder of the licence such notice, if any, of the board's intentions as may be practicable in the circumstances.

Supplementary

Notice of refusal of licence, etc.

144.—(1) This paragraph applies where an education and library board—

(a) refuses an application for a licence under this Part; or

(b) revokes such a licence; or

(c) in the case of a licence under Article 138—

(i) varies it otherwise than on the application of the holder, or

(ii) in granting it or in giving approval under paragraph (5)(a) of that Article imposes any conditions otherwise than with the consent of the applicant or holder;

(d) in the case of a licence under Article 143—

(i) varies it, or

(ii) in granting it, imposes any conditions otherwise than with the consent of the applicant.

(2) Where paragraph (1) applies, the education and library board shall serve a notice on the applicant or holder of the licence informing him of—

(a) the board's reasons for acting as described in paragraph (1); and

(b) his right of appeal under Article 145.

Appeal against refusal of licence, etc.

145.—(1) The applicant or holder of a licence may, where Article 144(1) applies, appeal to the court.

(2) An appeal shall not be brought under paragraph (1) by the

applicant or holder of a licence more than 28 days after the service on him of the notice required by Article 144(2).

Powers of entry

146.—(1) Where, on an application made by any person for a warrant under this Article, it appears to the court that there is reasonable cause to believe that the provisions of this Part or of any regulations made or licences granted under this Part are being contravened with respect to any child, the court may issue a warrant authorising any officer of an education and library board or any constable to enter, at any reasonable time within 48 hours of the issue of the warrant, any place in or in connection with which the child in question is, or is believed to be, employed or taking part in a performance, or being trained, and to make inquiries there with respect to that child.

(2) Any authorised officer of an education and library board or any constable may—

(*a*) at any time enter any place used—

(i) as a broadcasting studio or film studio; or

(ii) for the recording of a performance with a view to its use in a programme service or in a film intended for public exhibition,

and make inquiries there as to any children taking part in performances to which Article 137 applies;

(*b*) at any time during the currency of a licence granted under Article 138 or 143 enter any place (whether or not it is such a place as is mentioned in sub-paragraph (*a*)) where the child to whom the licence relates is authorised by the licence to take part in a performance or to be trained, and make inquiries there with respect to that child.

(3) A person (other than a constable in uniform) exercising any power of entry conferred by this Article shall, if so required, produce some duly authenticated document showing his authority to do so.

(4) An application for a warrant under this Article shall be made in the manner and form prescribed by rules of court.

Offences

147.—(1) Any person who employs a child in contravention of—

(*a*) Article 135; or

(*b*) regulations under Article 136,

and any person (other than the child) to whose act or default the contravention is attributable shall be guilty of an offence.

127

(2) Any person who—

    (*a*) causes or procures a child; or

    (*b*) being his parent, allows a child,

to take part in any performance in contravention of Article 137 or 141 or to be trained to take part in performances of a dangerous nature in contravention of Article 142 or 143 shall be guilty of an offence.

(3) In paragraph (2)(*b*) "parent" includes—

    (*a*) any person who is not a parent of the child but who has parental responsibility for him; and

    (*b*) any person who has care of the child.

(4) Any person who—

    (*a*) fails to observe—

        (i) any condition subject to which a licence under this Part is granted; or

        (ii) any condition prescribed under Article 137(3); or

    (*b*) in or in connection with an application for a licence under this Part or for the variation of a licence under Article 139, knowingly or recklessly makes any statement which is false in a material particular or in a material respect misleading;

    (*c*) fraudulently alters or uses, or permits to be fraudulently altered or used—

        (i) any licence under this Part; or

        (ii) any record which he is required to keep under Article 140;

    (*d*) fails to keep or produce any record which he is required to keep or produce under Article 140,

shall be guilty of an offence.

(5) Where the commission by any person of an offence under paragraph (1) is due to an act or default of some other person, that other person may be charged with and convicted of the offence whether or not proceedings are taken against the first-mentioned person.

(6) Any person who is guilty of an offence under paragraph (1), (2) or (4) shall be liable on summary conviction to a fine not exceeding level 3 on the standard scale.

(7) The court by which the holder or one of the holders of a licence under this Part is sentenced for an offence under paragraph (2) or (4) may revoke the licence.

(8) Any child who engages in street trading in contravention of Article 135(4) shall be guilty of an offence and liable on summary conviction to a fine not exceeding level 1 on the standard scale.

(9) Any person who intentionally obstructs any officer of an education and library board or any constable in the exercise of any

powers conferred on him by or under Article 146 shall be guilty of an offence and liable on summary conviction to a fine not exceeding level 2 on the standard scale.

Defences

148.—(1) Where a person is charged with the commission of an offence under Article 147(1) and it is proved—

(a) that the commission of the offence was due to an act or default of some other person; and

(b) that the person charged took all reasonable precautions and exercised all due diligence to avoid the commission of the offence by him or any person under his control,

then, subject to paragraph (2), the person charged shall be acquitted of the offence.

(2) The person charged as described in paragraph (1) shall not be entitled to be acquitted under that paragraph unless not more than 14 days after the date of the service of the summons on him nor less than seven days before the date of the hearing he has given notice in writing to the complainant of his intention to rely on the provisions of that paragraph, specifying the name and address of the person to whose act or default he alleges the commission of the offence was due, and has sent a like notice to that person; and that person shall be entitled to appear at the hearing and to give evidence.

(3) In any proceedings for an offence under Article 147(2) alleged to have been committed by causing, procuring or allowing a child to take part in a performance without a licence in contravention of Article 137, it shall be a defence to prove that the person charged believed that the condition specified in Article 137(3)(a) was satisfied and that he had reasonable grounds for that belief.

PART XIII

DEPARTMENT'S SUPERVISORY FUNCTIONS AND RESPONSIBILITIES

Inspection of children's homes, etc., by Department

149.—(1) The Department may cause to be inspected—

(a) any children's home;

(b) any premises in which a child who is being looked after by an authority is living;

(c) any premises in which a child who is being accommodated by or on behalf of an education and library board or voluntary organisation is living;

(d) any premises in which a privately fostered child, or child who is treated as a foster child by virtue of Article 114 (application of Part X to certain school children during holidays), is living or in which it is proposed that he will live;

(*e*) any premises on which any person is acting as a child minder;

(*f*) any premises with respect to which a person is registered under Article 118(1)(*b*) (day care);

(*g*) any of the following if used to accommodate children—

(i) a residential care home,

(ii) a nursing home,

(iii) a hospital (including a private hospital);

(*h*) any premises which are provided by an authority and in which any service is provided by that authority under Part IV;

(*i*) any school providing accommodation for any child.

(2) An inspection under this Article shall be conducted by a person authorised to do so by the Department.

(3) An officer of an authority shall not be so authorised except with the consent of that authority.

(4) The Department may require any person mentioned in paragraph (5) to furnish the Department with such information, or allow any person authorised by the Department to inspect such records (in whatever form they are held), relating to—

(*a*) any premises to which paragraph (1) applies;

(*b*) any child who is living in any such premises;

(*c*) any person who is living in or is employed in any such premises;

(*d*) the discharge by the Department of any of its functions under this Order; or

(*e*) the discharge by any authority of any of its functions under this Order,

as the Department may at any time direct.

(5) The persons are—

(*a*) any Board or Health and Social Services trust;

(*b*) any voluntary organisation;

(*c*) any person carrying on a children's home;

(*d*) any managers of a school;

(*e*) any person fostering any privately fostered child or providing accommodation for a child on behalf of an authority, an education and library board or a voluntary organisation;

(*f*) any education and library board providing accommodation for any child;

(*g*) any person employed in a school at which a child is accommodated by or on behalf of an authority or an education and library board;

(*h*) any person who is the occupier of any premises in which any person acts as a child minder (within the meaning of Part XI) or provides day care for young children (within the meaning of that Part);

(*i*) any person carrying on any home or hospital of a kind mentioned in paragraph (1)(*g*).

Powers of persons authorised by Department

150.—(1) Any person inspecting any home or other premises under Article 149 may—

(*a*) inspect the children there; and

(*b*) make such examination into the state and management of the home or premises and the treatment of the children there as he thinks fit.

(2) Any person authorised by the Department to exercise the power to inspect records conferred by Article 149(4)—

(*a*) shall be entitled at any reasonable time to have access to, and inspect and check the operation of, any computer and any associated apparatus or material which is or has been in use in connection with the records in question; and

(*b*) may require—

(i) the person by whom or on whose behalf the computer is or has been so used; or

(ii) any person having charge of, or otherwise concerned with the operation of, the computer, apparatus or material,

to afford him such reasonable assistance as he may require.

(3) A person authorised to inspect any premises under Article 149 may enter the premises for that purpose, and for any purpose specified in paragraph (4) of that Article, at any reasonable time.

(4) Any person exercising that power shall, if so required, produce some duly authenticated document showing his authority to do so.

(5) Any person who intentionally obstructs another in the exercise of that power shall be guilty of an offence and liable on summary conviction to a fine not exceeding level 3 on the standard scale.

Power to exempt children's homes, etc., from inspection

151.—(1) The Department may by order provide that Articles 149 and 150 shall not apply in relation to particular homes or premises specified in the order.

(2) Orders under paragraph (1) shall be subject to negative resolution.

Inquiries

152.—(1) The Department may cause local or other inquiries to be held in any cases where it appears to the Department to be advisable to do so in connection with—

(*a*) the functions of an authority or voluntary organisation, in so far as those functions relate to children;

(*b*) a children's home or voluntary home;

(*c*) any of the following, so far as they provide accommodation for children—

(i) a residential care home;

(ii) a hospital (including a private hospital);

(iii) a nursing home;

(iv) a school;

(v) any prescribed home or institution not falling within heads (i) to (iv) and not provided by the Secretary of State.

(2) Before an inquiry is begun, the Department may direct that it shall be held in private.

(3) Where no direction has been given, the person holding the inquiry may if he thinks fit hold it, or any part of it, in private.

(4) In paragraph (1)(*a*) "functions" includes powers and duties other than under a statutory provision.

Child care training

153.—(1) The Department shall keep under review the adequacy of the provision of child care training and may, subject to such conditions as it may determine—

(*a*) make grants towards any fees or expenses incurred by, or

(*b*) defray or contribute towards the cost of maintenance of,

persons undergoing child care training.

(2) The Department shall receive and consider any information from or representations made by—

(*a*) the Central Council for Education and Training in Social Work;

(*b*) any authority; or

(*c*) such other persons or organisations as appear to the Department to be appropriate,

concerning the provision of child care training.

(3) In this Article "child care training" means training for persons with a view to, or in the course of, their employment or the use of their services in the health and personal social services for the purposes of this Order or the Adoption Order or by a voluntary organisation for similar purposes.

Research and information

154.—(1) The Department may conduct or promote or assist (by grants or otherwise) any person in conducting research or investigations into any matter connected with the functions under this Order of the Department, authorities or, with the consent of the Department of Education, education and library boards.

(2) The Department of Education may conduct or promote or assist (by grants or otherwise) any person in conducting research or investigations into any matter connected with the functions under this Order of education and library boards.

(3) Every authority shall, at such times and in such form as the Department may direct, transmit to the Department such particulars as the Department may require with respect to—

(*a*) the performance by the authority of all or any of its functions—

(i) under this Order; or

(ii) in connection with the accommodation of children in residential care homes, nursing homes or private hospitals; and

(*b*) the children in relation to whom the authority has exercised those functions.

PART XIV

PARENTS NOT MARRIED TO EACH OTHER

Parents not being married to each other to have no effect in law on relationships

155.—(1) In this Order and in any statutory provision or any instrument passed or made after the commencement of this Article, references (however expressed) to any relationship between two persons shall be construed without regard to whether or not the father and mother of either of them or the father and mother of any person through whom the relationship is deduced, have or had been married to each other at any time.

(2) In this Order and in any statutory provision passed or made after the commencement of this Article—

(*a*) references to a person whose father and mother were married to each other at the time of his birth include, and

(*b*) references to a person whose father and mother were not married to each other at the time of his birth do not include,

references to any person to whom paragraph (3) applies.

(3) This paragraph applies to any person who—

(*a*) is treated as legitimate by virtue of section 1 of the Legitimacy Act (Northern Ireland) 1961;   1961 c. 5 (N.I.)

(b) is a legitimated person within the meaning of Article 32 of the Matrimonial and Family Proceedings (Northern Ireland) Order 1989;

(c) is an adopted child within the meaning of Part V of the Adoption Order; or

(d) is otherwise treated in law as legitimate.

(4) For the purpose of construing references falling within paragraph (2), the time of a person's birth shall be taken to include any time during the period beginning with—

(a) the insemination resulting in his birth; or

(b) where there was no such insemination, his conception,

and (in either case) ending with his birth.

(5) Paragraphs (1) and (2) have effect subject to any contrary intention.

Application of principle to certain existing statutory provisions

156. The Department of Finance and Personnel may by order make provision for the construction in accordance with Article 155 of such statutory provisions passed or made before the commencement of that Article as may be specified in the order, but an order under this Article shall so amend the statutory provisions to which it relates as to secure that (so far as practicable) they continue to have the same effect notwithstanding the making of the order.

Property rights

157. Schedule 6 (which contains provisions relating to property rights where the parents of a child were not married to each other at the time of his birth) shall have effect.

Repeal of Illegitimate Children (Affiliation Orders) Act (Northern Ireland) 1924

158. The Illegitimate Children (Affiliation Orders) Act (Northern Ireland) 1924 shall cease to have effect.

PART XV

GUARDIANS

Appointment by court

159.—(1) Where an application with respect to a child is made by any individual, the High Court or a county court may by order appoint that individual to be the child's guardian if—

(a) the child has no parent with parental responsibility for him; or

(b) a residence order has been made with respect to the child in favour of a parent or guardian of his who has died while the order was in force.

(2) The power conferred by paragraph (1) may also be exercised in any family proceedings by the High Court or a county court if it considers that the order should be made even though no application has been made for it.

(3) Paragraph (1) shall not apply if the residence order referred to in sub-paragraph (b) of that paragraph was also made in favour of a surviving parent of the child.

(4) A person appointed as a guardian under this Article shall have parental responsibility for the child concerned.

(5) Subject to any provision made by rules of court, the High Court shall not exercise its inherent jurisdiction to appoint a guardian of the fortune or estate of any child.

(6) Where rules are made under paragraph (5), they may prescribe the circumstances in which, and conditions subject to which, an appointment of such a guardian may be made.

(7) A guardian may only be appointed in accordance with the provisions of this Article or Article 160.

Appointment by parent or guardian

160.—(1) A parent who has parental responsibility for his child may appoint another individual to be the child's guardian in the event of his death.

(2) A guardian of a child may appoint another individual to take his place as the child's guardian in the event of his death.

(3) An appointment under paragraph (1) or (2) shall not have effect unless it is made—

(a) by will or by deed; or

(b) by a written and dated instrument which is signed—

(i) by the person making the appointment, or

(ii) at his direction, in his presence and in the presence of two witnesses each of whom attests the signature.

(4) A person appointed as a guardian under this Article shall have parental responsibility for the child concerned.

(5) Where—

(a) on the death of any person making an appointment under paragraph (1) or (2), the child concerned has no parent with parental responsibility for him; or

(b) immediately before the death of any person making such an appointment, a residence order in his favour was in force with respect to the child, the appointment shall take effect on the death of that person.

(6) Where, on the death of any person making an appointment under paragraph (1) or (2)—

(a) the child concerned has a parent with parental responsibility for him; and

(b) paragraph (5)(b) does not apply,

the appointment shall take effect when the child no longer has a parent who has parental responsibility for him.

(7) Paragraph (5) shall not apply if the residence order referred to in sub-paragraph (b) of that paragraph was also made in favour of a surviving parent of the child.

(8) Nothing in this Article shall be taken to prevent an appointment under paragraph (1) or (2) being made by two or more persons acting jointly.

Revocation of appointment by parent or guardian

161.—(1) An appointment under paragraph (1) or (2) of Article 160 revokes an earlier such appointment (including one made in an unrevoked will) made by the same person in respect of the same child, unless it is clear (whether as the result of an express provision in the later appointment or by any necessary implication) that the purpose of the later appointment is to appoint an additional guardian.

(2) An appointment under paragraph (1) or (2) of Article 160 (including one made in an unrevoked will) is revoked if the person who made the appointment revokes it by a written and dated instrument which is signed—

(a) by him; or

(b) at his direction, in his presence and in the presence of two witnesses each of whom attests the signature.

(3) An appointment under paragraph (1) or (2) of Article 160 (other than one made in a will) is revoked if, with the intention of revoking the appointment, the person who made it—

(a) destroys the instrument by which it was made; or

(b) has some other person destroy that instrument in his presence.

(4) An appointment under paragraph (1) or (2) of Article 160 made in a will is revoked if the will is revoked.

(5) An appointment under paragraph (1) or (2) of Article 160 (including one made in an unrevoked will) is revoked if—

(a) the marriage of the person who made the appointment is dissolved or annulled, and

(b) the person appointed is his former spouse.

(6) Paragraph (5) is subject to a contrary intention appearing from the appointment.

(7) In paragraph (5)—

"dissolved or annulled" means—

(a) dissolved by a decree of divorce or annulled by a decree of nullity of marriage granted under the law of any part of the United Kingdom or the Channel Islands or under the law of the Isle of Man, or

(b) dissolved or annulled in any country or territory outside the United Kingdom, the Channel Islands and the Isle of Man by a divorce or annulment which is entitled to be recognised as valid by the law of Northern Ireland;

"former spouse" means the person whose marriage with the person who made the appointment was so dissolved or annulled.

Disclaimer of appointment by parent or guardian

162.—(1) A person who is appointed as a guardian under paragraph (1) or (2) of Article 160 may disclaim his appointment by an instrument in writing signed by him and made within a reasonable time of his first knowing that the appointment has taken effect.

(2) Where regulations are made by the Department of Finance and Personnel prescribing the manner in which such disclaimers must be recorded, no such disclaimer shall have effect unless it is recorded in the prescribed manner.

Termination by court

163.—(1) Any appointment of a guardian under Article 159 or 160 may be brought to an end at any time by order of the court—

(a) on the application of any person who has parental responsibility for the child;

(b) on the application of the child concerned, with leave of the court; or

(c) in any family proceedings, if the court considers that it should be brought to an end even though no application has been made.

(2) In paragraph (1) "the court" means the High Court and, except in relation to any appointment of a guardian under Article 159 by the High Court, a county court.

PART XVI

JURISDICTION AND PROCEDURE

Jurisdiction

164.—(1) In this Order "the court" means the High Court, a county court or a court of summary jurisdiction.

(2) Paragraph (1) is subject to the provision made by or under Schedule 7 and to any express provision as to the jurisdiction of any court made by any other provision of this Order.

(3) A court of summary jurisdiction shall not be competent to entertain any application, or make any order, involving the administration or application of—

(*a*) any property belonging to or held in trust for a child; or

(*b*) the income of any such property.

(4) A juvenile court (that is to say, a court of summary jurisdiction constituted in accordance with Schedule 2 to the Children and Young Persons Act (Northern Ireland) 1968) sitting for the purpose of exercising any jurisdiction conferred by or under this Order may be known as a family proceedings court.

1968 c. 34 (N.I.)

(5) Schedule 7 which makes provision, including provision for the Lord Chancellor to make orders, principally with respect to the jurisdiction of courts in proceedings under this Order, shall have effect.

Rules of court

165.—(1) An authority having power to make rules of court may make such provision for giving effect to—

(*a*) this Order;

(*b*) the provisions of any regulations or order made under this Order; or

(*c*) any amendment made by this Order in any other statutory provision,

as appears to that authority to be necessary or expedient.

(2) The rules may, in particular, make provision—

(*a*) with respect to the procedure to be followed in any relevant proceedings (including the manner in which any application is to be made or other proceedings commenced);

(*b*) as to the persons entitled to participate in any relevant proceedings, whether as parties to the proceedings or by being given the opportunity to make representations to the court;

(*c*) with respect to the documents and information to be furnished, and notices to be given, in connection with any relevant proceedings;

(*d*) applying (with or without modification) statutory provisions which govern proceedings brought on a complaint made to a court of summary jurisdiction to relevant proceedings in such a court brought otherwise than on a complaint or disapplying or modifying such statutory provisions in relation to relevant proceedings in a court of summary jurisdiction which would otherwise be brought on a complaint;

(*e*) with respect to preliminary hearings;

(*f*) for the service outside Northern Ireland, in such circumstances and in such manner as may be prescribed, of any notice of proceedings in a court of summary jurisdiction;

(*g*) for the exercise by a court of summary jurisdiction, in such circumstances as may be prescribed, of such powers as may be prescribed (even though a party to the proceedings in question is or resides outside Northern Ireland);

(*h*) enabling the court, in such circumstances as may be prescribed, to proceed on any application even though the respondent has not been given notice of the proceedings;

(*i*) authorising a resident magistrate or a member of a juvenile court panel to discharge the functions of a court of summary jurisdiction with respect to such relevant proceedings as may be prescribed;

(*j*) authorising a court of summary jurisdiction to order any of the parties to such relevant proceedings as may be prescribed, in such circumstances as may be prescribed, to pay the whole or part of the costs of all or any of the other parties.

(3) In paragraph (2)—

"notice of proceedings" means a summons or such other notice of proceedings as is required; and "given", in relation to a summons, means "served";

"prescribed" means prescribed by the rules; and

"relevant proceedings" means any application made, or proceedings brought, under any of the provisions mentioned in sub-paragraphs (*a*) to (*c*) of paragraph (1) and any part of such proceedings.

(4) This Article and any other power in this Order to make rules of court are not to be taken as in any way limiting any other power of the authority in question to make rules of court.

(5) When making any rules under this Article an authority shall be subject to the same requirements as to consultation (if any) as apply when the authority makes rules under its general rule making power.

Appeals

166.—(1) Subject to any express provisions to the contrary made by or under this Order, an appeal shall lie to the High Court against—

(*a*) the making by a county court of any order under this Order; or

139

(*b*) any refusal by a county court to make such an order,

as if the decision had been made in the exercise of the jurisdiction conferred by Part III of the County Courts (Northern Ireland) Order 1980 and the appeal were brought under Article 60 of that Order.

1980 NI 3

(2) An appeal shall not lie to the High Court under paragraph (1)—

(*a*) on an appeal from a court of summary jurisdiction; or

(*b*) where the county court is a divorce county court exercising jurisdiction under the Matrimonial Causes (Northern Ireland) Order 1978 in the same proceedings.

1978 NI 15

(3) Subject to any express provisions to the contrary made by or under this Order, an appeal shall lie to the county court against—

(*a*) the making by a court of summary jurisdiction of any order under this Order; or

(*b*) any refusal by a court of summary jurisdiction to make such an order.

(4) If the court of summary jurisdiction referred to in paragraph (3) is a family proceedings court—

(*a*) the county court to which the appeal under that paragraph lies shall be such county court as may be specified for the purposes of this paragraph;

(*b*) section 178 of the Children and Young Persons Act (Northern Ireland) 1968 shall not apply where such a county court deals with such an appeal;

and in sub-paragraph (*a*) "specified" has the meaning given in paragraph 4(2) of Schedule 7.

(5) Where a court of summary jurisdiction has power, in relation to any proceedings under this Order, to decline jurisdiction because it considers that the case can more conveniently be dealt with by another court, no appeal shall lie against any exercise of that power by that court of summary jurisdiction.

(6) No appeal shall lie in relation to an interim order for periodical payments made under Schedule 1.

(7) In paragraphs (8) to (13) "appellate court" means the High Court or the county court as the case may be.

(8) On an appeal under this Article, the appellate court may make such orders as may be necessary to give effect to its determination of the appeal.

(9) Where an order is made under paragraph (8) the appellate court may also make such incidental or consequential orders as appear to it to be just.

(10) Where an appeal under this Article relates to an order for the making of periodical payments, the appellate court may order that its determination of the appeal shall have effect from such date as it

thinks fit to specify in the order.

(11) The date so specified must not be earlier than the earliest date allowed in accordance with rules of court made for the purposes of this Article.

(12) Where, on an appeal under this Article in respect of an order requiring a person to make periodical payments, the appellate court reduces the amount of those payments or discharges the order—

> (*a*) it may order the person entitled to the payments to pay to the person making them such sum in respect of payments already made as that court thinks fit; and

> (*b*) if any arrears are due under the order for periodical payments, it may remit payment of the whole, or part, of those arrears.

(13) Any order of the appellate court made on an appeal under this Article (other than one directing that an application be re-heard by the county court or a court of summary jurisdiction) shall, for the purposes—

> (*a*) of the enforcement of the order; and

> (*b*) of any power to vary, revive or discharge orders,

be treated as if it were an order of the court from which the appeal was brought and not an order of the appellate court.

(14) The Lord Chancellor may by order make provision as to the circumstances in which appeals may be made against decisions taken by courts on questions arising in connection with the transfer, or proposed transfer, of proceedings by virtue of any order under paragraph 2 of Schedule 7.

(15) Except to the extent provided for in any order made under paragraph (14), no appeal may be made against any decision of a kind mentioned in that paragraph.

Attendance of child and his parents, etc., at hearing under Part V or VI

167.—(1) In any proceedings in which a court is hearing an application for an order under Part V or VI, or is considering whether to make any such order, the court may order the child concerned to attend such stage or stages of the proceedings as may be specified in the order.

(2) In any proceedings in which a court is hearing an application for an order under Part V or VI, or is considering whether to make any such order, the court may order any person who is a parent of the child concerned or who has parental responsibility for or care of him to attend such stage or stages of the proceedings as may be specified in the order.

(3) The powers conferred by paragraphs (1) and (2) shall be exercised in accordance with rules of court.

(4) Paragraphs (5) to (7) apply where—

(a) an order under paragraph (1) has not been complied with; or

(b) the court has reasonable cause to believe that it will not be complied with.

(5) The court may make an order authorising a constable, or such person as may be specified in the order—

(a) to take charge of the child and to bring him to the court; and

(b) to enter and search any premises specified in the order if he has reasonable cause to believe that the child may be found on the premises.

(6) The court may order any person who is in a position to do so to bring the child to the court.

(7) Where the court has reason to believe that a person has information about the whereabouts of the child it may order him to disclose it to the court.

Power to clear court while child is giving evidence in certain proceedings

168.—(1) Where in any proceedings other than criminal proceedings the court considers that the evidence of a child is likely to involve matter of an indecent or immoral nature, the court may direct that during the taking of the evidence of that child all or any persons, not being members or officers of the court or parties to the case, their counsel or solicitors, or persons otherwise directly concerned in the case, be excluded from the court.

(2) The powers conferred on a court by paragraph (1) shall be in addition and without prejudice to any other powers of the court to hear proceedings in private or to exclude a witness until his evidence is required.

Evidence given by, or with respect to, children

169.—(1) Subject to paragraph (2), in relation to any oath administered to and taken by a child in any civil proceedings, section 1 of the Oaths Act 1978 shall have effect as if the words "I promise before Almighty God" were set out in it instead of the words "I swear by Almighty God that".

1978 c. 19

(2) Where, in any oath otherwise duly administered to and taken by any person in any civil proceedings, either of the forms mentioned in paragraph (1) is used instead of the other, the oath shall nevertheless be deemed to have been duly administered and taken.

(3) Paragraph (4) applies where a child who is called as a witness in any civil proceedings does not, in the opinion of the court, understand the nature of an oath.

(4) The child's evidence may be heard by the court if, in its opinion—

(a) he understands that it is his duty to speak the truth; and

(b) he has sufficient understanding to justify his evidence being heard.

(5) The Lord Chancellor may by order make provision for the admissibility of evidence which would otherwise be inadmissible under any rule of law relating to hearsay.

(6) An order under paragraph (5) may only be made with respect to—

(a) civil proceedings in general or such civil proceedings as may be prescribed; and

(b) evidence in connection with the upbringing, maintenance or welfare of a child.

(7) An order under paragraph (5)—

(a) may, in particular, provide for the admissibility of statements which are made orally or in a prescribed form or which are recorded by any prescribed method of recording; and

(b) may make such amendments and repeals in any statutory provision relating to evidence (other than in this Order) as the Lord Chancellor considers necessary or expedient in consequence of the provision made by the order.

(8) In this Article—

"civil proceedings" and "court" have the same meaning as they have in the Civil Evidence Act (Northern Ireland) 1971 by virtue of section 14 of that Act; and

1971 c. 36 (N.I.)

"prescribed" means prescribed by an order under paragraph (5).

Privacy for children involved in certain proceedings

170.—(1) Rules of court may make provision for the court to sit in private in proceedings in which any powers under this Order may be exercised by the court with respect to any child.

(2) No person shall publish any material which is intended, or likely, to identify—

(a) any child as being involved in any proceedings in which any power under this Order may be exercised by the court with respect to that or any other child; or

(b) an address or school as being that of a child involved in any such proceedings.

(3) In any proceedings for an offence under this Article it shall be a defence for a person to prove that he did not know, and had no reason to suspect, that the published material was intended, or likely, to identify the child.

(4) The court may, if satisfied that the welfare of the child requires

it, by order dispense with the requirements of paragraph (2) to such extent as may be specified in the order.

(5) The Lord Chancellor may, if satisfied that the welfare of the child requires it, make a direction dispensing with the requirements of paragraph (2) to such extent as may be specified in the direction.

(6) This paragraph applies to any proceedings other than criminal proceedings or proceedings to which paragraph (2) applies.

(7) In relation to any proceedings to which paragraph (6) applies, the court may direct that no person shall publish any material which is intended, or likely, to identify—

(a) any child as being involved in those proceedings; or

(b) an address or school as being that of a child involved in any such proceedings,

except in so far (if at all) as may be permitted by the direction of the court.

(8) For the purposes of this Article—

"publish" includes—

(a) include in a programme service (within the meaning of the Broadcasting Act 1990);

(b) cause to be published; and

"material" includes any picture or representation.

(9) Any person who contravenes this Article shall be guilty of an offence and liable on summary conviction to a fine not exceeding level 4 on the standard scale.

(10) Paragraph (1) is without prejudice to—

(a) the generality of any other power to make rules of court; or

(b) any other power of the court to sit in private.

(11) Articles 89 and 90 of the Magistrates' Courts (Northern Ireland) Order 1981 (domestic proceedings—sitting of court and newspaper reports) shall apply in relation to any proceedings to which this Article applies subject to the provisions of this Article.

1990 c. 42

1981 NI 26

Self-incrimination

171.—(1) In any proceedings in which a court is hearing an application for an order under Part V or VI, no person shall be excused from—

(a) giving evidence on any matter; or

(b) answering any question put to him in the course of his giving evidence,

on the ground that doing so might incriminate him or his spouse of an offence.

(2) A statement or admission made in such proceedings shall not

be admissible in evidence against the person making it or his spouse in proceedings for an offence other than perjury.

Legal aid, advice and assistance

172.—(1) The Legal Aid, Advice and Assistance (Northern Ireland) Order 1981 shall be amended in accordance with paragraphs (2) and (3).

(2) In Article 5 (representation in proceedings), after paragraph (4) there shall be inserted the following paragraph—

"(4A) Without prejudice to paragraphs (3) and (4), regulations may make provision in relation to assistance by way of representation for purposes corresponding to those of Article 10(5A) to (5E) (legal aid for proceedings under the Children (Northern Ireland) Order 1995).".

(3) In Article 10 (scope and general conditions of legal aid), after paragraph (5) there shall be inserted the following paragraphs—

"(5A) Legal aid shall not be available—

(*a*) to any Health and Social Services Board; or

(*b*) to any Health and Social Services trust; or

(*c*) to any other prescribed body; or

(*d*) to a guardian ad litem,

for the purposes of any proceedings under the Children (Northern Ireland) Order 1995.

(5B) Regardless of paragraphs (4) and (5) and Articles 9 and 12, legal aid must be granted where a child who is brought before a court under Article 44 of the Children (Northern Ireland) Order 1995 (secure accommodation) is not, but wishes to be, legally represented before the court.

(5C) Subject to paragraph (5A) but regardless of paragraphs (4) and (5) and Articles 9 and 12, legal aid must be granted to the child in respect of whom the application is made, to any parent of such a child and to any person with parental responsibility for him within the meaning of the Children (Northern Ireland) Order 1995 to cover proceedings relating to an application for the following orders under that Order—

(*a*) an order under Article 50 (a care or supervision order);

(*b*) an order under Article 62 (a child assessment order);

(*c*) an order under Article 63 (an emergency protection order); or

(*d*) an order under Article 64 (extension or discharge of an emergency protection order).

(5D) Subject to paragraphs (4) and (5) but regardless of Articles 9 and 12, legal aid must be granted to cover proceedings relating to an appeal against an order made under Article 50 of the

Children (Northern Ireland) Order 1995 to a person who has been granted legal aid by virtue of paragraph (5C).

(5E) Subject to paragraph (5A) and Articles 9 and 12 but regardless of paragraphs (4) and (5), legal aid must be granted where a person applies to be or has been joined as a party to any of the proceedings mentioned in paragraph (5C).".

(4) The Lord Chancellor may by order make—

(a) such further amendments in the Legal Aid, Advice and Assistance (Northern Ireland) Order 1981 as he considers necessary or expedient in consequence of any provision made by or under this Order;

(b) such transitional and saving provisions as appear to him to be necessary or expedient in consequence of any provision made by or under this Order in connection with the operation of any provisions of the Legal Aid, Advice and Assistance (Northern Ireland) Order 1981 (including any provision amended by this Article).

Restrictions on use of wardship jurisdiction

173.—(1) The court shall not exercise its inherent jurisdiction with respect to children—

(a) so as to require a child to be placed in the care, or put under the supervision, of a Board or Health and Social Services trust;

(b) so as to require a child to be accommodated by or on behalf of a Board or Health and Social Services trust;

(c) so as to make a child who is the subject of a care order a ward of court; or

(d) for the purpose of conferring on any Board or Health and Social Services trust power to determine any question which has arisen, or which may arise, in connection with any aspect of parental responsibility for a child.

(2) No application for any exercise of the court's inherent jurisdiction with respect to children may be made by an authority unless the authority has obtained the leave of the court.

(3) The court may only grant leave if it is satisfied that—

(a) the result which the authority wishes to achieve could not be achieved through the making of any order of a kind to which paragraph (4) applies; and

(b) there is reasonable cause to believe that if the court's inherent jurisdiction is not exercised with respect to the child he is likely to suffer significant harm.

(4) This paragraph applies to any order—

(a) made otherwise than in the exercise of the court's inherent jurisdiction; and

146

(b) which the authority is entitled to apply for (assuming, in the case of any application which may only be made with leave, that leave is granted).

(5) In this Article "the court" means the High Court.

PART XVII

MISCELLANEOUS AND GENERAL

Children accommodated in certain establishments

Children accommodated in hospitals

174.—(1) Where a child is provided with accommodation in a hospital administered by a Board—

(a) for a consecutive period of at least three months; or

(b) with the intention, on the part of the Board, of accommodating him for such a period,

the Board shall notify the responsible authority.

(2) Where a child is provided with accommodation in a hospital administered by a Health and Social Services trust—

(a) for a consecutive period of at least three months; or

(b) with the intention, on the part of the trust, of accommodating him for such a period,

the trust shall notify the responsible authority.

(3) Where paragraph (1) or (2) applies, the Board or trust shall also notify the responsible authority when the child ceases to be accommodated in the hospital.

(4) Paragraphs (1) to (3) shall not apply where the Board or trust is the responsible authority.

(5) In this Article "the responsible authority" means—

(a) the authority appearing to the Board or trust to be the authority within whose area the child was ordinarily resident immediately before being accommodated in that hospital; or

(b) where it appears to the Board or trust that the child was not resident within the area of any authority, the authority within whose area the hospital is situated.

(6) Where an authority has been notified under this Article or would but for paragraph (4) have been notified under this Article, it shall—

(a) take such steps as are reasonably practicable to enable it to determine whether the child's welfare is adequately safeguarded and promoted while he is accommodated by the Board or trust; and

(b) consider the extent to which (if at all) any functions under this Order should be exercised with respect to the child by it or another Board or trust.

(7) A person authorised by an authority may enter a hospital for the purpose of establishing whether the requirements of this Article have been complied with.

(8) Any person exercising the power conferred by paragraph (7) shall, if so required, produce some duly authenticated document showing his authority to do so.

Children accommodated in certain homes and in private hospitals

175.—(1) Where a child is provided with accommodation in any residential care home, nursing home or private hospital—

(a) for a consecutive period of at least three months; or

(b) with the intention, on the part of the person taking the decision to accommodate him, of accommodating him for such a period,

the person carrying on the home or hospital shall notify the authority within whose area the home or hospital is carried on.

(2) Where paragraph (1) applies with respect to a child, the person carrying on the home or hospital shall also notify that authority when he ceases to accommodate the child.

(3) Where an authority has been notified under this Article, it shall—

(a) take such steps as are reasonably practicable to enable it to determine whether the child's welfare is adequately safeguarded and promoted while he is accommodated in the home or hospital; and

(b) consider the extent to which (if at all) the authority should exercise any of its functions under this Order with respect to the child.

(4) If the person carrying on any home or hospital fails, without reasonable excuse, to comply with this Article he shall be guilty of an offence.

(5) A person authorised by an authority may enter any residential care home, nursing home or private hospital within the authority's area for the purpose of establishing whether the requirements of this Article have been complied with.

(6) Any person who intentionally obstructs another in the exercise of the power of entry shall be guilty of an offence.

(7) Any person exercising the power of entry shall, if so required, produce some duly authenticated document showing his authority to do so.

(8) Any person guilty of an offence under this Article shall be liable on summary conviction to a fine not exceeding level 3 on the standard scale.

Children accommodated in schools

176.—(1) It shall be the duty of the managers of any school which provides accommodation for any child to safeguard and promote the child's welfare.

(2) Where accommodation is provided for a child by a school within the area of an authority, the authority shall take such steps as are reasonably practicable to enable it to determine whether the child's welfare is adequately safeguarded and promoted while he is accommodated by the school.

(3) Where an authority is of the opinion that there has been a failure to comply with paragraph (1) in relation to a child provided with accommodation by a school within the authority's area, the authority shall notify both the Department and the Department of Education.

(4) Any person authorised by an authority may, for the purpose of enabling the authority to discharge its duty under this Article, enter at any reasonable time any school within the authority's area which provides accommodation for any child.

(5) Any person entering a school in exercise of the power conferred by paragraph (4) may carry out such inspection of premises, children and records as is prescribed by regulations made by the Department for the purposes of this Article after consultation with the Department of Education.

(6) Any person exercising that power shall, if asked to so do, produce some duly authenticated document showing his authority to do so.

(7) Any person authorised under this Article to inspect records—

(a) shall be entitled at any reasonable time to have access to, and inspect and check the operation of, any computer and any associated apparatus or material which is or has been in use in connection with the records in question; and

(b) may require—

(i) the person by whom or on whose behalf the computer is or has been so used; or

(ii) any person having charge of, or otherwise concerned with the operation of, the computer, apparatus or material,

to afford him such assistance as he may reasonably require.

(8) Any person who intentionally obstructs another in the exercise of any power conferred by this Article shall be guilty of an offence and liable on summary conviction to a fine not exceeding level 3 on the standard scale.

Children not accommodated in schools

177.—(1) Where a child is provided with accommodation by an education and library board—

(*a*) for a consecutive period of at least three months; or

(*b*) with the intention, on the part of the board, of accommodating him for such a period,

the education and library board shall notify the responsible authority.

(2) Paragraph (1) does not apply to accommodation to which Article 176(1) applies.

(3) Where paragraph (1) applies with respect to a child, the education and library board shall also notify the responsible authority when it ceases to accommodate the child.

(4) In this Article "the responsible authority" means—

(*a*) the authority appearing to the education and library board to be the authority within whose area the child was ordinarily resident immediately before being accommodated; or

(*b*) where it appears to the education and library board that the child was not ordinarily resident within the area of any authority, the authority within whose area the accommodation is situated.

(5) Where an authority has been notified under this Article, it shall—

(*a*) take such steps as are reasonably practicable to enable it to determine whether the child's welfare is adequately safeguarded and promoted while he is accommodated by the education and library board; and

(*b*) consider the extent to which (if at all) the authority should exercise any of its functions under this Order with respect to the child.

Search warrants

Police assistance in exercise of powers of search and inspection

178.—(1) Where, on an application made by any person for a warrant under this Article, it appears to the court—

(*a*) that a person attempting to exercise powers under any provision specified in paragraph (6) has been prevented from doing so by being refused entry to the premises concerned or refused access to the child concerned; or

(*b*) that any such person is likely to be so prevented from exercising any such powers,

it may issue a warrant authorising any constable to assist that person in the exercise of those powers, using reasonable force if necessary.

(2) Every warrant issued under this Article shall be addressed to, and executed by, a constable who shall be accompanied by the person applying for the warrant if—

(a) that person so desires; and

(b) the court by whom the warrant is issued does not direct otherwise.

(3) A court granting an application for a warrant under this Article may direct that the constable concerned may, in executing the warrant, be accompanied by a medical practitioner, registered nurse or registered health visitor if he so chooses.

(4) An application for a warrant under this Article shall be made in the manner and form prescribed by rules of court.

(5) Where—

(a) an application for a warrant under this Article relates to a particular child; and

(b) it is reasonably practicable to do so,

the application and any warrant granted on the application shall name the child; and where it does not name him it shall describe him as clearly as possible.

(6) The provisions referred to in paragraph (1) are—

(a) Articles 77, 93, 108, 130, 149, 175 and 176;

(b) paragraph 7(1)(b) or (2)(b) of Schedule 3;

(c) Article 34 of the Adoption Order (duty to secure that protected children are visited).

Effect and duration of orders, etc.

Effect and duration of orders, etc.

179.—(1) The making of a residence order with respect to a child who is the subject of a care order discharges the care order.

(2) The making of a care order with respect to a child who is the subject of any Article 8 order discharges the Article 8 order.

(3) The making of a care order with respect to a child who is the subject of a supervision order discharges the supervision order.

(4) The making of a care order with respect to a child who is a ward of court brings that wardship to an end.

(5) The making of a care order with respect to a child who is the subject of a school attendance order made under Part I of Schedule 13 to the Education and Libraries (Northern Ireland) Order 1986 discharges the school attendance order. 1986 NI 3

(6) Where an emergency protection order is made with respect to a child who is in care, the care order shall have effect subject to the emergency protection order.

(7) Any order made under Article 7(1) or 159(1) shall continue in force until the child reaches the age of 18, unless it is brought to an end earlier.

(8) Any—

(a) agreement under Article 7; or

(b) appointment under Article 160(1) or (2),

shall continue in force until the child reaches the age of 18, unless it is brought to an end earlier.

(9) An order under Schedule 1 has effect as specified in that Schedule.

(10) An Article 8 order shall, if it would otherwise still be in force, cease to have effect when the child reaches the age of 16, unless it is to have effect beyond that age by virtue of Article 9(6).

(11) Where an Article 8 order has effect with respect to a child who has reached the age of 16, it shall, if it would otherwise still be in force, cease to have effect when he reaches the age of 18.

(12) Any care order, other than an interim care order, shall continue in force until the child reaches the age of 18, unless it is brought to an end earlier.

(13) Any order made by a court under any other provision of this Order in relation to a child shall, if it would otherwise still be in force, cease to have effect when he reaches the age of 18.

(14) On disposing of any application for an order under this Order, the court may (whether or not it makes any other order in response to the application) order that no application for an order under this Order of any specified kind may be made with respect to the child concerned by any person named in the order without leave of the court.

(15) Where an application ("the previous application") has been made for—

(a) the discharge of a care order;

(b) the discharge of a supervision order;

(c) the discharge of an education supervision order;

(d) the substitution of a supervision order for a care order; or

(e) a child assessment order,

no further application of a kind mentioned in sub-paragraphs (a) to (e) may be made with respect to the child concerned, without leave of the court, unless the period between the disposal of the previous application and the making of the further application exceeds six months.

(16) Paragraph (15) does not apply to applications made in relation to interim orders.

(17) Where—

(a) a person has made an application for an order under Article 53;

(b) the application has been refused; and

(c) a period of less than six months has elapsed since the refusal,

that person may not make a further application for such an order with respect to the same child, unless he has obtained the leave of the court.

The Isle of Man and the Channel Islands

180.—(1) Where a child who is in the care of an authority is lawfully taken to live in the Isle of Man or any of the Channel Islands, the care order in question shall cease to have effect if the prescribed conditions are satisfied.

(2) The Department may make regulations providing for prescribed orders which—

(a) are made by a court in the Isle of Man or in any of the Channel Islands; and

(b) appear to the Department to correspond in their effect to orders which may be made under this Order,

to have effect in prescribed circumstances for prescribed purposes of this Order as if they were orders of a prescribed kind made under this Order.

Miscellaneous

Annual report

181. The Department shall, after consultation with the Lord Chancellor, the Department of Education and the Department of Finance and Personnel, cause an annual general report on the operation of this Order to be prepared and laid before the Assembly.

Temporary exercise of functions of authorities by Department

182.—(1) The Department may by regulations provide that until such date as may be prescribed the provisions to which paragraph (2) applies shall have effect as if for references to an authority there were substituted references to the Department.

(2) This paragraph applies to—

(a) Articles 78, 80 to 87, 94 and 96 to 103;

(b) regulations made for the purposes of Article 80(4) or 96(4);

(c) regulations made under Article 89(2)(j) or (k) or 105(2)(j) or (k); and

(d) such other provisions of this Order as may be prescribed.

(3) Regulations may make such modifications of this Order as appear to the Department to be necessary or expedient for the purposes of paragraph (1).

PART XVII

(4) Regulations under paragraph (1) shall not prescribe a date later than the expiration of six years from the commencement of this Article.

Regulations and orders

183.—(1) Subject to paragraphs (2) and (3), regulations under this Order shall be subject to negative resolution.

(2) Orders under Article 18(4) or 156 shall be subject to affirmative resolution.

1946 c. 36

(3) Regulations and orders under this Order made by the Lord Chancellor shall be subject to annulment in like manner as a statutory instrument and section 5 of the Statutory Instruments Act 1946 shall apply accordingly.

Transitional provisions and savings

184.—(1) The transitional provisions and savings set out in Schedule 8 shall have effect.

(2) An order under Article 1(2) may make such transitional provisions or savings as appear to the Secretary of State to be necessary or expedient in connection with the provisions brought into operation by the order, including—

(a) provisions adding to or modifying the provisions of Schedule 8; and

(b) such adaptations—

(i) of the provisions brought into operation by the order; and

(ii) of any provisions of this Order then in operation,

as appear to the Secretary of State necessary or expedient in consequence of the partial operation of this Order.

Amendments and repeals

185.—(1) The statutory provisions set out in Schedule 9 shall have effect subject to the amendments there specified.

(2) The statutory provisions set out in Schedule 10 are hereby repealed to the extent specified in the third column of that Schedule.

N. H. Nicholls
Clerk of the Privy Council

SCHEDULES

SCHEDULE 1

FINANCIAL PROVISION FOR CHILDREN

Interpretation

1.—(1) In this Schedule "child" includes, in any case where an application is made under paragraph 3 or 7 in relation to a person who has reached the age of 18, that person.

(2) In this Schedule, except paragraphs 3 and 17, "parent" includes any party to a marriage (whether or not subsisting) in relation to whom the child concerned is a child of the family; and for this purpose any reference to either parent or both parents shall be construed as references to any parent of his and to all of his parents.

(3) In this Schedule "maintenance assessment" means an assessment of maintenance made under the Child Support (Northern Ireland) Order 1991 and includes, except in circumstances prescribed for the purposes of the definition of that expression in Article 2(2) of that Order, an interim maintenance assessment within the meaning of that Order.

1991 NI 23

Orders for financial relief against parents

2.—(1) On an application made by a parent or guardian of a child, or by any person in whose favour a residence order is in force with respect to a child, the court may—

    (*a*) if it is the High Court or a county court, make one or more of the orders mentioned in sub-paragraph (2);

    (*b*) if it is a court of summary jurisdiction, make one or both of the orders mentioned in heads (*a*) and (*c*) of that sub-paragraph.

(2) The orders referred to in sub-paragraph (1) are—

    (*a*) an order requiring either or both parents of a child—

        (i) to make to the applicant for the benefit of the child; or

        (ii) to make to the child himself,

    such periodical payments, for such term, as may be specified in the order;

    (*b*) an order requiring either or both parents of a child—

        (i) to secure to the applicant for the benefit of the child; or

        (ii) to secure to the child himself,

    such periodical payments, for such term, as may be so specified;

    (*c*) an order requiring either or both parents of a child—

        (i) to pay to the applicant for the benefit of the child; or

        (ii) to pay to the child himself,

    such lump sum as may be so specified;

    (*d*) an order requiring a settlement to be made for the benefit of the child, and to the satisfaction of the court, of property—

        (i) to which either parent is entitled (either in possession or in reversion); and

        (ii) which is specified in the order;

    (*e*) an order requiring either or both parents of a child—

(i) to transfer to the applicant, for the benefit of the child; or

(ii) to transfer to the child himself,

such property to which the parent is, or the parents are, entitled (either in possession or in reversion) as may be specified in the order.

(3) The powers conferred by this paragraph may be exercised at any time.

(4) An order under sub-paragraph (2)(*a*) or (*b*) may be varied or discharged by a subsequent order made on the application of any person by or to whom payments were required to be made under the previous order.

(5) Where a court makes an order under this paragraph—

(*a*) it may at any time make a further such order under sub-paragraph (2)(*a*), (*b*) or (*c*) with respect to the child concerned if he has not reached the age of 18;

(*b*) it may not make more than one order under sub-paragraph (2)(*d*) or (*e*) against the same person in respect of the same child.

(6) On making, varying or discharging a residence order the court may exercise any of its powers under this Schedule even though no application has been made to it under this Schedule.

(7) Where a child is a ward of court, the High Court may exercise any of its powers under this Schedule even though no application has been made to it.

Orders for financial relief for persons over 18

3.—(1) If, on an application by a person who has reached the age of 18, it appears to the court—

(*a*) that the applicant is, will be or (if an order were made under this paragraph) would be receiving instruction at an educational establishment or undergoing training for a trade, profession or vocation, whether or not while in gainful employment; or

(*b*) that there are special circumstances which justify the making of an order under this paragraph,

the court may make one or both of the orders mentioned in sub-paragraph (2).

(2) The orders are—

(*a*) an order requiring either or both of the applicant's parents to pay to the applicant such periodical payments, for such term, as may be specified in the order;

(*b*) an order requiring either or both of the applicant's parents to pay to the applicant such lump sum as may be so specified.

(3) An application may not be made under this paragraph by any person if, immediately before he reached the age of 16, a periodical payments order was in force with respect to him.

(4) No order shall be made under this paragraph at a time when the parents of the applicant are living with each other in the same household.

(5) An order under sub-paragraph (2)(*a*) may be varied or discharged by a subsequent order made on the application of any person by or to whom payments were required to be made under the previous order.

(6) In sub-paragraph (3) "periodical payments order" means an order made under—

SCH. 1

    (*a*) this Schedule;

    (*b*) Article 25 or 29 of the Matrimonial Causes (Northern Ireland) Order 1978; or

1978 NI 15

    (*c*) the Domestic Proceedings (Northern Ireland) Order 1980;

1980 NI 5

for the making or securing of periodical payments.

(7) The powers conferred by this paragraph shall be exercisable at any time.

(8) Where the court makes an order under this paragraph it may while that order remains in force make further such orders.

Duration of orders for financial relief

4.—(1) The term to be specified in an order for periodical payments made under paragraph 2(2)(*a*) or (*b*) in favour of a child may begin with the date of the making of an application for the order in question or any later date or a date ascertained in accordance with sub-paragraph (8) or (10) but—

    (*a*) shall not in the first instance extend beyond the child's seventeenth birthday unless the court thinks it right in the circumstances of the case to specify a later date; and

    (*b*) shall not in any event extend beyond the child's eighteenth birthday.

(2) Head (*b*) of sub-paragraph (1) shall not apply in the case of a child if it appears to the court that—

    (*a*) the child is, or will be or (if an order were made without complying with that head) would be receiving instruction at an educational establishment or undergoing training for a trade, profession or vocation, whether or not while in gainful employment; or

    (*b*) there are special circumstances which justify the making of an order without complying with that head.

(3) An order for periodical payments made under paragraph 2(2)(*a*) or 3(2)(*a*) shall, notwithstanding anything in the order, cease to have effect on the death of the person liable to make payments under the order.

(4) Where an order is made under paragraph 2(2)(*a*) or (*b*) requiring periodical payments to be made or secured to the parent of a child, the order shall cease to have effect if—

    (*a*) any parent making or securing the payments; and

    (*b*) any parent to whom the payments are made or secured,

live together for a period of more than six months.

(5) An order for periodical payments made under paragraph 2(2)(*a*) or (*b*) in favour of a child to whom head (*a*) of sub-paragraph (2) applies shall cease to have effect in the event of his ceasing to receive instruction or undergo training as mentioned in that head.

(6) An order for periodical payments made under paragraph 3(2)(*a*) in favour of an applicant to whom head (*a*) of paragraph 3(1) applies shall cease to have effect in the event of his ceasing to receive instruction or undergo training as mentioned in that head.

(7) Where an order for periodical payments made under paragraph 2(2)(*a*) or (*b*) or paragraph 3(2)(*a*) ceases to have effect by virtue of sub-paragraph

(5) or (6), the person to whom the periodical payments are directed by the order to be made shall give notice of the event mentioned in sub-paragraph (5) or (6) to the court; and any person failing without reasonable excuse to give such a notice shall be guilty of an offence and liable on summary conviction to a fine not exceeding level 2 on the standard scale.

(8) Where—

    (a) a maintenance assessment ("the current assessment") is in force with respect to a child; and

    (b) before the end of the period of six months beginning with the date on which the current assessment was made, an application is made for an order under paragraph 2(2)(a) or (b) for periodical payments in favour of that child,

the term to be specified in any such order made on that application may be expressed to begin on, or at any time after, the earliest permitted date.

(9) For the purposes of sub-paragraph (8) "the earliest permitted date" is whichever is the later of—

    (a) the date six months before the application for the order was made; or

    (b) the date on which the current assessment took effect or, where successive maintenance assessments have been continuously in force with respect to that child, the first of those assessments took effect.

(10) Where—

    (a) a maintenance assessment ceases to have effect or is cancelled by or under any provision of the Child Support (Northern Ireland) Order 1991; and

    (b) before the end of the period of six months beginning with the relevant date, an application is made for an order for periodical payments under paragraph 2(2)(a) or (b) in favour of a child with respect to whom that maintenance assessment was in force immediately before it ceased to have effect or was cancelled,

1991 NI 23

the term to be specified in any such order, or in any interim order under paragraph 11, made on that application may begin with the relevant date or any later date.

(11) In sub-paragraph (10)(b) "the relevant date" means—

    (a) where the maintenance assessment ceased to have effect, the date on which it so ceased; and

    (b) where the maintenance assessment was cancelled, the later of—

        (i) the date on which the person who cancelled it did so; or

        (ii) the date from which the cancellation first had effect.

Matters to which court is to have regard in making orders for financial relief

5.—(1) In deciding whether to exercise its powers under paragraph 2 or 3, and if so in what manner, the court shall have regard to all the circumstances including—

    (a) the income, earning capacity, property and other financial resources which each person mentioned in sub-paragraph (4) has or is likely to have in the foreseeable future;

    (b) the financial needs, obligations and responsibilities which each person mentioned in sub-paragraph (4) has or is likely to have in the foreseeable future;

(c) the financial needs of the child;

(d) the income, earning capacity (if any), property and other financial resources of the child;

(e) any physical or mental disability of the child;

(f) the manner in which the child was being, or was expected to be, educated or trained.

(2) In deciding whether to exercise its powers under paragraph 2 against a person who is not the mother or father of the child, and if so in what manner, the court shall in addition have regard to—

(a) whether that person had assumed responsibility for the maintenance of the child and, if so, the extent to which and basis on which he assumed that responsibility and the length of the period during which he met that responsibility;

(b) whether he did so knowing that the child was not his child;

(c) the liability of any other person to maintain the child.

(3) Where the court makes an order under paragraph 2 against a person on the basis that he is not the father of the child, it shall record in the order that the order is made on that basis.

(4) The persons referred to in sub-paragraph (1) are—

(a) in relation to a decision whether to exercise its powers under paragraph 2, any parent of the child;

(b) in relation to a decision whether to exercise its powers under paragraph 3, the mother and father of the child;

(c) the applicant for the order;

(d) any other person in whose favour the court proposes to make the order.

Provisions relating to lump sums

6.—(1) Without prejudice to the generality of paragraph 2, an order under that paragraph for the payment of a lump sum may be made for the purpose of enabling any liabilities or expenses—

(a) incurred in connection with the birth of the child or in maintaining the child; and

(b) reasonably incurred before the making of the order,

to be met.

(2) The amount of any lump sum required to be paid by an order made by a court of summary jurisdiction under paragraph 2 or 3 shall not exceed £1000 or such larger amount as the Lord Chancellor may by order fix for the purposes of this sub-paragraph.

(3) The power of the court under paragraph 2 or 3 to vary or discharge an order for the making or securing of periodical payments by a parent shall include power to make an order under that provision for the payment of a lump sum by that parent.

(4) The amount of any lump sum which a parent may be required to pay by virtue of sub-paragraph (3) shall not, in the case of an order made by a court of summary jurisdiction, exceed the maximum amount that may at the time of the making of the order be required to be paid under sub-paragraph

(2), but a court of summary jurisdiction may make an order for the payment of a lump sum not exceeding that amount even though the parent was required to pay a lump sum by a previous order under this Order.

(5) An order made under paragraph 2 or 3 for the payment of a lump sum may provide for the payment of that sum by instalments.

(6) Where the court provides for the payment of a lump sum by instalments the court, on an application made either by the person liable to pay or the person entitled to receive that sum, shall have power to vary that order by varying—

(a) the number of instalments payable;

(b) the amount of any instalment payable;

(c) the date on which any instalment becomes payable.

Variation, etc., of orders for periodical payments

7.—(1) In exercising its powers under paragraph 2 or 3 to vary or discharge an order for the making or securing of periodical payments the court shall have regard to all the circumstances, including any change in any of the matters to which the court was required to have regard when making the order.

(2) The power of the court under paragraph 2 or 3 to vary an order for the making or securing of periodical payments shall include power to suspend any provision of the order temporarily and to revive any provision so suspended.

(3) Where on an application under paragraph 2 or 3 for the variation or discharge of an order for the making or securing of periodical payments the court varies the payments required to be made under that order, the court may provide that the payments as so varied shall be made from such date as the court may specify, except that, subject to sub-paragraph (11), the date shall not be earlier than the date of the making of the application.

(4) An application for the variation of an order made under paragraph 2 for the making or securing of periodical payments to or for the benefit of a child may, if the child has reached the age of 16, be made by the child himself.

(5) Where an order for the making or securing of periodical payments made under paragraph 2 ceases to have effect on the date on which the child reaches the age of 16, or at any time after that date but before or on the date on which he reaches the age of 18, the child may apply to the court which made the order for an order for its revival.

(6) If on such an application it appears to the court that—

(a) the child is, will be or (if an order were made under this subparagraph) would be receiving instruction at an educational establishment or undergoing training for a trade, profession or vocation, whether or not while in gainful employment; or

(b) there are special circumstances which justify the making of an order under this sub-paragraph,

the court shall have power by order to revive the order from such date as the court may specify, not being earlier than the date of the making of the application.

(7) Any order which is revived by an order under sub-paragraph (6) may

be varied or discharged under that sub-paragraph on the application of any person by whom or to whom payments are required to be made under the revived order.

(8) An order for the making or securing of periodical payments made under paragraph 2 may be varied or discharged, after the death of either parent, on the application of a guardian of the child concerned.

(9) An order for the making or securing of periodical payments made under paragraph 2 which is revived under sub-paragraph (6) in favour of a child to whom head (*a*) of that sub-paragraph applies shall cease to have effect in the event of his ceasing to receive instruction or undergo training as mentioned in that head.

(10) Where an order for the making or securing of periodical payments made under paragraph 2 ceases to have effect by virtue of sub-paragraph (9), the person to whom the periodical payments are directed by the order to be made shall give notice of the event mentioned in that sub-paragraph to the court; and any person failing without reasonable excuse to give such a notice shall be guilty of an offence and liable on summary conviction to a fine not exceeding level 2 on the standard scale.

(11) Sub-paragraph (12) applies where—

  (*a*) an order under paragraph 2(2)(*a*) or (*b*) for the making or securing of periodical payments in favour of more than one child ("the order") is in force;

  (*b*) the order requires payments specified in it to be made to or for the benefit of more than one child without apportioning those payments between them;

  (*c*) a maintenance assessment ("the assessment") is made with respect to one or more, but not all, of the children in whose favour those payments are to be made; and

  (*d*) an application is made, before the end of the period of six months beginning with the date on which the assessment was made, for the variation or discharge of the order.

(12) Where this sub-paragraph applies, the court may, in exercise of its powers under paragraph 2 to vary or discharge the order, direct that the variation or discharge shall take effect from the date on which the assessment took effect or any later date.

Variation of orders for periodical payments etc. made by court of summary jurisdiction

8.—(1) Subject to sub-paragraphs (7) and (8), the power of a court of summary jurisdiction—

  (*a*) under paragraph 2 or 3 to vary an order for the making of periodical payments, or

  (*b*) under paragraph 6(6) to vary an order for the payment of a lump sum by instalments,

shall include power, if the court is satisfied that payment has not been made in accordance with the order, to exercise one of its powers under sub-paragraphs (*a*) to (*d*) of Article 85(3) of the Magistrates' Courts (Northern Ireland) Order 1981.

1981 NI 26

(2) In any case where—

  (*a*) a court of summary jurisdiction has made an order under this

Schedule for the making of periodical payments or for the payment of a lump sum by instalments, and

(b) payments under the order are required to be made by any method of payment falling within Article 85(7) of the Magistrates' Courts (Northern Ireland) Order 1981 (standing order, etc.),

any person entitled to make an application under this Schedule for the variation of the order (in this paragraph referred to as "the applicant") may apply to the clerk of petty sessions for the order to be varied as mentioned in sub-paragraph (3).

(3) Subject to sub-paragraph (5), where an application is made under sub-paragraph (2), the clerk, after serving written notice of the application on any interested party and allowing that party, within the period of 14 days from the date of the serving of that notice, an opportunity to make written representations, may vary the order to provide that payments under the order shall be made to the collecting officer.

(4) The clerk may proceed with an application under sub-paragraph (2) notwithstanding that any such interested party as is referred to in sub-paragraph (3) has not received written notice of the application.

(5) Where an application has been made under sub-paragraph (2), the clerk may, if he considers it inappropriate to exercise his power under sub-paragraph (3), refer the matter to the court which, subject to sub-paragraphs (7) and (8), may vary the order by exercising one of its powers under sub-paragraphs (a) to (d) of Article 85(3) of the Magistrates' Courts (Northern Ireland) Order 1981.

(6) Paragraph (5) of Article 85 of the Magistrates' Courts (Northern Ireland) Order 1981 (power of court to order that account be opened) shall apply for the purposes of sub-paragraphs (1) and (5) as it applies for the purposes of that Article.

(7) Before varying the order by exercising one of its powers under sub-paragraphs (a) to (d) of Article 85(3) of the Magistrates' Courts (Northern Ireland) Order 1981, the court shall have regard to any representations made by the parties to the application.

(8) If the court does not propose to exercise its power under sub-paragraph (c) or (d) of paragraph (3) of Article 85 of the Magistrates' Courts (Northern Ireland) Order 1981, the court shall, unless upon representations expressly made in that behalf by the applicant for the order it is satisfied that it is undesirable to do so, exercise its power under sub-paragraph (b) of that paragraph.

(9) None of the powers of the court, or of the clerk of petty sessions, conferred by this paragraph shall be exercisable in relation to an order under this Schedule for the making of periodical payments, or for the payment of a lump sum by instalments, which is not a qualifying maintenance order (within the meaning of Article 85 of the Magistrates' Courts (Northern Ireland) Order 1981).

(10) In sub-paragraphs (3) and (4) "interested party", in relation to an application made by the applicant under sub-paragraph (2), means a person who would be entitled to be a party to an application for the variation of the order made by the applicant under any other provision of this Schedule if such an application were made.

Variation of orders for secured periodical payments after death of parent

9.—(1) Where the parent liable to make payments under a secured periodical payments order has died, the persons who may apply for the variation or discharge of the order shall include the personal representatives of the deceased parent.

(2) No application for the variation of the order shall, except with the permission of the court, be made after the end of the period of six months from the date on which representation in regard to the estate of that parent is first taken out.

(3) The personal representatives of a deceased person against whom a secured periodical payments order was made shall not be liable for having distributed any part of the estate of the deceased after the end of the period of six months referred to in sub-paragraph (2) on the ground that they ought to have taken into account the possibility that the court might permit an application for variation to be made after that period by the person entitled to payments under the order.

(4) Sub-paragraph (3) shall not prejudice any power to recover any part of the estate so distributed arising by virtue of the variation of an order in accordance with this paragraph.

(5) Where an application to vary a secured periodical payments order is made after the death of the parent liable to make payments under the order, the circumstances to which the court is required to have regard under paragraph 7(1) shall include the changed circumstances resulting from the death of the parent.

(6) In considering for the purposes of sub-paragraph (2) the question when representation was first taken out, a grant limited to part of the estate of the deceased shall be left out of account unless a grant limited to the remainder of the estate has previously been made or is made at the same time.

(7) In this paragraph "secured periodical payments order" means an order for secured periodical payments under paragraph 2(2)(*b*).

Financial relief under other statutory provisions

10.—(1) This paragraph applies where a residence order is made with respect to a child at a time when there is in force an order ("the financial relief order") made under any statutory provision other than this Order and requiring a person to contribute to the child's maintenance.

(2) Where this paragraph applies, the court may, on the application of—

(*a*) any person required by the financial relief order to contribute to the child's maintenance; or

(*b*) any person in whose favour a residence order with respect to the child is in force,

make an order revoking the financial relief order, or varying it by altering the amount of any sum payable under that order or by substituting the applicant for the person to whom any such sum is otherwise payable under that order.

Interim orders

11.—(1) Where an application is made under paragraph 2 or 3 the court may, at any time before it disposes of the application, make an interim order—

163

SCH. 1

(*a*) requiring either or both parents to make such periodical payments, at such times and for such term as the court thinks fit; and

(*b*) giving any direction which the court thinks fit.

(2) An interim order made under this paragraph may provide for payments to be made from such date as the court may specify, except that, subject to paragraph 4(8) and (10), the date shall not be earlier than the date of the making of the application under paragraph 2 or 3.

(3) An interim order made under this paragraph shall cease to have effect when the application is disposed of or, if earlier, on the date specified for the purposes of this paragraph in the interim order.

(4) An interim order in which a date has been specified for the purposes of sub-paragraph (3) may be varied by substituting a later date.

Alteration of maintenance agreements

12.—(1) In this paragraph and in paragraph 13 "maintenance agreement" means any agreement in writing made with respect to a child (including an agreement made before the commencement of this paragraph) which—

(*a*) is or was made between the father and mother of the child; and

(*b*) contains provision with respect to the making or securing of payments, or the disposition or use of any property, for the maintenance or education of the child,

and any such provisions are in this paragraph and paragraph 13 referred to as "financial arrangements".

(2) Where a maintenance agreement is for the time being subsisting and each of the parties to the agreement is for the time being either domiciled or resident in Northern Ireland, then either party may apply to the court for an order under this paragraph.

(3) If the court to which the application is made is satisfied either—

(*a*) that, by reason of a change in the circumstances in the light of which any financial arrangements contained in the agreement were made (including a change foreseen by the parties when making the agreement), the agreement should be altered so as to make different financial arrangements; or

(*b*) that the agreement does not contain proper financial arrangements with respect to the child,

then that court may by order make such alterations in the agreement by varying or revoking any financial arrangements contained in it as may appear to the court to be just having regard to all the circumstances.

(4) If the maintenance agreement is altered by an order under this paragraph, the agreement shall have effect thereafter as if the alteration had been made by agreement between the parties and for valuable consideration.

(5) Where a court decides to make an order under this paragraph altering the maintenance agreement—

(*a*) by inserting provision for the making or securing by one of the parties to the agreement of periodical payments for the maintenance of the child; or

(*b*) by increasing the rate of periodical payments required to be made or secured by one of the parties for the maintenance of the child,

then, in deciding the term for which under the agreement as altered by the order the payments or (as the case may be) the additional payments attributable to the increase are to be made or secured for the benefit of the child, the court shall apply the provisions of sub-paragraphs (1) and (2) of paragraph 4 as if the order were an order under paragraph 2(2)(a) or (b).

(6) A court of summary jurisdiction shall not entertain an application under sub-paragraph (2) unless both the parties to the agreement are resident in Northern Ireland and at least one of the parties is resident within the county court division which includes the petty sessions district for which the court sits, and shall not have power to make any order on such an application except—

(a) in a case where the agreement contains no provision for periodical payments by either of the parties, an order inserting provision for the making by one of the parties of periodical payments for the maintenance of the child;

(b) in a case where the agreement includes provision for the making by one of the parties of periodical payments, an order increasing or reducing the rate of, or terminating, any of those payments.

(7) Nothing in this paragraph affects any power of a court before which any proceedings between the parties to a maintenance agreement are brought under any other statutory provision to make an order containing financial arrangements or any right of either party to apply for such an order in such proceedings.

13.—(1) Where a maintenance agreement provides for the continuation, after the death of one of the parties, of payments for the maintenance of a child and that party dies domiciled in Northern Ireland, the surviving party or the personal representatives of the deceased party may apply to the High Court or a county court for an order under paragraph 12.

(2) If a maintenance agreement is altered by a court on an application under this paragraph, the agreement shall have effect thereafter as if the alteration had been made, immediately before the death, by agreement between the parties and for valuable consideration.

(3) An application under this paragraph shall not, except with leave of the High Court or a county court, be made after the end of the period of six months from the day on which representation in regard to the estate of the deceased is first taken out.

(4) In considering for the purposes of sub-paragraph (3) the question when representation was first taken out, a grant limited to part of the estate of the deceased shall be left out of account unless a grant limited to the remainder of the estate has previously been made or is made at the same time.

(5) A county court shall not entertain an application under this paragraph, or an application for leave to make an application under this paragraph, unless it would have jurisdiction to hear and determine proceedings for an order under Article 4 of the Inheritance (Provision for Family and Dependants) (Northern Ireland) Order 1979 in relation to the deceased's estate by virtue of Article 24 of that Order.

1979 NI 8

(6) The provisions of this paragraph shall not render the personal representatives of the deceased liable for having distributed any part of the estate of the deceased after the expiry of the period of six months referred to in sub-paragraph (3) on the ground that they ought to have taken into account the possibility that a court might grant leave for an application by virtue of

this paragraph to be made by the surviving party after that period.

(7) Sub-paragraph (6) shall not prejudice any power to recover any part of the estate so distributed arising by virtue of the making of an order in pursuance of this paragraph.

Notice of change of address

14.—(1) Any person for the time being under an obligation to make payments in pursuance of any order for the payment of money made by a court of summary jurisdiction under this Schedule shall give notice of any change of address to such person (if any) as may be specified in the order.

(2) Any person failing without reasonable excuse to give such a notice shall be guilty of an offence and liable on summary conviction to a fine not exceeding level 2 on the standard scale.

Direction for settlement of instrument by conveyancing counsel

15. Where the High Court or a county court decides to make an order under this Schedule for the securing of periodical payments or for the transfer or settlement of property, it may direct that the matter be referred to a conveyancing counsel appointed by the court to settle a proper instrument to be executed by all necessary parties.

Financial provision for child resident in country outside Northern Ireland

16.—(1) Where one parent of a child lives in Northern Ireland and the child lives outside Northern Ireland with—

   (a) another parent of his;

   (b) a guardian of his; or

   (c) a person in whose favour a residence order is in force with respect to the child,

the court shall have power, on an application made by any of the persons mentioned in heads (a) to (c), to make one or both of the orders mentioned in paragraph 2(2)(a) and (b) against the parent living in Northern Ireland.

(2) Any reference in this Order to the powers of the court under paragraph 2(2) or to an order made under paragraph 2(2) shall include a reference to the powers which the court has by virtue of sub-paragraph (1) or (as the case may be) to an order made by virtue of sub-paragraph (1).

Contribution by an authority to child's maintenance

17.—(1) Where a child lives, or is to live, with a person as the result of a residence order, an authority may make contributions to that person towards the cost of the accommodation and maintenance of the child.

(2) Sub-paragraph (1) does not apply where the person with whom the child lives, or is to live, is a parent of the child or the husband or wife of a parent of the child.

Article 18(2).

SCHEDULE 2

PROVISION OF SERVICES FOR FAMILIES: SPECIFIC POWERS AND DUTIES

Identification of children in need

1. Every authority shall take reasonable steps to identify the extent to which there are children in need within the authority's area.

Provision of information

2.—(1) Every authority shall publish information—

(a) about services provided by the authority under Articles 18, 19, 21, 35 and 36; and

(b) where the authority considers it appropriate, about the provision by others (including, in particular, voluntary organisations) of services which the authority has power to provide under those Articles.

(2) Every authority shall take such steps as are reasonably practicable to ensure that those who might benefit from the services receive the information relevant to them.

Maintenance of register of disabled children

3.—(1) Every authority shall open and maintain a register of disabled children within the authority's area.

(2) The register may be kept by means of a computer.

Assessment of children's needs

4. Where it appears to an authority that a child within the authority's area is in need, the authority may assess his needs for the purposes of this Order at the same time as any assessment of his needs is made under—

(a) the Chronically Sick and Disabled Persons (Northern Ireland) Act 1978;

(b) the Education and Libraries (Northern Ireland) Order 1986;

(c) the Disabled Persons (Northern Ireland) Act 1989; or

(d) any other statutory provision.

1978 c. 53

1986 NI 3

1989 c. 10

Prevention of neglect and abuse

5.—(1) Every authority shall take reasonable steps, through the provision of services under Part IV, to prevent children within the authority's area suffering ill-treatment or neglect.

(2) Where an authority believes that a child who is at any time within the authority's area—

(a) is likely to suffer harm; but

(b) lives or proposes to live in the area of another authority,

the authority shall inform that other authority.

(3) When informing that other authority the authority shall specify—

(a) the harm that it believes the child is likely to suffer; and

(b) (if it can) where the child lives or proposes to live.

Provision of accommodation for another person to protect child

6.—(1) Where—

(a) it appears to an authority that a child who is living on particular premises is suffering, or is likely to suffer, ill-treatment at the hands of another person who is living on those premises; and

(b) that other person proposes to move from the premises,

the authority may assist that other person to obtain alternative accommodation.

(2) Assistance given under this paragraph may be in cash.

(3) Paragraphs (7) to (9) of Article 18 shall apply in relation to assistance given under this paragraph as they apply in relation to assistance given under that Article.

Services for disabled children

7. Every authority shall provide services designed—

(a) to minimise the effect on disabled children within the authority's area of their disabilities; and

(b) to give such children the opportunity to lead lives which are as normal as possible.

Steps to reduce need for care proceedings, etc.

8. Every authority shall take reasonable steps designed—

(a) to reduce the need to bring—

(i) proceedings for care or supervision orders with respect to children within the authority's area;

(ii) criminal proceedings against such children;

(iii) any family or other proceedings with respect to such children which might lead to them being placed in the authority's care; or

(iv) proceedings under the inherent jurisdiction of the High Court with respect to children;

(b) to encourage children within the authority's area not to commit criminal offences; and

(c) to avoid the need for children within the authority's area to be placed in secure accommodation.

Provision for children living with their families

9. Every authority shall make such provision as the authority considers appropriate for the following services to be available with respect to children in need within the authority's area while they are living with their families—

(a) advice, guidance and counselling;

(b) occupational, social, cultural or recreational activities;

(c) home help (which may include laundry facilities);

(d) facilities for, or assistance with, travelling to and from home for the purpose of taking advantage of any other service provided under this Order or of any similar service;

(e) assistance to enable the child concerned and his family to have a holiday.

Family centres

10.—(1) Every authority shall provide such family centres as the authority considers appropriate in relation to children within its area.

(2) "Family centre" means a centre at which any of the persons mentioned in sub-paragraph (3) may—

(a) attend for occupational, social, cultural or recreational activities;

(b) attend for advice, guidance or counselling; or

(c) be provided with accommodation while he is receiving advice, guidance or counselling.

(3) The persons are—

(a) a child;

(b) his parents;

(c) any person who is not a parent of his but who has parental responsibility for him;

(d) any other person who is looking after him.

Maintenance of the family home

11. Every authority shall take such steps as are reasonably practicable, where any child within the authority's area who is in need and whom the authority is not looking after is living apart from his family—

(a) to enable him to live with his family; or

(b) to promote contact between him and his family,

if, in the opinion of the authority, it is necessary to do so in order to safeguard or promote his welfare.

Duty to consider racial groups to which children in need belong

12. Every authority shall, in making any arrangements—

(a) for the provision of day care within the authority's area; or

(b) designed to encourage persons to act as authority foster parents,

have regard to the different racial groups to which children within the authority's area who are in need belong.

SCHEDULE 3

Article 54(2).

SUPERVISION ORDERS

Meaning of "responsible person"

1. In this Schedule, "the responsible person", in relation to a supervised child, means—

(a) any person who has parental responsibility for the child; and

(b) any other person with whom the child is living.

Power of supervisor to give directions to supervised child

2.—(1) A supervision order may require the supervised child to comply with any directions given by the supervisor which require him to do all or any of the following things—

(a) to live at any place specified in the directions for any period so specified;

(b) to present himself to any person specified in the directions at any place and on any day so specified;

(c) to participate in activities specified in the directions on any day so specified.

(2) It shall be for the supervisor to decide whether, and when, and to what extent, he exercises his power to give directions and to decide the form of any directions which he gives.

(3) Sub-paragraph (1) does not confer on a supervisor power to give directions in respect of any medical or psychiatric examination or treatment (which are matters dealt with in paragraphs 4 and 5).

Imposition of obligations on responsible person

3.—(1) With the consent of any responsible person, a supervision order may include a requirement—

    (*a*) that he take all reasonable steps to ensure that the supervised child complies with any direction given by the supervisor under paragraph 2;

    (*b*) that he take all reasonable steps to ensure that the supervised child complies with any requirement included in the order under paragraph 4 or 5;

    (*c*) that he comply with any directions given by the supervisor requiring him to attend at a place specified in the directions for the purpose of taking part in activities so specified.

(2) A direction given under sub-paragraph (1)(*c*) may specify the time at which the responsible person is to attend and whether or not the supervised child is required to attend with him.

(3) A supervision order may require any person who is a responsible person in relation to the supervised child to keep the supervisor informed of his address, if it differs from the child's.

Psychiatric and medical examinations

4.—(1) A supervision order may require the supervised child—

    (*a*) to submit to a medical or psychiatric examination; or

    (*b*) to submit to any such examination as directed by the supervisor.

(2) Any such examination shall be required to be conducted—

    (*a*) by, or under the direction of, such medical practitioner as may be specified in the order;

    (*b*) at a place specified in the order and at which the supervised child is to attend as a non-resident patient; or

    (*c*) at a hospital at which the supervised child is, or is to attend as, a resident patient.

(3) A requirement of a kind mentioned in sub-paragraph (2)(*c*) shall not be included unless the court is satisfied, on the evidence of a medical practitioner, that—

    (*a*) the child may be suffering from a physical or mental condition that requires, and may be susceptible to, treatment; and

    (*b*) a period as a resident patient is necessary if the examination is to be carried out properly.

(4) No court shall include a requirement under this paragraph in a supervision order unless it is satisfied—

    (*a*) where the child has sufficient understanding to make an informed decision, that he consents to its inclusion; and

    (*b*) that satisfactory arrangements have been, or can be, made for the examination.

(5) In this paragraph and paragraph 5 "hospital" does not include special accommodation within the meaning of the Mental Health (Northern Ireland) Order 1986.

1986 NI 4

170

Psychiatric and medical treatment

5.—(1) Where a court which proposes to make or vary a supervision order is satisfied, on the evidence of a medical practitioner appointed for the purposes of Part II of the Mental Health (Northern Ireland) Order 1986, that the mental condition of the supervised child—

(*a*) is such as requires, and may be susceptible to, treatment; but

(*b*) is not such as to warrant his detention in pursuance of a hospital order under Part III of that Order,

the court may include in the order a requirement that the supervised child shall, for a period specified in the order, submit to such treatment as is so specified.

(2) The treatment specified in accordance with sub-paragraph (1) must be—

(*a*) by, or under the direction of, such medical practitioner as may be specified in the order;

(*b*) as a non-resident patient at such a place as may be so specified; or

(*c*) as a resident patient in a hospital.

(3) Where a court which proposes to make or vary a supervision order is satisfied, on the evidence of a medical practitioner, that the physical condition of the supervised child is such as requires, and may be susceptible to, treatment, the court may include in the order a requirement that the supervised child shall, for a period specified in the order, submit to such treatment as is so specified.

(4) The treatment specified in accordance with sub-paragraph (3) must be—

(*a*) by, or under the direction of, such medical practitioner as may be specified in the order;

(*b*) as a non-resident patient at such place as may be so specified; or

(*c*) as a resident patient in a hospital.

(5) No court shall include a requirement under this paragraph in a supervision order unless it is satisfied—

(*a*) where the child has sufficient understanding to make an informed decision, that he consents to its inclusion; and

(*b*) that satisfactory arrangements have been, or can be, made for the treatment.

(6) If a medical practitioner by whom or under whose direction a supervised child is being treated in pursuance of a requirement included in a supervision order by virtue of this paragraph is unwilling to continue to treat or direct the treatment of the supervised child or is of the opinion that—

(*a*) the treatment should be continued beyond the period specified in the order;

(*b*) the supervised child needs different treatment;

(*c*) he is not susceptible to treatment; or

(*d*) he does not require further treatment,

the practitioner shall make a report in writing to that effect to the supervisor.

(7) On receiving a report under this paragraph the supervisor shall refer it to the court, and on such a reference the court may make an order cancelling or varying the requirement.

SCH. 3

Life of supervision order

6.—(1) Subject to sub-paragraph (2) and Article 179 (effect and duration of orders, etc.), a supervision order shall cease to have effect at the end of the period of one year beginning with the date on which it was made.

1985 c. 60

(2) A supervision order shall also cease to have effect if an event mentioned in section 25(1)(*a*) or (*b*) of the Child Abduction and Custody Act 1985 (termination of existing orders) occurs with respect to the child.

(3) Where the supervisor applies to the court to extend, or further extend, a supervision order the court may extend the order for such period as it may specify.

(4) A supervision order may not be extended so as to run beyond the end of the period of three years beginning with the date on which it was made.

Information to be given to supervisor, etc.

7.—(1) A supervision order may require the supervised child—

(*a*) to keep the supervisor informed of any change in his address; and

(*b*) to allow the supervisor to visit him at the place where he is living.

(2) The responsible person in relation to any child with respect to whom a supervision order is made shall—

(*a*) if asked by the supervisor, inform him of the child's address (if it is known to him); and

(*b*) if he is living with the child, allow the supervisor reasonable contact with the child.

Selection of supervisor

8. A supervision order shall not designate an authority as the supervisor unless—

(*a*) the authority agrees; or

(*b*) the supervised child lives or will live within the authority's area.

Effect of supervision order on earlier orders

9. The making of a supervision order with respect to any child brings to an end any earlier care or supervision order which—

(*a*) was made with respect to that child; and

(*b*) would otherwise continue in force.

Regulations

10. The Department may make regulations with respect to the exercise by an authority of its functions where a child has been placed under its supervision by a supervision order.

Article 55(8).

SCHEDULE 4

EDUCATION SUPERVISION ORDERS

Interpretation

1. In this Schedule—

"1986 Order" means the Education and Libraries (Northern Ireland) Order 1986;

1986 NI 3

"parent" has the meaning assigned to it by Article 2(2D) of the 1986 Order.

Effect of orders

2.—(1) Where an education supervision order is in force with respect to a child, it shall be the duty of the supervisor—

(*a*) to advise, assist and befriend, and give directions to—

(i) the supervised child; and

(ii) his parents,

in such a way as will, in the opinion of the supervisor, secure that he is properly educated;

(*b*) where any such directions given to—

(i) the supervised child; or

(ii) a parent of his,

have not been complied with, to consider what further steps to take in the exercise of the supervisor's powers under this Order.

(2) Before giving any directions under sub-paragraph (1) the supervisor shall, so far as is reasonably practicable, ascertain the wishes and feelings of—

(*a*) the child; and

(*b*) his parents,

including, in particular, their wishes as to the place at which the child should be educated.

(3) When settling the terms of any such directions, the supervisor shall give due consideration—

(*a*) having regard to the child's age and understanding, to such wishes and feelings of his as the supervisor has been able to ascertain; and

(*b*) to such wishes and feelings of the child's parents as he has been able to ascertain.

(4) Directions may be given under this paragraph at any time while the education supervision order is in force.

3.—(1) Where an education supervision order is in force with respect to a child, the duties of the child's parents under Article 45 of, and Schedule 13 to, the 1986 Order (duty to secure education of children and to secure regular attendance of registered pupils) shall be superseded by their duty to comply with any directions in force under the education supervision order.

(2) Where an education supervision order is made with respect to a child—

(*a*) any school attendance order—

(i) served under paragraph 1(2) of Schedule 13 to the 1986 Order with respect to the child; and

(ii) in force immediately before the making of the education supervision order,

shall cease to have effect; and

(*b*) while the education supervision order remains in force, the following provisions shall not apply with respect to the child—

(i) Article 44 of the 1986 Order (pupils to be educated in accordance with wishes of their parents);

(ii) Part I of Schedule 13 to the 1986 Order (school attendance orders);

1989 NI 20

        (iii) Articles 36 and 37 of the Education Reform (Northern Ireland) Order 1989 (parental preference and appeals against admission decisions);

(c) a probation order made with respect to the child, while the education supervision order is in force, may not include any requirement relating to the child's attendance at school;

(d) any such requirement which was in force with respect to the child immediately before the making of the education supervision order shall cease to have effect.

Effect where child also subject to other orders

4.—(1) This paragraph applies where—

(a) an education supervision order; and

(b) a supervision order, a probation order or an order under section 74(1)(c) of the Children and Young Persons Act (Northern Ireland) 1968 (power of court to make supervision order on finding of guilt),

1968 c. 34 (N.I.)

are in force at the same time with respect to the same child.

(2) Any failure to comply with a direction given by the supervisor under the education supervision order shall be disregarded if it would not have been reasonably practicable to comply with it without failing to comply with a direction given under the other order.

Duration of orders

5.—(1) An education supervision order shall have effect for a period of one year, beginning with the date on which it is made.

(2) An education supervision order shall not expire if, before it would otherwise have expired, the court has (on the application of the education and library board in whose favour the order was made) extended the period during which it is in force.

(3) Such an application may not be made earlier than three months before the date on which the order would otherwise expire.

(4) The period during which an education supervision order is in force may be extended under sub-paragraph (2) on more than one occasion.

(5) No one extension may be for a period of more than three years.

(6) An education supervision order shall cease to have effect on—

(a) the child's ceasing to be of compulsory school age; or

(b) the making of a care order with respect to the child;

and sub-paragraphs (1) to (4) are subject to this sub-paragraph.

Information to be given to supervisor, etc.

6.—(1) An education supervision order may require the child—

(a) to keep the supervisor informed of any change in his address; and

(b) to allow the supervisor to visit him at the place where he is living.

(2) A person who is the parent of a child with respect to whom an education supervision order has been made shall—

(a) if asked by the supervisor, inform him of the child's address (if it is known to him); and

(b) if he is living with the child, allow the supervisor reasonable contact with the child.

Discharge of orders

7.—(1) The court may discharge any education supervision order on the application of—

(a) the child concerned;

(b) a parent of his; or

(c) the education and library board concerned.

(2) On discharging an education supervision order, the court may direct the authority within whose area the child lives, or will live, to investigate the circumstances of the child.

Offences

8.—(1) If a parent of a child with respect to whom an education supervision order is in force persistently fails to comply with a direction given under the order he shall be guilty of an offence.

(2) It shall be a defence for any person charged with such an offence to prove that—

(a) he took all reasonable steps to ensure that the direction was complied with;

(b) the direction was unreasonable; or

(c) he had complied with—

(i) a requirement included in a supervision order made with respect to the child; or

(ii) directions given under such a requirement,

and that it was not reasonably practicable to comply both with the direction and with the requirement or directions mentioned in this paragraph.

(3) A person guilty of an offence under this paragraph shall be liable on summary conviction to a fine not exceeding level 3 on the standard scale.

Persistent failure of child to comply with directions

9.—(1) Where a child with respect to whom an education supervision order is in force persistently fails to comply with any direction given under the order, the education and library board concerned shall notify the appropriate authority.

(2) Where an authority has been notified under sub-paragraph (1) it shall investigate the circumstances of the child.

(3) In this paragraph "the appropriate authority" means—

(a) in the case of a child who is being provided with accommodation by or on behalf of an authority, that authority;

(b) in any other case, the authority in whose area the child lives, or will live.

SCHEDULE 5

Article 91(4).

Foster Parents: Limits on Number of Foster Children

Interpretation

1. For the purposes of this Schedule, a person fosters a child if—

SCH. 5

    (a) he is an authority foster parent in relation to the child;

    (b) he is a foster parent with whom the child has been placed by a voluntary organisation; or

    (c) he fosters the child privately.

The usual fostering limit

2. Subject to what follows, a person shall not foster more than three children ("the usual fostering limit").

Siblings

3. A person may exceed the usual fostering limit if the children concerned are all siblings with respect to each other.

Exemption by an authority

4.—(1) A person may exceed the usual fostering limit if he is exempted from it by the authority within whose area he lives.

(2) In considering whether to exempt a person, an authority shall have regard, in particular, to—

    (a) the number of children whom the person proposes to foster;

    (b) the arrangements which the person proposes for the care and accommodation of the fostered children;

    (c) the intended and likely relationship between the person and the fostered children;

    (d) the period of time for which he proposes to foster the children; and

    (e) whether the welfare of the fostered children (and of any other children who are or will be living in the accommodation) will be safeguarded and promoted.

(3) Where an authority exempts a person, the authority shall inform him by notice in writing—

    (a) that he is so exempted;

    (b) of the children, described by name, whom he may foster; and

    (c) of any condition to which the exemption is subject.

(4) An authority may at any time by notice in writing—

    (a) vary or cancel an exemption; or

    (b) impose, vary or cancel a condition to which the exemption is subject,

and, in considering whether to do so, the authority shall have regard in particular to the considerations mentioned in sub-paragraph (2).

(5) The Department may make regulations amplifying or modifying the provisions of this paragraph in order to provide for cases where children need to be placed with foster parents as a matter of urgency.

Effects of exceeding fostering limit

5.—(1) A person shall cease to be treated as fostering and shall be treated as carrying on a children's home if—

    (a) he exceeds the usual fostering limit; or

    (b) where he is exempted under paragraph 4—

        (i) he fosters any child not named in the exemption; and

        (ii) in so doing, he exceeds the usual fostering limit.

(2) Sub-paragraph (1) shall not apply if the children concerned are all siblings in respect of each other.

Complaints, etc.

6.—(1) Every authority shall establish a procedure for considering any representations (including any complaint) made to the authority about the discharge of its functions under paragraph 4 by a person exempted or seeking to be exempted under that paragraph.

(2) In carrying out any consideration of representations under sub-paragraph (1), an authority shall comply with any regulations made by the Department for the purposes of this paragraph.

SCHEDULE 6

PROPERTY RIGHTS WHERE PARENTS NOT MARRIED TO EACH OTHER

Succession on intestacy

1.—(1) In Part II of the Administration of Estates Act (Northern Ireland) 1955 (which deals with the distribution of the estate of an intestate), references (however expressed) to any relationship between two persons shall be construed in accordance with Article 155.

(2) For the purposes of sub-paragraph (1) and that Part of that Act, a person whose father and mother were not married to each other at the time of his birth shall be presumed not to have been survived by his father, or by any person related to him only through his father, unless the contrary is shown.

(3) In section 19(1) of that Act (which relates to the construction of documents), the reference to Part II of that Act, or to the foregoing provisions of that Part, shall in relation to an instrument inter vivos made, or a will coming into operation, after the commencement of this paragraph (but not in relation to instruments inter vivos made or wills coming into operation earlier) be construed as including references to this paragraph.

(4) This paragraph does not affect any rights under the intestacy of a person dying before the commencement of this paragraph.

Dispositions of property

2.—(1) In the following dispositions, namely—

(a) dispositions inter vivos made after the commencement of this paragraph; and

(b) dispositions by will where the will is made after the commencement of this paragraph,

references (whether express or implied) to any relationship between two persons shall be construed in accordance with Article 155.

(2) The use, without more, of the word "heir" or "heirs" or any expression which is used to create an entailed interest in real or personal property does not show a contrary intention for the purposes of Article 155 as applied by sub-paragraph (1).

(3) In relation to the dispositions mentioned in sub-paragraph (1), section 34 of the Trustee Act (Northern Ireland) 1958 (which specifies the trust implied by a direction that income is to be held on protective trusts for the benefit of any person) shall have effect as if any reference (however ex-

SCH. 6

pressed) to any relationship between two persons were construed in accordance with Article 155.

(4) Where under any disposition of real or personal property, any interest in such property is limited (whether subject to any preceding limitation or charge or not) in such a way that it would, apart from this paragraph, devolve (as nearly as the law permits) along with a dignity or title of honour, then—

(a) whether or not the disposition contains an express reference to the dignity or title of honour; and

(b) whether or not the property or some interest in the property may in some event become severed from it,

nothing in this paragraph shall operate to sever the property or any interest in it from the dignity or title, but the property or interest shall devolve in all respects as if this paragraph had not come into operation.

(5) This paragraph is without prejudice to Article 42 of the Adoption Order (construction of dispositions in cases of adoption).

(6) In this paragraph "disposition" means a disposition, including an oral disposition, of real or personal property whether inter vivos or by will.

(7) Notwithstanding any rule of law, a disposition made by will executed before the date on which this paragraph comes into operation shall not be treated for the purposes of this paragraph as made on or after that date by reason only that the will is confirmed by a codicil executed on or after that date.

No special protection for trustees and personal representatives

1977 NI 17

3. Article 6 of the Family Law Reform (Northern Ireland) Order 1977 (which enables trustees and personal representatives to distribute property without having ascertained that no person whose parents were not married to each other at the time of his birth, or who claims through such a person, is or may be entitled to an interest in the property) shall cease to have effect.

Entitlement to grant of probate, etc.

4.—(1) For the purpose of determining the person or persons who would in accordance with rules of court be entitled to a grant of probate or administration in respect of the estate of a deceased person, the deceased shall be presumed, unless the contrary is shown, not to have been survived—

(a) by any person related to him whose father and mother were not married to each other at the time of his birth; or

(b) by any person whose relationship with him is deduced through such a person as is mentioned in head (a).

(2) This paragraph does not apply in relation to the estate of a person dying before the commencement of this paragraph.

Article 164(5).

SCHEDULE 7

JURISDICTION

Commencement of proceedings

1.—(1) The Lord Chancellor may by order specify proceedings under this Order which may only be commenced in—

(*a*) a specified level of court;

(*b*) a court which falls within a specified class of court; or

(*c*) a particular court determined in accordance with, or specified in, the order.

(2) The Lord Chancellor may by order specify circumstances in which specified proceedings under this Order (which might otherwise be commenced elsewhere) may only be commenced in—

(*a*) a specified level of court;

(*b*) a court which falls within a specified class of court; or

(*c*) a particular court determined in accordance with, or specified in, the order.

(3) Sub-paragraphs (1) and (2) shall also apply in relation to proceedings—

(*a*) under Article 28 of the Child Support (Northern Ireland) Order 1991 (reference to court for declaration of parentage); or   1991 NI 23

(*b*) which are to be dealt with in accordance with an order made under Article 42 of that Order (jurisdiction of courts in certain proceedings under that Order).

(4) The Lord Chancellor may by order make provision by virtue of which, where specified proceedings with respect to a child under—

(*a*) this Order;

(*b*) Article 22 (appeals) or 28 (reference to court for declaration of parentage) of the Child Support (Northern Ireland) Order 1991; or

(*c*) the High Court's inherent jurisdiction with respect to children,

have been commenced in or transferred to any court (whether or not by virtue of an order under this Schedule), any other specified family proceedings which may affect, or are otherwise connected with, the child may, in specified circumstances, only be commenced in that court.

(5) A class of court specified in an order under this Schedule may be described by reference to a description of proceedings and may include different levels of court.

Transfer of proceedings

2.—(1) The Lord Chancellor may by order provide that in specified circumstances the whole, or any specified part of, specified proceedings to which this paragraph applies shall be transferred to—

(*a*) a specified level of court;

(*b*) a court which falls within a specified class of court; or

(*c*) a particular court determined in accordance with, or specified in, the order.

(2) Any order under this paragraph may provide for the transfer to be made at any stage, or specified stage, of the proceedings and whether or not the proceedings, or any part of them, have already been transferred.

(3) The proceedings to which this paragraph applies are—

(*a*) any proceedings under this Order;

(*b*) any proceedings under Article 22 (appeals) or 28 (reference to court for declaration of parentage) of the Child Support (Northern Ireland) Order 1991;

(c) any other proceedings which—

    (i) are family proceedings for the purposes of this Order, other than proceedings under the inherent jurisdiction of the High Court; and

    (ii) may affect, or are otherwise connected with, the child concerned.

(4) Proceedings to which this paragraph applies by virtue of sub-paragraph (3)(c) may only be transferred in accordance with the provisions of an order made under this paragraph for the purpose of consolidating them with proceedings under—

    (a) this Order; or

    (b) the High Court's inherent jurisdiction with respect to children.

(5) An order under this paragraph may make such provision as the Lord Chancellor thinks appropriate for excluding proceedings to which this paragraph applies from the operation of any statutory provision which would otherwise govern the transfer of those proceedings, or any part of them.

Emergency protection orders

3. In such circumstances as the Lord Chancellor may by order specify, the jurisdiction of a court of summary jurisdiction to make an emergency protection order may be exercised by a resident magistrate or a member of a juvenile court panel.

General

4.—(1) For the purposes of this Schedule—

    (a) the commencement of proceedings under this Order includes the making of any application under this Order in the course of proceedings (whether or not those proceedings are proceedings under this Order); and

    (b) there are three levels of court, that is to say the High Court, a county court and a court of summary jurisdiction.

(2) In this Schedule "specified" means specified by an order made under this Schedule.

(3) Any order under paragraph 1 may make provision as to the effect of commencing proceedings in contravention of any of the provisions of the order.

(4) The Lord Chancellor may by order specify county courts for the purposes of Article 166(4).

(5) An order under paragraph 2 may make provision as to the effect of a failure to comply with any of the provisions of the order.

(6) An order under this Schedule may—

    (a) make such consequential, incidental or transitional provision as the Lord Chancellor considers expedient, including provision amending any other statutory provision so far as it concerns the jurisdiction of any court or person exercising the powers of a court under any statutory provision;

    (b) make provision for treating proceedings which are—

        (i) in part proceedings of a kind mentioned in head (a) of paragraph 2(3); and

(ii) in part proceedings of a kind mentioned in head (*b*) of paragraph 2(3),

as consisting entirely of proceedings of one or other of those kinds, for the purposes of the application of any order made under paragraph 2.

(7) Except to the extent that the Lord Chancellor by order otherwise provides, the jurisdiction of any specified county court under this Order shall be exercisable throughout Northern Ireland (and accordingly Article 3(3)(*b*) of the County Courts (Northern Ireland) Order 1980 (jurisdiction exercisable throughout county court division) shall not apply).

1980 NI 3

SCHEDULE 8

Article 184(1).

TRANSITIONALS AND SAVINGS

Pending proceedings, etc.

1.—(1) Subject to sub-paragraphs (2) and (5), nothing in any provision of this Order (other than the repeals mentioned in sub-paragraph (3)) shall affect any proceedings which are pending immediately before the commencement of that provision.

(2) Proceedings in the exercise of the High Court's inherent jurisdiction with respect to children which are pending in relation to a child who has been placed or allowed to remain in the care of the Department or an authority shall not be treated as pending proceedings after the expiration of one year from the commencement of this sub-paragraph if no final order has been made by then in the exercise of the High Court's inherent jurisdiction in respect of the child's care.

(3) The repeals are those of—

(*a*) Article 45(3) of the Matrimonial Causes (Northern Ireland) Order 1978 (declaration by court that party to marriage unfit to have custody of children of family);

1978 NI 15

(*b*) section 12 of the Criminal Law Amendment Act 1885 (power to divest person of authority over girl in cases of seduction or prostitution);

1885 c. 69

(*c*) section 1(4) of the Punishment of Incest Act 1908 (power to divest person of authority over girl in cases of incest).

1908 c. 45

(4) For the purposes of the following provisions of this Schedule, any reference to an order in force immediately before the commencement of a provision of this Order shall be construed as including a reference to an order made after that commencement in proceedings pending before that commencement.

(5) Sub-paragraph (4) is not to be read as making the order in question have effect from a date earlier than that on which it was made.

(6) An order under Article 169(5) (orders for admissibility of hearsay) may make such provision with respect to the application of the order in relation to proceedings which are pending when the order comes into operation as the Lord Chancellor considers appropriate.

2. Where, immediately before the commencement of Part V, there was in force an order under section 94(4) of the Children and Young Persons Act (Northern Ireland) 1968 (order directing the Department to bring a child or

1968 c. 34 (N.I.)

young person before a juvenile court under subsection (1) of that section), the order shall cease to have effect on the commencement of that Part.

CUSTODY ORDERS, ETC.

Cessation of declarations of unfitness, etc.

3. Where, immediately before the commencement of Parts II and III, there was in force—

1978 NI 15

(a) a declaration under Article 45(3) of the Matrimonial Causes (Northern Ireland) Order 1978 (declaration by court that party to marriage unfit to have custody of children of family); or

1885 c. 69
1908 c. 45

(b) an order under section 12 of the Criminal Law Amendment Act 1885 or section 1(4) of the Punishment of Incest Act 1908 divesting a person of authority over a girl;

the declaration or, as the case may be, the order shall cease to have effect on the commencement of those Parts.

Orders to which paragraphs 5 to 10 apply

4.—(1) In paragraphs 5 to 10 "an existing order" means any order which—

(a) is in force immediately before the commencement of Parts II and III;

(b) was made under any statutory provision mentioned in sub-paragraph (2);

(c) determines all or any of the following—

(i) who is to have custody of a child;

(ii) who is to have care and control of a child;

(iii) who is to have access to a child;

(iv) any matter with respect to a child's education or upbringing; and

(d) is not an order of a kind mentioned in paragraph 11(3).

(2) The statutory provisions are—

1980 NI 5

(a) the Domestic Proceedings (Northern Ireland) Order 1980;

(b) the Matrimonial Causes (Northern Ireland) Order 1978;

1945 c. 14 (N.I.)

(c) the Summary Jurisdiction (Separation and Maintenance) Act (Northern Ireland) 1945;

1939 c. 13 (N.I.)

(d) the Matrimonial Causes Act (Northern Ireland) 1939;

1886 c. 27

(e) the Guardianship of Infants Act 1886.

(3) For the purposes of this paragraph and paragraphs 5 to 10 "custody" includes legal custody, joint as well as sole custody, and parental rights and duties retained under an order under Article 10(4) of the Domestic Proceedings (Northern Ireland) Order 1980, but does not include access.

Parental responsibility of parents

5.—(1) Where—

(a) a child's father and mother were married to each other at the time of his birth; and

(b) there is an existing order with respect to the child,

each parent shall have parental responsibility for the child in accordance with Article 5 as modified by sub-paragraph (3).

(2) Where—

(*a*) a child's father and mother were not married to each other at the time of his birth; and

(*b*) there is an existing order with respect to the child,

Article 5 shall apply as modified by sub-paragraphs (3) and (4).

(3) The modification is that for Article 5(7) there shall be substituted—

"(7) The fact that a person has parental responsibility for a child does not entitle him to act in a way which would be incompatible with any existing order or any order made under this Order with respect to the child.".

(4) The modifications are that—

(*a*) for the purposes of Article 5(2), where the father has custody or care and control of the child by virtue of any existing order, the court shall be deemed to have made (at the commencement of that Article) an order under Article 7(1) giving him parental responsibility for the child; and

(*b*) where by virtue of head (*a*) a court is deemed to have made an order under Article 7(1) in favour of a father who has care and control of a child by virtue of an existing order, the court shall not bring the order under Article 7(1) to an end at any time while he has care and control of the child by virtue of the order.

Persons who are not parents but who have custody or care and control

6.—(1) Where a person who is not the parent or guardian of a child has custody or care and control of him by virtue of an existing order, that person shall have parental responsibility for him so long as he continues to have that custody or care and control by virtue of the order.

(2) Where sub-paragraph (1) applies, Parts II, III and V shall have effect as modified by this paragraph.

(3) The modifications are that—

(*a*) for Article 5(7) there shall be substituted—

"(7) The fact that a person has parental responsibility for a child does not entitle him to act in a way which would be incompatible with any existing order or with any order made under this Order with respect to the child.";

(*b*) at the end of Article 10(4) there shall be inserted—

"(*c*) any person who has custody or care and control of a child by virtue of any existing order"; and

(*c*) at the end of Article 53(1)(*c*) there shall be inserted—

"(*cc*) where immediately before the care order was made there was an existing order by virtue of which a person had custody or care and control of the child, that person;".

Persons who have care and control

7.—(1) Sub-paragraphs (2) to (6) apply where a person has care and control of a child by virtue of an existing order, but they shall cease to apply when that order ceases to have effect.

(2) Article 10 shall have effect as if for paragraph (5)(*c*)(i) there were substituted—

"(i) in any case where by virtue of an existing order any person or persons has or have care and control of the child, has the consent of that person or each of those persons;".

(3) Article 22 shall have effect as if for paragraph (3)(*a*) there were substituted—

"(*a*) who has care and control of the child by virtue of an existing order; or".

(4) Article 27 shall have effect as if for paragraph (4)(*c*) there were substituted—

"(*c*) where the child is in care and immediately before the care order was made there was an existing order by virtue of which a person had care and control of the child, that person.".

(5) Articles 159 and 160 shall have effect as if—

(*a*) for any reference to a residence order in favour of a parent or guardian there were substituted a reference to any existing order by virtue of which the parent or guardian has care and control of the child;

(*b*) for Article 159(3) there were substituted—

"(3) Paragraph (1) shall not apply if the existing order referred to in sub-paragraph (*b*) of that paragraph was one by virtue of which a surviving parent of the child also had care and control of him.";

(*c*) for Article 160(7) there were substituted—

"(7) Paragraph (5) shall not apply if the existing order referred to in sub-paragraph (*b*) of that paragraph was one by virtue of which a surviving parent also had care and control of him.".

(6) In Schedule 1, paragraphs 2(1) and 16(1) shall have effect as if for the words "in whose favour a residence order is in force with respect to the child" there were substituted the words "who has been given care and control of the child by virtue of an existing order".

Persons who have access

8.—(1) Sub-paragraphs (2) to (4) apply where a person has access by virtue of an existing order.

(2) Article 10 shall have effect as if after paragraph (5) there were inserted—

"(5A) Any person who has access to a child by virtue of an existing order is entitled to apply for a contact order.".

(3) Article 16(2) shall have effect as if after sub-paragraph (*b*) there were inserted—

"(*bb*) any person who has access to the child by virtue of an existing order;".

(4) Articles 62(11), 63(13) and 65(10) shall have effect as if in each case after sub-paragraph (*d*) there were inserted—

"(*dd*) any person who has been given access to him by virtue of an existing order;".

Enforcement of certain existing orders

9.—(1) Sub-paragraph (2) applies in relation to any existing order which, but for the repeal by this Order of Article 37 of the Domestic Proceedings (Northern Ireland) Order 1980 (enforcement of custody orders) might have been enforced as if it were an order requiring a person to give up a child to another person.   1980 NI 5

(2) Where this sub-paragraph applies, the existing order may, after the repeal mentioned in sub-paragraph (1), be enforced under Article 14 as if—

   (*a*) any reference to a residence order were a reference to the existing order; and

   (*b*) any reference to a person in whose favour the residence order is in force were a reference to a person to whom actual custody of the child is given by an existing order which is in force.

(3) In sub-paragraph (2) "actual custody", in relation to a child, means the actual possession of his person.

Discharge of existing orders

10.—(1) The making of a residence order or care order with respect to a child who is the subject of an existing order discharges the existing order.

(2) Where the court makes any Article 8 order (other than a residence order) with respect to a child with respect to whom any existing order is in force, the existing order shall have effect subject to the Article 8 order.

(3) The court may discharge an existing order which is in force with respect to a child—

   (*a*) in any family proceedings relating to the child or in which any question arises with respect to the child's welfare; or

   (*b*) on the application of—

      (i) any parent or guardian of the child;

      (ii) the child himself; or

      (iii) any person named in the order.

(4) A child may not apply for the discharge of an existing order except with the leave of the court.

(5) The power in sub-paragraph (3) to discharge an existing order includes the power to discharge any part of the order.

(6) In considering whether to discharge an order under the power conferred by sub-paragraph (3) the court shall, if the discharge of the order is opposed by any party to the proceedings, have regard in particular to the matters mentioned in Article 3(3).

CHILDREN IN CARE

Children in compulsory care

11.—(1) Sub-paragraph (2) applies where, immediately before the commencement of Part V—

   (*a*) a person is in the care of the Department or an authority by virtue of any order mentioned in sub-paragraph (3); or

   (*b*) there is in force a parental rights order under section 104 of the Children and Young Persons Act (Northern Ireland) 1968 with respect to a person.   1968 c. 34 (N.I.)

(2) Where this sub-paragraph applies, then, on and after the commencement of Part V—

(a) the order in question shall be deemed to be a care order;

(b) if the person was in the care of an authority immediately before that commencement, that authority shall be deemed to be the authority designated in that deemed care order, or if the person was in the care of the Department, the authority in whose area he is immediately before that commencement shall be deemed to be the authority designated in that deemed care order; and

(c) any reference to a child in the care of an authority shall include a reference to a person who is the subject of such a deemed care order,

and the provisions of this Order shall apply accordingly, subject to paragraph 12.

(3) The orders referred to in sub-paragraph (1)(a) are—

(a) an order committing a person to the care of a fit person under section 66, 74, 95, 96, 97, 143 or 144 of the Children and Young Persons Act (Northern Ireland) 1968;

1989 c. 41

(b) an order which by virtue of regulations under section 101 of the Children Act 1989 has effect as if it were an order under section 95(1)(b) of the Children and Young Persons Act (Northern Ireland) 1968 committing a person to the care of an authority;

(c) an order under—

1968 c. 49

(i) section 74 of the Social Work (Scotland) Act 1968;

1969 c. 54

(ii) section 25 of the Children and Young Persons Act 1969;

(d) an order under—

1978 NI 15

(i) Article 46 of the Matrimonial Causes (Northern Ireland) Order 1978;

1980 NI 5

(ii) Article 12 of the Domestic Proceedings (Northern Ireland) Order 1980;

(iii) Article 27(1)(b) of the Adoption Order;

(e) an order of the High Court in the exercise of its inherent jurisdiction with respect to children.

12.—(1) This sub-paragraph applies to a child who has been placed or allowed to remain in the care of the Department or an authority in the exercise of the High Court's inherent jurisdiction and who immediately before the expiration of one year from the commencement of paragraph 1(2) is still in the care of the Department or an authority.

(2) Where in respect of a child to whom sub-paragraph (1) applies proceedings have ceased by virtue of paragraph 1(2) to be treated as pending, paragraph 11(2) shall apply on the expiration of one year from the commencement of paragraph 1(2) as if the child was in care pursuant to an order specified in paragraph 11(3)(e).

(3) Sub-paragraphs (4) and (5) only apply where a child who is the subject of a care order by virtue of paragraph 11(2) is a person falling within sub-paragraph (3)(d) or (e) of that paragraph.

(4) Subject to sub-paragraph (5), where a court, on making the order, or at any time thereafter, gave directions under—

(a) Article 46(5)(a) of the Matrimonial Causes (Northern Ireland) Order 1978; or

(b) in the exercise of the High Court's inherent jurisdiction with respect to children,

as to the exercise by the Department or an authority of any powers, those directions shall, subject to the provisions of Article 44 and regulations made under that Article, continue to have effect (regardless of any conflicting provision in this Order other than Article 44 or in such regulations) until varied or discharged by a court under this sub-paragraph.

(5) Where directions referred to in sub-paragraph (4) are to the effect that a child be placed in accommodation provided for the purpose of restricting liberty, then the directions shall cease to have effect upon the expiry of the maximum period specified by regulations under Article 44(3)(a) in relation to children of his description, calculated from the commencement of that Article.

Cessation of wardship where child is in care

13.—(1) Where a child who is a ward of court is in the care of the Department or an authority by virtue of an order made in the exercise of the High Court's inherent jurisdiction with respect to children, he shall, on the commencement of Part V, cease to be a ward of court.

(2) Where immediately before the commencement of Part V a child was in the care of the Department or an authority and as a result of an order made in the exercise of the High Court's inherent jurisdiction with respect to children continued to be in the care of the Department or an authority and was made a ward of court, he shall, on the commencement of Part V, cease to be a ward of court.

(3) Sub-paragraphs (1) and (2) do not apply in proceedings which are pending.

Children placed with parent, etc., while in compulsory care

14.—(1) This paragraph applies where a child is deemed by paragraph 11 to be in the care of the Department or an authority under an order which is deemed by that paragraph to be a care order.

(2) If, immediately before the commencement of Part IV, the child was allowed to be under the control of—

(a) a parent or guardian under section 105(3) or 145(1) of the Children and Young Persons Act (Northern Ireland) 1968; or

(b) a person who, before the child was in the care of the Department or an authority, had care and control of the child by virtue of an order falling within paragraph 4,

on and after that commencement the provision made by and under Article 27(5) shall apply as if the child had been placed with the person in question in accordance with that provision.

Children in voluntary care

15.—(1) This paragraph applies where, immediately before the commencement of Part IV, a child—

(a) was in the care of the Department or an authority under section 103 of the Children and Young Persons Act (Northern Ireland) 1968; or

187

(*b*) was deemed by virtue of subsection (7) of that section to have come within the care of the Department or an authority.

(2) Where this paragraph applies, the child shall, after the commencement of Part IV, be treated for the purposes of this Order as a child who is provided with accommodation under Part IV, but he shall cease to be so treated once he ceases to be so accommodated in accordance with the provisions of that Part.

Boarded out children

16.—(1) Where, immediately before the commencement of Part IV, a child in the care of the Department or an authority—

(*a*) was—

(i) boarded out with a person under section 114(1)(*a*) of the Children and Young Persons Act (Northern Ireland) 1968; or

(ii) allowed to be under the control of a person under section 105(3) or 145(1) of that Act; and

(*b*) the person with whom he was boarded out or, as the case may be, under whose control he was allowed to be was not a person falling within paragraph 14(2)(*a*) or (*b*),

after the commencement of that Part, he shall be treated (subject to sub-paragraph (2)) as having been placed with an authority foster parent and shall cease to be so treated when he ceases to be placed with that person in accordance with the provisions of this Order.

(2) Regulations made under Article 27(2)(*a*) shall not apply in relation to a person who is an authority foster parent by virtue of sub-paragraph (1) before the end of the period of twelve months beginning with the commencement of Part IV and accordingly that person, if the child was boarded out with him as mentioned in sub-paragraph (1)(*a*)(i), shall for that period be subject to terms and regulations mentioned in section 114(1)(*a*) of the Children and Young Persons Act (Northern Ireland) 1968 as if that section had not been repealed by this Order.

Children in care to qualify for advice and assistance

17. Any reference in Part IV to a person qualifying for advice and assistance shall be construed as including a reference to a person within the area of the authority in question who is under 21 and who was, at any time after reaching the age of 16 but while still a child a person falling within paragraph 11(1), 15(1) or 30(1).

Emigration of children in care

18. Where the Head of the Department is considering whether to give his consent under section 118 of the Children and Young Persons Act (Northern Ireland) 1968 to arrangements for the emigration of a child in the care of the Department but immediately before the repeal of that section by this Order he has not decided whether to give his consent, that section shall continue to apply (regardless of that repeal) until the Head of the Department has determined whether to give his consent.

Contributions for maintenance of children in care

19.—(1) Where, immediately before the commencement of Part IV, there was in force an order made (or having effect as if made) under any of the provisions mentioned in sub-paragraph (2), then, after the commencement of that Part—

(a) the order shall have effect as if made under Article 41(2) against a person liable to contribute; and

(b) Articles 38 to 43 shall apply to the order, subject to the modifications in sub-paragraph (3).

(2) The provisions referred to in sub-paragraph (1) are—

(a) Article 13(4) of the Domestic Proceedings (Northern Ireland) Order 1980;

(b) Article 27(2) of the Adoption Order;

(c) section 156 of the Children and Young Persons Act (Northern Ireland) 1968,

(provisions empowering the court to make an order requiring a person to make periodical payments to the Department or an authority in respect of a child in care).

(3) The modifications are that in Article 41—

(a) in paragraph (4), sub-paragraph (a) shall be omitted;

(b) for paragraph (6) there shall be substituted—

"(6) Where—

(a) a contribution order is in force;

(b) the authority serves a contribution notice under Article 40; and

(c) the contributor and the authority reach an agreement under Article 40(7) in respect of the contribution notice,

the effect of the agreement shall be to discharge the order from the date on which it is agreed that the agreement shall take effect."; and

(c) at the end of paragraph (10) there shall be inserted—

"and

(c) where the order is against a person who is not a parent of the child, shall be made with due regard to—

(i) whether that person had assumed responsibility for the maintenance of the child, and, if so, the extent to which and basis on which he assumed that responsibility and the length of the period during which he met that responsibility;

(ii) whether he did so knowing that the child was not his child;

(iii) the liability of any other person to maintain the child.".

Supervision orders

Orders under the 1968 Act

20.—(1) This paragraph applies to any supervision order made under the Children and Young Persons Act (Northern Ireland) 1968—

(a) which places a child under the supervision of the Department or an authority; and

189

(b) which is in force immediately before the commencement of Part V.

(2) On and after the commencement of Part V, the order shall be deemed to be a supervision order made under Article 50 and—

    (a) any requirement of the order that the child reside with a named individual shall continue to have effect while the order remains in force, unless the court otherwise directs;

    (b) any other requirement imposed by the court, or directions given by the supervisor, shall be deemed to have been imposed or given under the appropriate provisions of Schedule 3.

(3) Where, immediately before the commencement of Part V, the order had been in force for a period of more than six months, it shall cease to have effect at the end of the period of six months from the commencement of that Part unless—

    (a) the court directs that it shall cease to have effect at the end of a different period (which shall not exceed three years);

    (b) it ceases to have effect earlier in accordance with Article 179 (effect and duration of orders, etc.); or

    (c) it would have ceased to have had effect earlier had this Order not been made.

(4) Where sub-paragraph (3) applies, paragraph 6 of Schedule 3 shall not apply.

(5) Where, immediately before the commencement of Part V, the order had been in force for a period of six months or less it shall cease to have effect in accordance with Article 179 (effect and duration of orders, etc.) and paragraph 6 of Schedule 3 unless—

    (a) the court directs that it shall cease to have effect at the end of a different period (which shall not exceed three years); or

    (b) it would have ceased to have had effect earlier had this Order not been made.

21.—(1) This paragraph applies to any supervision order made under the Children and Young Persons Act (Northern Ireland) 1968—

    (a) which places a child under the supervision of an education and library board; and

    (b) which is in force immediately before the commencement of Part V.

(2) On and after the commencement of Part V, the order shall be deemed to be an education supervision order made under Article 55 and—

    (a) any requirement of the order that the child reside with a named individual shall continue to have effect while the order remains in force, unless the court otherwise directs;

    (b) any other requirement imposed by the court, or directions given by the supervisor, shall be deemed to be directions under Schedule 4.

(3) Where, immediately before the commencement of Part V, the order had been in force for a period of more than six months, it shall continue to have effect until the end of the period of six months from the commencement of that Part unless—

    (a) the court directs that it shall continue to have effect until a different date (which shall not be later than either the date on which the child ceases to be of compulsory school age or the end of the period of three years from the making of the order);

(b) it ceases to have effect earlier in accordance with sub-paragraph (4); or

(c) it would have ceased to have effect earlier had this Order not been made.

(4) The order shall cease to have effect on the making of a care order.

(5) Where sub-paragraph (3) applies, paragraph 5 of Schedule 4 shall not apply.

(6) Where, immediately before the commencement of Part V, the order had been in force for a period of six months or less, it shall cease to have effect in accordance with paragraph 5 of Schedule 4 unless—

(a) the court directs that it shall continue to have effect until a different date (which shall not be later than either the date on which the child ceases to be of compulsory school age or the end of the period of three years from the making of the order);

(b) it would have ceased to have effect earlier had this Order not been made.

Other supervision orders

22.—(1) This paragraph applies to any order for the supervision of a child which was in force immediately before the commencement of Part V and was made under—

(a) Article 47 of the Matrimonial Causes (Northern Ireland) Order 1978;

1978 NI 15

(b) Article 11 of the Domestic Proceedings (Northern Ireland) Order 1980;

1980 NI 5

(c) Article 27(1)(a) of the Adoption Order.

(2) The order shall not be deemed to be a supervision order made under any provision of this Order but shall nevertheless continue in force for a period of one year from the commencement of Part V unless—

(a) the court directs that it shall cease to have effect at the end of a lesser period, or

(b) it would have ceased to have had effect earlier had this Order not been made.

Place of safety orders

23.—(1) This paragraph applies to—

(a) any order or warrant authorising the taking or removal of a child to a place of safety which—

(i) was made, or issued, under any of the provisions mentioned in sub-paragraph (2); and

(ii) was in force immediately before the commencement of Part V; and

(b) any interim order made under section 101(1) of the Children and Young Persons Act (Northern Ireland) 1968.

1968 c. 34 (N.I.)

(2) The provisions referred to in sub-paragraph (1)(a)(i) are—

(a) section 8 of the Children and Young Persons Act (Northern Ireland) 1968 (children improperly kept);

191

(b) section 18(1) of that Act (detention of child in place of safety);

(c) section 32 of that Act (warrant to search for or remove child);

(d) Article 35 of the Adoption Order (removal of protected child from unsuitable surroundings).

(3) The order or warrant shall continue to have effect as if this Order were not in operation.

(4) Any statutory provision repealed by this Order shall continue to have effect in relation to the order or warrant so far as is necessary for the purposes of securing that the effect of the order is what it would have been if this Order were not in operation.

(5) Sub-paragraph (4) does not apply to the power to make an interim order or further interim order given by section 101 of the Children and Young Persons Act (Northern Ireland) 1968.

(6) Where, immediately before section 32 or 99 of the Children and Young Persons Act (Northern Ireland) 1968 is wholly or partly repealed by this Order, a child is being detained under the powers granted by that section, he may continue to be detained in accordance with that section.

Voluntary homes

24.—(1) This paragraph applies to a voluntary home which is registered in the register kept for the purposes of section 127 of the Children and Young Persons Act (Northern Ireland) 1968 by the Department.

(2) Where a voluntary home to which this paragraph applies is being carried on immediately before the commencement of Part VIII, that home shall be deemed to have been registered under that Part by the authority in whose area the home is situated on the last anniversary of the original registration to fall before the commencement of that Part.

Foster children

25.—(1) This paragraph applies where—

(a) immediately before the commencement of Part IX, a person is providing a child to whom section 1 of the Children and Young Persons Act (Northern Ireland) 1968 applies with care and maintenance; and

(b) the circumstances of the case are such that, had Parts IX and X then been in operation, he would have been treated for the purposes of this Order as a child who was being provided with accommodation in a children's home and not as a child who was being privately fostered.

(2) If the child continues to be cared for and maintained as before, Article 95(1) and (3) shall not apply in relation to him if—

(a) an application for registration of the home in question is made under Article 96 before the end of the period of three months beginning with the day on which Part IX comes into operation; and

(b) the application has not been refused or, if it has been refused—

(i) the period for an appeal against the decision has not expired; or

(ii) an appeal against the refusal has been made but has not been determined or abandoned.

(3) While Article 95(1) and (3) do not apply, the child shall be treated as a privately fostered child for the purposes of Part X.

SCH. 8

Child minders

26.—(1) Sub-paragraph (2) applies where, immediately before the commencement of Part XI, any premises are registered under section 11 of the Children and Young Persons Act (Northern Ireland) 1968 (registration of premises of child minders).

(2) During the transitional period, the provisions of that Act shall continue to have effect with respect to those premises to the exclusion of Part XI.

(3) Nothing in sub-paragraph (2) shall prevent an authority from registering any person under Part XI with respect to the premises.

(4) In this paragraph "the transitional period" means the period ending with—

(a) the first anniversary of the commencement of Part XI; or

(b) if earlier, the date on which an authority registers any person under Part XI with respect to the premises.

Guardians

Existing guardians to be guardians under this Order

27.—(1) Any appointment of a person as guardian for a child which—

(a) was made—

    (i) under section 3 or 6 of the Guardianship of Infants Act 1886;   1886 c. 27

    (ii) under section 12 of the Criminal Law Amendment Act 1885;   1885 c. 69

    (iii) section 6 of the Tenures Abolition Act (Ireland) 1662; or   1662 c. 19

    (iv) under the High Court's inherent jurisdiction with respect to children; and

(b) has taken effect before the commencement of Part XV,

shall (subject to sub-paragraph (2)) be deemed, after the commencement of that Part, to be an appointment made and having effect under Article 159 or 160 as the case may be.

(2) Where an appointment of a person as guardian of a child has effect under that Part by virtue of sub-paragraph (1)(a)(ii), the appointment shall not have effect for a period which is longer than any period directed by the court.

Appointment of guardian not yet in effect

28. Any appointment of a person to be a guardian of a child—

(a) which was made as mentioned in paragraph 27(1)(a)(i) or (iii); but

(b) which, immediately before the commencement of Part XV, had not taken effect,

shall take effect in accordance with that Part (as modified, where it applies, by paragraph 7(5)).

Children accommodated in certain establishments

29. In calculating, for the purposes of Article 174(1)(a) or (2)(a) or Article 175(1)(a) or 177(1)(a) the period of time for which a child has been accommodated any part of that period which fell before commencement of that Article shall be disregarded.

Training school orders

30.—(1) This paragraph applies where, immediately before the commencement of Part V, a person was under the care of the managers of a training school by virtue of a training school order under section 95, 108(*a*) or 143(6)(*b*) of the Children and Young Persons Act (Northern Ireland) 1968.

(2) If, on the commencement of Part V, the person has reached the age of 18, the training school order shall cease to have effect.

(3) If, on the commencement of Part V, the person has not reached the age of 18, then, on and after the commencement of that Part—

(*a*) the training school order shall be deemed to be a care order;

(*b*) the authority in whose area the person is ordinarily resident shall be deemed to be the authority designated in that deemed care order; and

(*c*) any reference to a child in the care of an authority shall include a reference to a person who is the subject of such a deemed care order,

and the provisions of this Order shall apply accordingly, subject to sub-paragraphs (4) and (5).

(4) The deemed care order shall not continue to have effect beyond the date on which the training school order would have ceased to have effect by virtue of section 87(1) of the Children and Young Persons Act (Northern Ireland) 1968.

(5) Before the expiration of the period of six months beginning with the commencement of Part V, the authority referred to in sub-paragraph (3)(*b*) shall review the case of any person in relation to whom it is the authority designated in the deemed care order in accordance with Article 45 (reviews where child is looked after by an authority).

Miscellaneous

Marriage consents

31.—(1) In the circumstances mentioned in sub-paragraph (2), section 1 of, and the Schedule to, the Marriages Act (Northern Ireland) 1954 (consent to marriage of minors) shall continue to have effect regardless of the amendments and repeals of provisions of that Act contained in Schedules 9 and 10.

1954 c. 21 (N.I.)

(2) The circumstances are that—

(*a*) immediately before the commencement of paragraph 10 of Schedule 9 there is in force—

(i) an existing order, as defined in paragraph 4(1); or

(ii) an order of a kind mentioned in paragraph 11(1)(*b*) or (3); and

(*b*) section 1 of, and the Schedule to, the Marriages Act (Northern Ireland) 1954 would, but for this Order, have applied to the marriage of the child who is the subject of the order.

Affiliation orders, etc.

32.—(1) This paragraph applies to the following orders—

(*a*) any affiliation order in force immediately before the commencement of Article 158;

(b) any order which is enforceable in like manner as an affiliation order and is in force immediately before the commencement of Article 158;

(c) any order made in relation to an order described in head (a) or (b).

(2) The repeal by this Order of any statutory provision relating to affiliation orders shall not affect any order to which this paragraph applies.

(3) Where—

(a) an application is made to the High Court or a county court for an order under paragraph 2 of Schedule 1 in respect of a child whose parents were not married to each other at the time of his birth; and

(b) an affiliation order providing for periodical payments is in force in respect of the child by virtue of this Schedule,

the court may direct that the affiliation order shall cease to have effect on such date as may be specified in the direction.

Property rights where parents not married to each other

33.—(1) In this paragraph "the 1977 Order" means the Family Law Reform (Northern Ireland) Order 1977.

1977 NI 17

(2) The repeal by this Order of Article 3 of the 1977 Order (rights on intestacy) shall not affect any rights arising under the intestacy of a person who dies before the repeal comes into operation.

(3) The repeal by this Order of Article 4 of the 1977 Order (presumption in dispositions of property) shall not affect, or affect the operation of section 3 of the Legitimacy Act (Northern Ireland) 1928 or section 34 of the Trustee Act (Northern Ireland) 1958 in relation to—

1928 c. 5 (N.I.)
1958 c. 23 (N.I.)

(a) any disposition inter vivos made before the date on which the repeal comes into operation; or

(b) any disposition by will executed before that date.

(4) The repeal by this Order of Article 6 of the 1977 Order shall not affect the liability of trustees or personal representatives in respect of any conveyance or distribution made before the repeal comes into operation.

Attendance of child before court

34. Section 170 of the Children and Young Persons Act (Northern Ireland) 1968 (power to enforce attendance of child before court) shall apply in relation to any provision of that Act repealed by this Order as if this Order had not been made.

Employment of children

35.—(1) This paragraph (which in effect re-enacts a saving relating to section 37(2)(a) of the Children and Young Persons Act (Northern Ireland) 1968 in Part I of Schedule 2 to the Manual Handling Operations Regulations (Northern Ireland) 1992) applies only in relation to such employment as is permitted under section 1(2) of the Employment of Women, Young Persons and Children Act 1920.

S.R. 1992 No. 535

1920 c. 65

(2) Article 135 (general restrictions on the employment of children) shall have effect as if for paragraphs (2) and (3) there were substituted the following paragraphs—

"(2) No child shall be employed—

SCH. 8

(a) to lift, carry or move anything so heavy as to be likely to cause injury to the child; or

(b) in any occupation likely to be injurious to his life, limb, health or education, regard being had to his physical condition.

(3) If any education and library board serves on the employer of any child a copy of a certificate signed by a medical practitioner—

(a) that the lifting, carrying or moving of any specified weight is likely to cause injury to the child; or

(b) that any specified occupation is likely to be injurious to the life, limb, health or education of the child,

the certificate shall be admissible as evidence in any subsequent proceedings against the employer in respect of the employment of the child.".

Saving for certain amendments of 1968 Act

1972 NI 14

36. Notwithstanding the repeal by this Order of Part I of Schedule 16 to the Health and Personal Social Services (Northern Ireland) Order 1972, the Children and Young Persons Act (Northern Ireland) 1968 shall continue to have effect subject to the amendments made by paragraphs 2, 4, 7 and 13 of that Schedule.

Article 185(1).

SCHEDULE 9

AMENDMENTS

The Offences Against the Person Act 1861 (c. 100)

1. In section 53 (abduction with intent of girl under 18 from parent or person having lawful care or charge of her), for "the lawful care or charge of" substitute "parental responsibility for or care of".

2. In section 55 (abduction of girl under 16 from parent or person having lawful care or charge of her), for "the lawful care or charge of" substitute "parental responsibility for or care of".

The Criminal Law Amendment Act 1885 (c. 69)

3. In section 7 (abduction with intent of girl under 18 from parent or person having lawful care or charge of her), for "the lawful care or charge of" substitute "parental responsibility for or care of".

4. In section 10 (power of search for woman or girl detained for immoral purposes)—

(a) for ", relative, or guardian" in the first place where it occurs substitute "or relative, or any other person having parental responsibility for or care";

(b) for "guardians" substitute "any other person having parental responsibility for or care of her";

(c) for "the lawful care or charge" substitute "parental responsibility for or care".

The Maintenance Orders (Facilities for Enforcement) Act 1920 (c. 33)

5. In section 4A(3) (variation and revocation of maintenance orders)—

(a) for "defendant to a complaint" substitute "respondent to an application";

(*b*) for "the complaint" substitute "the application (where it would not have such jurisdiction apart from this subsection)";

(*c*) for "defendant" in the second place where it occurs substitute "respondent".

6. In section 11 (application to Ireland)—

(*a*) immediately before paragraph (*a*) insert the following paragraph—

> "(*za*) In section 3(1), (3) and (6) for the words "England and Wales" there shall be substituted the words "Northern Ireland" and for subsection (7) of that section there shall be substituted the following subsection—
>
> > "(7) Where paragraph (1) of Article 86 of the Magistrates' Courts (Northern Ireland) Order 1981 (revocation, variation, etc., of orders for periodical payment) applies in relation to an order made under this section which has been confirmed, that paragraph shall have effect as if for the words "by order on complaint" there were substituted the words "on an application being made, by order"."";";

(*b*) in paragraph (*b*), immediately before paragraph (*a*) of subsection (6A) of section 4 there shall be inserted in that subsection the following paragraph—

> "(*za*) as if in paragraph (1) for the words "by order on complaint" there were substituted "on an application being made, by order";";

(*c*) for paragraph (*c*) substitute the following paragraphs—

> "(*c*) In section 6 (mode of enforcing orders), in the proviso to subsection (2), for the words from "in like manner" to the end substitute "as an order to which Article 98 of the Magistrates' Courts (Northern Ireland) Order 1981 applies, the order shall be so enforceable subject to the modifications of that Article specified in subsection (3ZA) of section 18 of the Maintenance Orders Act 1950 (enforcement of registered orders)";
>
> (*cc*) In section 7 (application of Summary Jurisdiction Acts), after subsection (2) there shall be added the following subsection—
>
> > "(3) Without prejudice to the generality of the power to make rules under Article 13 of the Magistrates' Courts (Northern Ireland) Order 1981 (magistrates' courts rules), for the purpose of giving effect to this Act such rules may make, in relation to any proceedings brought under or by virtue of this Act, any provision which—
> >
> > > (*a*) falls within paragraph (2) of Article 165 of the Children (Northern Ireland) Order 1995, and
> > >
> > > (*b*) may be made in relation to relevant proceedings under that Article.".".

The Employment of Women, Young Persons, and Children Act 1920 (c. 65)

7. In section 1(6)(*a*) (restrictions on employment in industrial undertakings)—

SCH. 9

(a) for sub-paragraph (iii) substitute the following sub-paragraph—

"(iii) Articles 146(1) and (3), 147(1), (5), (6) and (9) and 148(1) and (2) of the Children (Northern Ireland) Order 1995,"; and

(b) for "Part III of that Act of 1968" substitute "Part XII of that Order of 1995".

The Legitimacy Act (Northern Ireland) 1928 (c. 5)

8. After section 8 (provisions as to persons legitimated by extraneous law) insert the following section—

"Legitimation of adopted child.

8A.—(1) Article 40 of the Adoption (Northern Ireland) Order 1987 does not prevent an adopted child being legitimated under section 1 or 8 if either natural parent is the sole adoptive parent.

(2) Where an adopted child (with a sole adoptive parent) is legitimated—

(a) paragraph (2) of Article 40 shall not apply after the legitimation to the natural relationship with the other natural parent; and

(b) revocation of the adoption order in consequence of the legitimation shall not affect Articles 40 to 42 as they apply to any instrument made before the date of legitimation.".

The Children and Young Persons Act (Northern Ireland) 1950 (c. 5)

9. In section 13(3) (amendments of the Criminal Law Amendment Act 1885), after "six" insert "and".

The Marriages Act (Northern Ireland) 1954 (c. 21)

10. In section 1 (consent to marriage of minors)—

(a) in subsection (1)—

(i) for "minor" substitute "child";

(ii) for "the Schedule to this Act" substitute "subsection (1A) of this section";

(b) after subsection (1) insert the following subsection—

"(1A) The consents are—

(a) subject to paragraphs (b) to (d) of this subsection, the consent of—

(i) each parent (if any) of the child who has parental responsibility for him; and

(ii) each guardian (if any) of the child;

(b) where a residence order is in force with respect to the child, the consent of the person or persons with whom he lives, or is to live, as a result of the order (in substitution for the consents mentioned in paragraph (a) of this subsection);

(c) where a care order is in force with respect to the child, the consent of the Health and Social Services Board or Health and Social Services trust designated in the order (in addition to the consents mentioned in paragraph (a) of this subsection);

198

(*d*) where neither paragraph (*b*) nor paragraph (*c*) of this subsection applies but a residence order was in force with respect to the child immediately before he reached the age of 16, the consent of the person or persons with whom he lived, or was to live, as a result of the order (in substitution for the consents mentioned in paragraph (*a*) of this subsection).".

11. In section 2 (order dispensing with consent)—

(*a*) for "minor" wherever it occurs substitute "child";

(*b*) in subsection (1), for paragraphs (*a*) to (*c*) substitute the following paragraphs—

"(*a*) it is not reasonably practicable to obtain the consent of any person whose consent is required; or

(*b*) any person whose consent is required withholds or refuses his consent; or".

12. In section 6 (interpretation)—

(*a*) in subsection (1), insert before the definition of "contravention" the following definition—

" "child" means a person over the age of 16, and under the age of 18, years;";

(*b*) after subsection (1), insert the following subsection—

"(1A) In this Act "care order", "guardian of a child", "Health and Social Services trust", "parental responsibility" and "residence order" have the same meaning as in the Children (Northern Ireland) Order 1995.".

The Administration of Justice Act 1960 (c. 65)

13. In Schedule 2, in the entry relating to section 12, for "For paragraph (*b*) of subsection (1)" substitute the following—

"(1) For paragraph (*a*) of subsection (1) there shall be substituted the following paragraph:—

(*a*) where the proceedings—

(i) relate to the exercise of the inherent jurisdiction of the High Court with respect to minors;

(ii) are brought under the Children (Northern Ireland) Order 1995; or

(iii) otherwise relate wholly or mainly to the maintenance or upbringing of a minor.

(2) For paragraph (*b*) of that subsection".

The Legitimacy Act (Northern Ireland) 1961 (c. 5)

14.—(1) In subsection (1) of section 2 (legitimacy of children of certain void marriages), for "act of intercourse resulting in the birth" substitute "insemination resulting in the birth or, where there was no such insemination, the child's conception".

(2) After subsection (2) insert the following subsections—

"(2A) Without prejudice to the generality of subsection (1), that subsection applies notwithstanding that the belief that the marriage was valid was due to a mistake of law.

(2B) In relation to a child born after the commencement of paragraph 14 of Schedule 9 to the Children (Northern Ireland) Order 1995, it shall be presumed for the purposes of subsection (1), unless the contrary is shown, that one of the parties to the void marriage reasonably believed at the time of the insemination resulting in the birth or, where there was no such insemination, the child's conception (or at the time of the celebration of the marriage if later) that the marriage was valid.".

The Factories Act (Northern Ireland) 1965 (c. 20)

15. In section 176(1) (interpretation), in the definition of "parent", for the words from "or guardian" to "young person" where it first occurs substitute "of a child or young person or any person who is not a parent of his but who has parental responsibility for him (within the meaning of the Children (Northern Ireland) Order 1995)".

The Maintenance and Affiliation Orders Act (Northern Ireland) 1966 (c. 35)

16. In section 10(2) (orders to which Part II applies), after paragraph (g) insert the following paragraph—

"(h) Article 41 of, or Schedule 1 to, the Children (Northern Ireland) Order 1995;".

17. In section 13 (variation of orders), for subsection (3) substitute the following subsection—

"(3) Article 165 of the Children (Northern Ireland) Order 1995 shall apply for the purposes of giving effect to this section as it applies for the purposes of giving effect to that Order, except that in the application of that Article by virtue of this subsection "relevant proceedings" means any application made under subsection (2).".

The Children and Young Persons Act (Northern Ireland) 1968 (c. 34)

18. In section 20 (cruelty to persons under 16)—

(a) in subsection (1), for "the custody, charge or care of" substitute "responsibility for";

(b) in subsection (2)(a), after "young person" insert ", or the legal guardian of a child or young person".

19. In section 21(1) (causing or encouraging seduction or prostitution of girl under 17), for "the custody, charge or care of" substitute "responsibility for".

20. In section 23 (allowing children or young persons to be in brothels), for "the custody, charge or care of" substitute "responsibility for".

21. In section 24 (causing or allowing persons under 16 to be used for begging)—

(a) in subsection (1), for "the custody, charge or care of" substitute "responsibility for";

(b) in subsection (2), for "the custody, charge or care of" substitute "responsibility for".

22. In section 29(1) (exposing children under 12 to risk of burning), for "the custody, charge or care of" substitute "responsibility for".

23. In section 33(2) (mode of charging offences), for the words from the beginning to "charge him" where it first occurs substitute "The same complaint or summons may charge any person".

24. For section 35 (notification of Department as to proceedings under Part II) substitute the following section—

"Notification as to proceedings under Part II

35.—(1) Where on the complaint of any person charging an offence under this Part with respect to a child or young person a summons or warrant is issued, the complainant shall as soon as reasonably practicable notify to the appropriate authority—

(*a*) the nature of the charge, and

(*b*) the name and address of the child, so far as known to the complainant.

(2) Subsection (1) shall not apply where the complainant is the appropriate authority.

(3) In this section "the appropriate authority" means the authority within whose area the child's address is or, if that is not known, the authority within whose area the offence is alleged to have been committed, and "authority" and "area" have the same meaning as in the Children Order.".

25. For section 36 (interpretation of Part II) substitute the following section—

"Interpretation of Part II.

36.—(1) For the purposes of this Part, the following shall be presumed to have responsibility for a child or young person—

(*a*) any person who—

(i) has parental responsibility for him (within the meaning of the Children Order); or

(ii) is otherwise legally liable to maintain him; and

(*b*) any person who has care of him.

(2) A person who is presumed to be responsible for a child or young person by virtue of subsection (1)(*a*) shall not be taken to have ceased to be responsible for him by reason only that he does not have care of him.".

26. In section 48 (general considerations), for the words from ", either as" to ", otherwise," substitute "in any proceedings against him or any other person for any offence".

27. In section 52 (attendance at court of parents of child or young person brought before court)—

(*a*) in subsection (1) for the words from "charged" to "before a court" substitute "is brought before a court in any proceedings against him or any other person for any offence";

(*b*) in subsection (7) after the words "supervision order" insert "(including a supervision order under Part V of the Children Order)";

(*c*) after subsection (7) insert the following subsection—

"(7A) If it appears that at the time of his arrest the child or young person is being provided with accommodation by or on behalf of a Board or HSS trust under Article 21 of the Children Order, that Board or HSS trust shall also be informed as described in subsection (3) as soon as it is reasonably practicable to do so.".

28. For section 53 (notices of charges against and applications relating to children and young persons) substitute the following section—

"Notices of charges against children and young persons.

53.—(1) Where a child or young person is to be brought before a court in respect of an offence alleged to have been committed by him, the complainant shall as soon as reasonably practicable notify the day and hour when, and the nature of the charge on which, the child or young person is to be brought before the court—

(a) to a probation officer appointed for or assigned to the petty sessions district in which the court will sit; and

(b) to the appropriate authority.

(2) Subsection (1)(b) shall not apply where the complainant is the appropriate authority.

(3) Where the appropriate authority receives a notification under subsection (1) or itself charges any child or young person with any offence, it shall, except in cases which appear to it to be of a trivial nature, make such investigations and render available to the court such information as to the home surroundings, school record, physical and mental health and character of the child or young person and, in proper cases, as to the availability of accommodation at training schools, as appears to the authority to be likely to assist the court.

(4) The appropriate authority shall be under no obligation under subsection (3) to make investigations as to the home surroundings of children or young persons in any petty sessions district in which arrangements have been made for such investigations to be made by a probation officer.

(5) In this section "the appropriate authority" means the authority within whose area the child or young person is ordinarily resident or, if that is not known, the authority within whose area the child or young person is, and "authority" and "area" have the same meaning as in the Children Order.".

29. In section 55(1) (power to clear court while child or young person is giving evidence in certain cases), for "proceedings" substitute "criminal proceedings".

30. In section 56 (form of oath for use in juvenile courts and by children and young persons in other courts)—

(a) in subsection (1), for "subsection (2)" substitute "subsections (2) and (3)";

(b) after subsection (2) add the following subsection—

"(3) This section shall not apply in proceedings to which Article 169 of the Children Order applies (civil proceedings).".

31. In section 59(1) (power to prohibit publication of certain matter in newspapers and broadcasts), for "proceedings" where it first occurs substitute "criminal proceedings".

32. In section 68 (restrictions on newspaper and broadcast reports of proceedings in juvenile courts and on appeal therefrom)—

(a) in subsection (1)(a), for "proceedings" where it first occurs substitute "criminal proceedings";

(b) in subsection (4), for "as they apply in relation to" substitute "in criminal proceedings as they apply in relation to such".

33. In section 81 (general provisions as to supervision orders), for subsection (4) substitute the following subsection—

"(4) An officer or a member of a Board or HSS trust or an education and library board shall not be appointed under subsection (1) in his capacity as such an officer or member.".

34. In section 88(3) (conveyance of children or young persons to training school)—

(a) for "Ministry" substitute "Secretary of State";

(b) for "Parliament" substitute "the Parliament of the United Kingdom".

35. In section 89 (supervision and recall after expiration of order)—

(a) in subsection (3), for "Minister" wherever it occurs substitute "Secretary of State";

(b) in subsection (4)(a), for "Minister" substitute "Secretary of State";

(c) in subsection (5), for "Ministry" in both places where it occurs and "Minister's" substitute in each case "Secretary of State".

36. In section 90 (extension of period of detention in training schools)—

(a) in subsection (1), for "Minister" substitute "Secretary of State";

(b) in subsection (2), for "Minister" substitute "Secretary of State".

37. In section 91(4) (provisions as to making, duration and effect of fit person orders) for "the same rights and powers" substitute "parental responsibility for him".

38. For section 96(1) (powers of other courts), substitute the following subsections—

"(1) Where it appears to any court by or before which a person is convicted of having committed in respect of a child or young person any of the offences mentioned in Schedule 1 (not being an offence which resulted in the death of the child or young person) that it may be appropriate for a care or supervision order to be made with respect to him under the Children Order, the court may direct the appropriate Board or HSS trust to undertake an investigation of the child's circumstances.

(1A) Paragraphs (2) to (6) of Article 56 of the Children Order (power of court in family proceedings to direct investigation into child's circumstances) shall have effect where the court gives a direction under this section as they have effect where a court gives a direction under that Article.".

39. For section 97(3) (power of probation officer, etc., to bring child or young person before court) substitute the following subsection—

"(3) The Magistrates' Courts (Northern Ireland) Order 1981 shall apply in relation to recognizances under subsection (2)(*b*) as it applies in relation to recognizances to be of good behaviour, and where such a recognizance is ordered to be estreated, the court, instead of ordering the person bound by the recognizance to pay the sum in which he is bound or part of the sum, may remit payment of it.".

40. In section 101(3) (provisions supplemental to section 100) for "or justice of the peace who" substitute "which".

41. After section 132 (provision of remand homes) insert the following section—

"Appeals.   **132A.**—(1) Where under subsection (5) of section 132 it is proposed to remove a remand home from the register, the person having charge of or control over the premises may within twenty-eight days from the service of the notice under that subsection appeal to a tribunal (in this section called "an Appeal Tribunal") constituted in accordance with the provisions of Schedule 4 against the proposal; and the home shall not be removed from the register before the determination of the appeal.

(2) An appeal under this section shall be brought by notice served on the Secretary of State requiring him to refer the proposal to an Appeal Tribunal.

(3) On an appeal under this section an Appeal Tribunal may—

(*a*) confirm the proposal, or

(*b*) direct that the home shall be registered,

and the Secretary of State shall comply with the direction.

(4) The Secretary of State may—

(*a*) pay to members of Appeal Tribunals such fees and allowances as he, with the approval of the Treasury, may determine;

(*b*) defray the expenses of such tribunals up to such amount as he, with the approval of the Treasury, may determine.

(5) An Appeal Tribunal may—

(*a*) by summons require any person to attend, at such time and place as is set forth in the summons, to give evidence or to produce any documents or articles in his custody or under his control which relate to any appeal or other matter pending before the Tribunal;

(*b*) hear, receive and examine evidence on oath and for that purpose may administer oaths, or instead of administering an oath require the person examined to make and subscribe a declaration of the truth of the matter respecting which he is examined; and

(*c*) also exercise the powers conferred by Schedule 4.

(6) Every person who—

204

(a) refuses or wilfully neglects to attend in obedience to a summons issued under subsection (5) or to give evidence; or

(b) wilfully alters, suppresses, cancels or destroys or refuses to produce any document or article which he may be required to produce by virtue of that subsection,

shall be guilty of an offence and liable on summary conviction to a fine not exceeding level 3 on the standard scale or to imprisonment for a term not exceeding six months or to both.

(7) Any person entitled to appeal to an Appeal Tribunal may appear and be heard on any such appeal either in person or by counsel or solicitor.".

42. In section 137 (approval of training schools), after subsection (5) add the following subsections—

"(6) At the request of the managers of a training school, the Secretary of State shall amend the certificate of approval of the school to exclude any premises on which it is proposed to carry on a voluntary home, and the amendment shall take effect on the date of the registration of the home under the Children Order or on such other date as the Secretary of State may specify.

(7) Nothing in any statutory provision or any deed or other instrument passed or made before the making of the Children Order shall prevent the managers of a training school from carrying on a voluntary home.".

43. In section 141 (effect of training school order where certain other orders are in force), for subsections (2) and (3) substitute the following subsections—

"(2) Where a person is subject to a care order under the Children Order and while the care order is in force a training school order is made with respect to that person, the care order shall be of no effect while he is under the care of the managers of the training school.

(3) Where a person has ceased to be in the care of a Board or HSS trust by virtue of subsection (1) or (2), the Board or HSS trust may, while the person is under the care of the managers of the training school but not out under supervision, cause him to be visited and befriended, and may, in exceptional circumstances, make payments for his welfare.".

44. In section 142 (general provisions as to children and young persons committed to the care of fit persons)—

(a) in subsection (2), for "Ministry" substitute "Secretary of State";

(b) in subsection (3)—

(i) for the words from the beginning to "think fit" substitute "The Secretary of State may board out children and young persons committed to his care for such periods and on such terms as to payment and otherwise as he thinks fit";

(ii) in paragraph (b), for "the Ministry of Home Affairs" substitute "the Secretary of State";

(c) in subsection (4), for "the Ministry of Home Affairs" and "the Ministry" substitute in each case "the Secretary of State".

45. In section 143 (variation and discharge of orders committing children and young persons to care)—

(a) in subsection (1), for "Minister" substitute "Secretary of State";

(b) in subsection (2), for "Minister" in each place where it occurs substitute "Secretary of State";

(c) in subsection (6)—

    (i) for "The Ministry of Home Affairs who are" substitute "The Secretary of State, if he is";

    (ii) for "their" substitute "his";

    (iii) for "his interests" substitute "the interests of the child or young person";

(d) for subsection (7) substitute the following subsection—

    "(7) Sections 99 to 101 shall apply where an application with respect to a child or young person is or is about to be made to a juvenile court under subsection (4) or (6) as they apply where a person is or is about to be brought before a juvenile court under section 97 and as if the references in sections 99 and 101(1) to section 97 were references to subsection (4) or (6).".

46. In section 144(2) (escapes from care of fit persons)—

(a) for "the Ministry of Home Affairs" substitute "the Secretary of State";

(b) for "he" substitute "the child or young person";

(c) for "the Ministry direct" substitute "the Secretary of State directs".

47. In section 145 (return to family of persons committed to care of Department or Secretary of State)—

(a) in subsection (1)—

    (i) for "the Ministry of Home Affairs" and in each place where it occurs "the Ministry" substitute "the Secretary of State";

    (ii) for "they otherwise determine" substitute "he otherwise determines";

(b) in subsection (2), for "the Ministry of Home Affairs" and in each place where it occurs "the Ministry" substitute "the Secretary of State";

(c) in subsection (3), for "the Ministry of Home Affairs" and "the Ministry" substitute "the Secretary of State";

(d) in subsection (4)—

    (i) in paragraph (a), for "the Ministry of Home Affairs" and "the Ministry" substitute "the Secretary of State";

    (ii) in paragraph (b), for "the Ministry at any time determine under subsection (1) that he" substitute "the Secretary of State at any time determines under subsection (1) that the first-mentioned person";

    (iii) in paragraph (c), for "the Ministry with respect to his return to the Ministry" substitute "the Secretary of State with respect to the return of the first-mentioned person to the Secretary of State";

    (iv) for "the Ministry" in the last place where it occurs substitute "the Secretary of State".

48. For section 147 (acquisition of land) and section 147A (power to enter
on lands) substitute the following sections—

"Acquisition of   **147.**—(1) For the purposes of this Act the Secretary of
land.   State may acquire land by agreement or compulsorily.

(2) Where the Secretary of State desires to acquire land
compulsorily the provisions of Article 48 of and Schedule
7 to the Health and Personal Social Services (Northern
Ireland) Order 1972 with respect to the acquisition of land
shall apply as if any reference to the Department of
Health and Social Services were a reference to the
Secretary of State and as if any reference to that Order
were a reference to this Act.

Power to enter on **147A.** Article 49 of the Health and Personal Social
lands.   Services (Northern Ireland) Order 1972 shall apply for the
purposes of this Act as if any reference to the Department
of Health and Social Services were a reference to the
Secretary of State and as if any reference to that Order
were a reference to this Act.".

49. In section 148 (expenses)—

(a) for "Parliament" substitute "the Parliament of the United
Kingdom";

(b) for "Ministry" in both places where it occurs substitute "Secretary of
State".

50. In section 151 (grants for training in child care)—

(a) in subsection (1), for "Ministry with the consent of the Ministry of
Finance" and "the Ministry" substitute respectively "Secretary of
State with the consent of the Treasury" and "him";

(b) in subsection (2), for "Ministry" where it first occurs and "it may
with the consent of the Ministry of Finance" substitute respectively
"Secretary of State" and "he may with the consent of the Treasury".

51. In section 163 (duty of police to notify Department in certain
circumstances)—

(a) in subsection (1) for "the Ministry of Home Affairs" substitute "the
appropriate authority";

(b) for subsection (2) substitute the following subsections—

"(2) Where an authority is notified under subsection (1) that a
child or young person may be in need of advice, guidance or
assistance, it shall make or cause to be made such enquiries as it
considers necessary to enable it to decide whether it should take
any action to safeguard or promote the child's welfare.

(3) In this section "the appropriate authority" means the
authority within whose area the child is ordinarily resident or, if
that is not known, the authority within whose area the child is,
and "authority" and "area" have the same meaning as in the
Children Order.".

52. For section 167 (inquiries and investigations) and section 168 (power of
inspection) substitute the following sections—

"Inquiries and investigations.

167. The Secretary of State may cause an inquiry to be held or an investigation to be made in any case where it appears to him advisable to do so in connection with any matter arising under this Act.

Power of inspection.

168.—(1) An authorised person may, on production of his credentials, at any reasonable time enter any premises in which a person under the age of eighteen is maintained under this Act and—

(*a*) inspect the premises; and

(*b*) make such examination into the state and management of the premises and the condition and treatment of such persons there as he thinks requisite.

(2) A person who wilfully obstructs an authorised person in the execution of his duties under this section shall be guilty of an offence and liable on summary conviction to a fine not exceeding level 3 on the standard scale.

(3) In this section "an authorised person" means a person authorised by the Secretary of State.".

53. In section 180(1) (interpretation)—

(*a*) after the definition of "the Act of 1950" insert the following definition—

" "Board" means a Health and Social Services Board;";

(*b*) for the definition of "child" substitute the following definitions—

" "child" means a person under the age of fourteen;
"Children Order" means the Children (Northern Ireland) Order 1995;";

(*c*) in the definition of "guardian", for "charge of or control over" substitute "care of";

(*d*) for the definition of "HSS home" and "HSS trust" substitute the following definition—

" "HSS trust" means a Health and Social Services trust established under the Health and Personal Social Services (Northern Ireland) Order 1991;";

(*e*) in the definition of "legal guardian", for the words from "a person" to "his guardian" substitute "a guardian of a child as defined in the Children Order";

(*f*) for the definition of "parental rights order" substitute the following definition—

" "parental responsibility" has the same meaning as in the Children Order;";

(*g*) after the definition of "remand home" insert the following definition—

" "responsibility" shall be construed in accordance with section 36;".

54. In Schedule 1 (offences against children and young persons with respect to which special provisions of the Act apply)—

(*a*) in the entry relating to sections 20, 21, 22, 23, 24, 29 and 42 of the Act for ", 29 and 42" substitute "and 29";

(*b*) at the end add the following entry—

"Any offence under Article 147(2) of the Children Order in respect of a contravention of Article 141 of that Order.".

55. In Schedule 3 (supervision orders), at the end of paragraph 3 add the following sub-paragraph—

"(3) Without prejudice to its power under sub-paragraph (1), where the person under supervision is subject to a care order under Part V of the Children Order, the juvenile court may discharge the supervision order on the application of a Board or HSS trust or, where the care order is revoked, without any application.".

56. In Schedule 4 (Appeal Tribunals)—

(*a*) in paragraph 1 for "Minister" substitute "Secretary of State";

(*b*) renumber paragraph 2 as paragraph 2(1) and at the end add the following sub-paragraph—

"(2) In this paragraph "government department" includes a department of the Government of the United Kingdom.";

(*c*) in paragraph 5 for "Ministry" and "its" substitute "Secretary of State" and "his";

(*d*) in paragraph 6 for "Ministry" in each place where it occurs substitute "Secretary of State".

57. In Schedule 5 (provisions as to administration of training schools and treatment of persons sent there), in paragraph 14, for sub-paragraph (1) substitute the following sub-paragraphs—

"(1) While a person is under the care of the managers of a training school they shall—

(*a*) have parental responsibility for him; and

(*b*) have the power (subject to sub-paragraph (1A)) to determine the extent to which a parent of that person may meet his parental responsibility for him.

(1A) The managers may only exercise the power in sub-paragraph (1)(*b*) where—

(*a*) a person out under supervision from a training school is lawfully living with his parents or either of them; and

(*b*) the managers are satisfied that it is necessary to exercise the power in order to safeguard or promote the welfare of that person.".

The Mines Act (Northern Ireland) 1969 (c. 6)

58. In section 158(1) (interpretation), in the definition of "parent", for the words from "or guardian" to "young person" where it first occurs substitute "of a young person or any person who is not a parent of his but who has parental responsibility for him (within the meaning of the Children (Northern Ireland) Order 1995)".

The Adoption (Hague Convention) Act (Northern Ireland) 1969 (c. 22)

59. In section 4(3) (definition of "foreign adoption"), for "section 4(3) of the Adoption Act 1968" substitute "section 72(2) of the Adoption Act 1976".

60. In section 5 (recognition of foreign determinations in adoption proceedings)—

(a) in subsection (1) for "other than Northern Ireland" substitute "outside the United Kingdom";

(b) in subsection (2) for "section 4(3) of the Adoption Act 1968" substitute "section 72(2) of the Adoption Act 1976".

61. In section 7(4) (certain supplementary provisions), in the definition of "notified provision" for "section 7(4) of the Adoption Act 1968" substitute "section 54(4) of the Adoption Act 1976".

62. In section 8(4) (registration), for "section 30 of the Births and Deaths Registration Act (Northern Ireland) 1967" substitute "Article 19 of the Births and Deaths Registration (Northern Ireland) Order 1976".

63. In section 9(1) (nationality), for "section 9(1) of the Adoption Act 1968" substitute "section 70(1) of the Adoption Act 1976".

64. In section 12 (interpretation), in the definition of "United Kingdom national" for "section 11(1) of the Adoption Act 1968" substitute "section 72(1) of the Adoption Act 1976".

The Civil Evidence Act (Northern Ireland) 1971 (c. 36)

65.—(1) Section 8 (which relates to the admissibility in civil proceedings of the fact that a person has been adjudged to be the father of a child in affiliation proceedings) shall be amended as provided by sub-paragraphs (2) to (4).

(2) In subsection (1), for paragraph (b) substitute the following paragraph—

"(b) the fact that a person has been found to be the father of a child in relevant proceedings before any court in Northern Ireland or England and Wales or has been adjudged to be the father of a child in affiliation proceedings before any court in the United Kingdom;".

(3) In subsection (2)—

(a) for "to have been adjudged" substitute "to have been found or adjudged";

(b) for "matrimonial or affiliation proceedings" substitute "other proceedings".

(4) In subsection (3), after "matrimonial" insert "or relevant".

(5) In subsection (5), after the definition of "matrimonial proceedings" insert the following definition—

" " relevant proceedings" means—

(a) proceedings under Article 101 of the Health and Personal Social Services (Northern Ireland) Order 1972 or section 101 of the Social Security Administration (Northern Ireland) Act 1992;

(b) proceedings under Article 28 of the Child Support (Northern Ireland) Order 1991;

(c) proceedings under the Children (Northern Ireland) Order 1995;

(d) proceedings under section 5A of the Guardianship of

Infants Act 1886 or section 27 of the Judicature (Northern Ireland) Act 1978;

(e) proceedings which are relevant proceedings as defined in section 12(5) of the Civil Evidence Act 1968;".

The Maintenance Orders (Reciprocal Enforcement) Act 1972 (c. 18)

66. In section 3 (power to make provisional maintenance order), for subsection (7) substitute the following subsection—

"(7) In the application of this section to Northern Ireland—

(a) for subsection (1) there shall be substituted—

"(1) Where an application is made to a magistrates' court against a person residing in a reciprocating country and the court would have jurisdiction to determine the application under the Domestic Proceedings (Northern Ireland) Order 1980 or the Children (Northern Ireland) Order 1995 if that person—

(a) were residing in Northern Ireland, and

(b) received reasonable notice of the date of the hearing of the application,

the court shall (subject to subsection (2) below) have jurisdiction to determine the application.";

(b) in subsection (4), for references to the High Court there shall be substituted references to the High Court of Justice in Northern Ireland.".

67. In section 5 (variation and revocation of maintenance order made in United Kingdom) after subsection (3A) insert the following subsection—

"(3B) Where paragraph (1) of Article 86 of the Magistrates' Courts (Northern Ireland) Order 1981 applies in relation to a maintenance order to which this section applies, that paragraph shall have effect as if for the words "by order on complaint," there were substituted "on an application being made, by order".

68. In section 8 (enforcement of maintenance order registered in United Kingdom court), in subsection (4) for the words from "if it were" to "any Act" substitute "an order made by that court to which that Article applies".

69. In section 9 (variation and revocation of maintenance order registered in United Kingdom court), immediately before subsection (1ZB)(a) insert the following paragraph—

"(za) as if in paragraph (1) for the words "by order on complaint," there were substituted "on an application being made, by order";".

70. In section 17 (proceedings in magistrates' courts), for subsection (6) substitute the following subsection—

"(6) Where the respondent to an application for the variation or revocation of—

(a) a maintenance order made by a magistrates' court in Northern Ireland, being an order to which section 5 of this Act applies; or

(b) a registered order which is registered in such a court,

is residing in a reciprocating country, a magistrates' court in Northern

Ireland shall have jurisdiction to hear the application (where it would not have jurisdiction apart from this subsection) if it would have had jurisdiction to hear it had the respondent been residing in Northern Ireland.".

71. In section 18 (magistrates' courts rules), after subsection (2) insert the following subsection—

"(2A) For the purpose of giving effect to this Part of this Act, rules made in accordance with Article 13 of the Magistrates' Courts (Northern Ireland) Order 1981 may make, in relation to any proceedings brought under or by virtue of this Part of this Act, any provision not covered by subsection (2) above which—

(a) falls within paragraph (2) of Article 165 of the Children (Northern Ireland) Order 1995, and

(b) may be made in relation to relevant proceedings under that Article.".

72. For sections 28C, 29 and 29A substitute the following sections—

"Applications for recovery of maintenance in Northern Ireland.

28C.—(1) This section applies to any application which—

(a) is received by the Lord Chancellor from the appropriate authority in a convention country, and

(b) is an application by a person in that country for the recovery of maintenance from another person who is for the time being residing in Northern Ireland.

(2) Subject to sections 28D to 29B of this Act, an application to which this section applies shall be treated for the purposes of any enactment as if it were an application for a maintenance order under the relevant Order, made at the time when the application was received by the Lord Chancellor.

(3) In the case of an application for maintenance for a child (or children) alone, the relevant Order is the Children (Northern Ireland) Order 1995.

(4) In any other case, the relevant Order is the Domestic Proceedings (Northern Ireland) Order 1980.

(5) In subsection (3) above, "child" means the same as in Schedule 1 to the Children (Northern Ireland) Order 1995.

Sending application to the appropriate magistrates' court.

28D.—(1) On receipt of an application to which section 28C of this Act applies, the Lord Chancellor shall send it, together with any accompanying documents, to the clerk of a magistrates' court acting for the petty sessions district in which the respondent is residing.

(2) Subject to subsection (4) below, if notice of the hearing of the application by a magistrates' court having jurisdiction to hear it cannot be duly served on the respondent, the clerk of the court shall return the application and the accompanying documents to the Lord Chancellor with a statement giving such information as he possesses as to the whereabouts of the respondent.

(3) If the application is returned to the Lord Chancellor under subsection (2) above, then, unless he is satisfied that the respondent is not residing in the United Kingdom, he shall deal with it in accordance with subsection (1) above or section 27B of this Act or send it to the Secretary of State to be dealt with in accordance with section 31 of this Act (as the circumstances of the case require).

(4) If the clerk of a court to whom the application is sent under this section is satisfied that the respondent is residing within the petty sessions district for which another magistrates' court acts, he shall send the application and accompanying documents to the clerk of that other court and shall inform the Lord Chancellor that he has done so.

(5) If the application is sent to the clerk of a court under subsection (4) above, he shall proceed as if it had been sent to him under subsection (1) above.

Applications to which section 28C applies: general.

28E.—(1) This section applies where a magistrates' court makes an order on an application to which section 28C of this Act applies.

(2) Article 85 of the Magistrates' Courts (Northern Ireland) Order 1981 ("the 1981 Order") (orders for periodical payment: means of payment) shall not apply.

(3) The court shall, at the same time that it makes the order, exercise one of its powers under subsection (4) below.

(4) Those powers are—

(a) the power to order that payments under the order be made directly to the collecting officer;

(b) the power to order that payments under the order be made to the collecting officer, by such method of payment falling within Article 85(7) of the 1981 Order (standing order, etc.) as may be specified;

(c) the power to make an attachment of earnings order under Part IX of the 1981 Order to secure payments under the order;

and in this subsection "collecting officer" means the officer mentioned in Article 85(4) of the 1981 Order.

(5) In deciding which of the powers under subsection (4) above it is to exercise, the court shall have regard to any representations made by the person liable to make payments under the order.

(6) Paragraph (5) of Article 85 of the 1981 Order (power of court to require debtor to open account) shall apply for the purposes of subsection (4) above as it applies for the purposes of that Article, but as if for sub-paragraph (a) there were substituted—

"(a) the court proposes to exercise its power under paragraph (*b*) of section 28E(4) of the Maintenance Orders (Reciprocal Enforcement) Act 1972, and".

(7) The clerk of the court shall register the order in the prescribed manner in the court.

Applications by spouses under the Domestic Proceedings (Northern Ireland) Order 1980.

29.—(1) The magistrates' court hearing an application which by virtue of section 28C of this Act is to be treated as if it were an application for a maintenance order under the Domestic Proceedings (Northern Ireland) Order 1980 may make any order on the application which it has power to make under Article 4 or 20(1) of that Order.

(2) That Order shall apply in relation to such an application, and to any order made on such an application, with the following omissions—

(*a*) Articles 8 to 10, 18, 19, 21, 22A, 25(1), 27 to 29 and 30(1A),

(*b*) in Article 32(1) the words "either the applicant or", and

(*c*) Article 36(1).

(3) Subsections (1) and (2) above do not apply where section 29A of this Act applies.

Applications by former spouses under the Domestic Proceedings (Northern Ireland) Order 1980.

29A.—(1) This section applies where in the case of any application which by virtue of section 28C of this Act is to be treated as if it were an application for a maintenance order under the Domestic Proceedings (Northern Ireland) Order 1980 ("the 1980 Order")—

(*a*) the applicant and respondent were formerly married,

(*b*) their marriage was dissolved or annulled in a country or territory outside the United Kingdom by a divorce or annulment which is recognised as valid by the law of Northern Ireland;

(*c*) an order for the payment of maintenance for the benefit of the applicant or a child of the family has, by reason of the divorce or annulment, been made by a court in a convention country, and

(*d*) where the order for the payment of maintenance was made by a court of a different country from that in which the divorce or annulment was obtained, either the applicant or the respondent was resident in the convention country whose court made that order at the time that order was applied for.

(2) Any magistrates' court that would have jurisdiction to hear the application under Article 32 of the 1980 Order (as modified in accordance with subsection (6) below) if the applicant and the respondent were still married shall have jurisdiction to hear it notwithstanding the dissolution or annulment of the marriage.

(3) If the magistrates' court hearing the application is satisfied that the respondent has failed to comply with the

provisions of any order such as is mentioned in subsection (1)(c) above, it may (subject to subsections (4) and (5) below) make any order which it has power to make under Article 4 or 20(1) of the 1980 Order.

(4) The court shall not make an order for the making of periodical payments for the benefit of the applicant or any child of the family unless the order made in the convention country provides for the making of periodical payments for the benefit of the applicant or, as the case may be, that child.

(5) The court shall not make an order for the payment of a lump sum for the benefit of the applicant or any child of the family unless the order made in the convention country provides for the payment of a lump sum to the applicant or, as the case may be, to that child.

(6) The 1980 Order shall apply in relation to the application, and to any order made on the application, with the following modifications—

(a) Article 3 shall be omitted,

(b) for the reference in Article 4(1) to any ground mentioned in Article 3 there shall be substituted a reference to non-compliance with any such order as is mentioned in subsection (1)(c) of this section,

(c) for the references in Article 5(2) and (3) to the occurrence of the conduct which is alleged as the ground of the application there shall be substituted references to the breakdown of the marriage,

(d) the reference in Article 6(2) to the subsequent dissolution or annulment of the marriage of the parties affected by the order shall be omitted,

(e) Articles 8 to 10, 18, 19, 21, 22A, 25(1) and 27 to 30 shall be omitted,

(f) in Article 32(1), the words "either the applicant or" shall be omitted, and

(g) Article 36(1) shall be omitted.

(7) A divorce or annulment obtained in a country or territory outside the United Kingdom shall be presumed for the purposes of this section to be one the validity of which is recognised by the law of Northern Ireland, unless the contrary is proved by the respondent.

(8) In this section "child of the family" has the meaning given in Article 2(2) of the 1980 Order.

Applications under the Children (Northern Ireland) Order 1995.

29B. No provision of an order made under Schedule 7 to the Children (Northern Ireland) Order 1995 requiring or enabling a court to transfer proceedings from a magistrates' court to a county court or the High Court shall apply in relation to an application which by virtue of section 28C of this Act is to be treated as if it were an application for a maintenance order under that Order.".

73. In section 33 (enforcement of orders), in subsection (3) for the words from "if it were" to "any Act" substitute "an order made by that court to which that Article applies".

74.—(1) In section 34 (variation and revocation of orders), in subsection (1) after "Subject to" insert "subsection (3B) below and".

(2) After subsection (3A) insert the following subsection—

"(3B) Where paragraph (1) of Article 86 of the Magistrates' Courts (Northern Ireland) Order 1981 (revocation, variation etc. of orders for periodical payment) applies in relation to a registered order, that paragraph shall have effect as if for the words "by order on complaint," there were substituted "on an application being made, by order"."

75. For section 35A substitute the following section—

"Further provisions with respect to variation etc. of orders by magistrates' courts in Northern Ireland.

35A.—(1) Notwithstanding anything in section 29(2) or 29A(6)(*e*) of this Act, a magistrates' court in Northern Ireland shall have jurisdiction to hear an application—

(*a*) for the variation or revocation of a registered order registered in that court, and

(*b*) made by the person against whom or on whose application the order was made,

notwithstanding that the person by or against whom the application is made is residing outside Northern Ireland.

(2) None of the powers of the court, or of the clerk, under section 34B of this Act shall be exercisable in relation to such an application.

(3) Where the respondent to an application for the variation or revocation of a registered order which is registered in a magistrates' court in Northern Ireland does not appear at the time and place appointed for the hearing of the application, but the court is satisfied—

(*a*) that the respondent is residing outside Northern Ireland, and

(*b*) that the prescribed notice of the making of the application and of the time and place appointed for the hearing has been given to the respondent in the prescribed manner,

the court may proceed to hear and determine the application at the time and place appointed for the hearing or for any adjourned hearing in like manner as if the respondent had appeared at that time and place.".

76. In section 36 (admissibility of evidence given in convention country), in subsection (1) for "received by the Lord Chancellor as mentioned in section 28C(1) of this Act" substitute "to which section 28C(1) of this Act applies".

77.—(1) In section 38A, after subsection (3) add the following subsection—

"(4) For the purpose of giving effect to this Part of this Act, rules made under Article 13 of the Magistrates' Courts (Northern Ireland) Order 1981 may make, in relation to any proceedings brought under or by virtue of this Part of this Act, any provision not covered by subsection (1) above which—

(a) falls within paragraph (2) of Article 165 of the Children (Northern Ireland Order) 1995, and

(b) may be made in relation to relevant proceedings under that Article.".

*The Health and Personal Social Services (Northern Ireland) Order 1972
(NI 14)*

78. In Article 2(2) (interpretation)—

(a) in the definition of "parent", for the words from "the guardian" to "custody" substitute "any person who has parental responsibility for or care";

(b) after that definition insert the following definition—

" "parental responsibility" has the same meaning as in the Children (Northern Ireland) Order 1995;";

(c) in the definition of "personal social services", for the words from "including" to "Article 72" substitute "(including services provided under the Adoption (Northern Ireland) Order 1987 or the Children (Northern Ireland) Order 1995)".

79. In Article 52 (powers of Department in emergency), for paragraph (2) substitute the following paragraph—

"(2) In this Article and Article 53 "the health and personal social services legislation" means—

(a) this Order;

(b) the Adoption (Northern Ireland) Order 1987;

(c) the Health and Personal Social Services (Special Agencies) (Northern Ireland) Order 1990;

(d) the 1991 Order;

(e) the Health and Personal Social Services (Northern Ireland) Order 1994; and

(f) the Children (Northern Ireland) Order 1995.".".

80. In Article 54 (inquiries), ιoι 'the health and personal social services legislation" substitute "any Order specified in sub-paragraph (a), (c), (d) or (e) of Article 52(2)".

81. In Article 87 (expenses of Boards, etc.), for paragraphs (2) and (2A) substitute the following paragraph—

"(2) In relation to expenditure under the Adoption (Northern Ireland) Order 1987 or the Children (Northern Ireland) Order 1995, paragraph (1) shall have effect with the omission of the words "being expenditure approved by the Ministry".".

82. In Article 100 (liability to maintain spouse and children), for paragraph (2) substitute the following paragraph—

"(2) Any reference in paragraph (1) to a person's children shall be construed in accordance with Article 155 of the Children (Northern Ireland) Order 1995.".

The Births and Deaths Registration (Northern Ireland) Order 1976 (NI 14)

83. In Article 2 (interpretation)—

(*a*) in paragraph (2), after the definition of "occupier" insert—

" "parental responsibility" and "parental responsibility agreement" have the same meanings as in the Children (Northern Ireland) Order 1995;";

(*b*) after that paragraph insert the following paragraph—

"(2A) Any reference in this Order to a child whose father and mother were or were not married to each other at the time of his birth shall be construed in accordance with Article 155 of the Children (Northern Ireland) Order 1995.".

84. For Article 14 substitute the following Article—

"Registration of father where parents not married

14.—(1) This Article applies in the case of a child whose father and mother were not married to each other at the time of his birth.

(2) The father of the child shall not as such be under any duty to give any information under this Part concerning the birth of the child.

(3) A registrar shall not enter the name of any person as the father of the child in such a case unless—

(*a*) the mother and the person stating himself to be the father of the child jointly request him to do so and in that event the mother and that person shall sign the register in the presence of each other; or

(*b*) the mother requests him to do so and produces—

(i) a declaration in the prescribed form made by her stating that that person is the father of the child; and

(ii) a statutory declaration made by that person stating himself to be the father of the child; or

(*c*) that person requests him to do so and produces—

(i) a declaration in the prescribed form by that person stating himself to be the father of the child; and

(ii) a statutory declaration made by the mother stating that that person is the father of the child; or

(*d*) the mother or that person requests him to do so and produces—

(i) a copy of a parental responsibility agreement made between them in relation to the child; and

(ii) a declaration in the prescribed form by the person making the request stating that the agreement was made in compliance with Article 7 of the Children (Northern Ireland) Order 1995 and has not been brought to an end by an order of a court; or

(*e*) the mother or that person requests him to do so and produces—

(i) a certified copy of an order under Article 7 of the Children (Northern Ireland) Order 1995 giving that person parental responsibility for the child; and

(ii) a declaration in the prescribed form by the person making the request stating that the order has not been brought to an end by an order of a court; or

(*f*) the mother or that person requests him to do so and produces—

(i) a certified copy of an order under paragraph 2 of Schedule 1 to the Children (Northern Ireland) Order 1995 which requires

218

that person to make any financial provision for the child and which is not an order falling within paragraph 5(3) of that Schedule; and

(ii) a declaration in the prescribed form by the person making the request stating that the order has not been discharged by an order of a court; or

(g) the mother or that person requests him to do so and produces—

(i) a certified copy of any of the orders which are mentioned in paragraph (4) which has been made in relation to the child; and

(ii) a declaration in the prescribed form by the person making the request stating that the order has not been brought to an end or discharged by an order of a court.

(4) The orders are—

(a) an order under section 5A of the Guardianship of Infants Act 1886 giving that person custody of the child;

(b) an order under the Illegitimate Children (Affiliation Orders) Act (Northern Ireland) 1924 adjudging that person to be the putative father of the child.

(5) Where a person stating himself to be the father of the child makes a request to the registrar in accordance with any of sub-paragraphs (c) to (g) of paragraph (3)—

(a) that person shall be treated as a qualified informant concerning the birth of the child for the purposes of this Part; and

(b) on the giving of the required information concerning the birth of the child by that person and the signing of the register by him in the presence of the registrar every other qualified informant shall cease to be under the duty imposed by Article 10(4).".

85. In Article 18 (re-registration of births)—

(a) in paragraph (1), for the words from "(b)" to "Article 14(3)" substitute the following sub-paragraph—

"(b) in the case of a child whose parents were not married to each other at the time of his birth—

(i) the birth was registered as if they were so married; or

(ii) no particulars relating to his father have been entered in the register.";

(b) after paragraph (1) insert the following paragraph—

"(1A) Re-registration under sub-paragraph (b)(ii) shall not be authorised otherwise than in accordance with Article 14(3).".

86. In Article 19(3)(c) (re-registration of births of legitimated persons), after "1868" insert "or Article 32 of the Matrimonial and Family Proceedings (Northern Ireland) Order 1989".

87. After Article 19 insert the following Article—

"Re-registration after declaration of parentage

19A.—(1) Where, in the case of a person whose birth has been registered under this Order (or any earlier statutory provision referred to in Article 19(1))—

(a) the Registrar General receives, by virtue of Article 32(4) of the Matrimonial and Family Proceedings (Northern Ireland) Order 1989, a notification of the making of a declaration of parentage in respect of that person; and

(b) it appears to him that the birth of that person should be re-registered,

he shall give his written authority for the re-registration of the birth of that person.

(2) Any re-registration under paragraph (1) shall be effected in the prescribed manner and at such place as may be prescribed.

(3) This Article shall apply with such modifications as the Department may, by regulations made subject to affirmative resolution, prescribe in relation to births at sea of which the Registrar General receives a return under any statutory provision.".

88. In Article 37(7) (qualified applicant for registration or alteration of child's name), for sub-paragraphs (a) to (d) substitute the following sub-paragraphs—

"(a) the father and mother of the child if—

(i) they were married to each other at the time of his birth; or

(ii) they were not married to each other at the time of his birth but the father has parental responsibility for the child;

(b) the mother of the child if his parents were not married to each other at the time of his birth and the father does not have parental responsibility for the child;

(c) the surviving parent if either of the parents of the child is deceased and the surviving parent has parental responsibility for the child;

(d) the guardian of the child or any other person who has parental responsibility for him if—

(i) both his parents are deceased; or

(ii) either of his parents is deceased and the surviving parent does not have parental responsibility for him;".

The Family Law Reform (Northern Ireland) Order 1977 (NI 17)

89. In Article 8 (power of court to require use of tests to determine paternity), after paragraph (1) insert the following paragraphs—

"(1A) An application for a direction under this Article shall specify who is to carry out the tests.

(1B) A direction under this Article shall—

(a) specify, as the person who is to carry out the tests, the person specified in the application; or

(b) where the court considers that it would be inappropriate to specify that person (whether because to specify him would be incompatible with any provision made by or under Article 10 or for any other reason), decline to give the direction applied for.".

The Judicature (Northern Ireland) Act 1978 (c. 23)

90. In section 26 (wards of court), after subsection (2) insert the following subsection—

"(2A) Subsection (2) does not apply with respect to a child who is the subject of a care order (as defined by Article 2(2) of the Children (Northern Ireland) Order 1995).".

91. In section 29(2)(c) (co-ordination of exercise of jurisdiction in relation to persons under disability), for "care, custody or control" substitute "upbringing".

92. In section 35(2)(g)(i) (leave not required for appeal to Court of Appeal where liberty of subject or custody of minors concerned), for "custody of" substitute "residence of, or contact with,".

The Matrimonial Causes (Northern Ireland) Order 1978 (NI 15)

93. In Article 2(2) (interpretation)—

(a) in the definition of "child", for the words from "an illegitimate" to "both parties" substitute "a child whose father and mother were not married to each other at the time of his birth within the meaning of Article 155 of the Children (Northern Ireland) Order 1995";

(b) in the definition of "child of the family", for "has been boarded-out with those parties by or on behalf of the Department of Health and Social Services" substitute "is placed with those parties as foster parents by an authority within the meaning of the Children (Northern Ireland) Order 1995".

94. In Article 29 (financial provision orders in case of neglect by party to marriage to maintain other party or child of the family), for paragraph (8) substitute the following paragraph—

"(8) Where a periodical payments order made under this Article in favour of a child ceases to have effect on the date on which the child attains the age of 16, or at any time after that date but before or on the date on which he attains the age of 18, then if, on an application made to the court for an order under this paragraph, it appears to the court that—

(a) the child is, or will be, or if an order were made under this paragraph would be, receiving instruction at an educational establishment or undergoing training for a trade, profession or vocation, whether or not he is, will be or would be, also in gainful employment; or

(b) there are special circumstances which justify the making of an order under this paragraph,

the court shall have power by order to revive the first-mentioned order from such date as the court may specify, not being earlier than the date of the making of the application, and to exercise its powers under Article 33 in relation to any order so revived.".

95. For Article 44 (restrictions on decrees for dissolution, annulment or separation affecting children) substitute the following Article—

"Restrictions on decrees for dissolution, annulment or separation affecting children

44.—(1) In any proceedings for a decree of divorce or nullity of marriage, or a decree of judicial separation, the court shall consider—

(a) whether there are any children of the family to whom this Article applies; and

(b) where there are any such children, whether (in the light of the

SCH. 9   arrangements which have been, or are proposed to be, made for their upbringing and welfare) it should exercise any of its powers under the Children (Northern Ireland) Order 1995 with respect to any of them.

(2) Where, in any case to which this Article applies, it appears to the court that—

(a) the circumstances of the case require it, or are likely to require it, to exercise any of its powers under the Children (Northern Ireland) Order 1995 with respect to any such child;

(b) it is not in a position to exercise that power or (as the case may be) those powers without giving further consideration to the case; and

(c) there are exceptional circumstances which make it desirable in the interests of the child that the court should give a direction under this Article,

it may direct that the decree of divorce or nullity is not to be made absolute, or that the decree of judicial separation is not to be granted, until the court orders otherwise.

(3) This Article applies to—

(a) any child of the family who has not attained the age of 16 at the date when the court considers the case in accordance with the requirements of this Article; and

(b) any child of the family who has attained that age at that date and in relation to whom the court directs that this Article shall apply.".

96. In Article 48(9) (provision for appeals to Court of Appeal), after "40)" insert "or of the Children (Northern Ireland) Order 1995".

97. In Schedule 1 (proceedings in divorce, etc., stayed by reference to proceedings in another jurisdiction), in paragraph 11(1)—

(a) at the end of the definition of "lump sum" add "or an order made in equivalent circumstances under Schedule 1 to the Children (Northern Ireland) Order 1995 and of a kind mentioned in paragraph 2(2)(c) of that Schedule";

(b) in the definition of "relevant order"—

(i) at the end of paragraph (b) add "or an order made in equivalent circumstances under Schedule 1 to the Children (Northern Ireland) Order 1995 and of a kind mentioned in paragraph 2(2)(a) or (b) of that Schedule";

(ii) in paragraph (c), after "children)" insert "or an Article 8 order under the Children (Northern Ireland) Order 1995";

(iii) in paragraph (d), for "custody, care or control" substitute "care".

98. In paragraph 11(3) of that Schedule, for "the custody of a child and the education of a child" substitute "or any provision which could be made by an Article 8 order under the Children (Northern Ireland) Order 1995".

The Rehabilitation of Offenders (Northern Ireland) Order 1978 (NI 27)

99. In Article 6(11)(b) (rehabilitation periods for particular sentences), for "care order in England and Wales" substitute "supervision order imposing a residence requirement as mentioned in section 12AA of that Act".

100. In Article 8(2) (limitations on rehabilitation under that Order), for

sub-paragraph (c) substitute the following sub-paragraphs—

"(c) in any proceedings relating to adoption, the marriage of any minor, the exercise of the inherent jurisdiction of the High Court with respect to minors or the provision by any person of accommodation, care or schooling for minors;

(cc) in any proceedings brought under the Children (Northern Ireland) Order 1995;".

The Domestic Proceedings (Northern Ireland) Order 1980 (NI 5)

101. In Article 2(2) (interpretation)—

(a) in the definition of "child", for the words from "an illegitimate" to "both parties" substitute "a child whose father and mother were not married to each other at the time of his birth within the meaning of Article 155 of the Children (Northern Ireland) Order 1995";

(b) in the definition of "child of the family", for "being boarded out with those parties by the Department" substitute "placed with those parties as foster parents by an authority within the meaning of the Children (Northern Ireland) Order 1995".

102. For Article 10 (orders for the custody of, or access to, children) substitute the following Article—

"Restrictions on making of orders: welfare of children

10. Where an application is made by a party to a marriage for an order under Article 4, 8 or 9, then, if there is a child of the family who is under the age of 18, the court shall not dismiss or make a final order on the application until it has decided whether to exercise any of its powers under the Children (Northern Ireland) Order 1995 with respect to the child.".

103. In Article 20(3A)(b) (interim maintenance orders, etc.), for "paragraphs (2) and" substitute "paragraph".

104. In Article 22 (variation, revival and revocation of orders for periodical payments), for paragraph (12) substitute the following paragraph—

"(12) An application under this Article may be made—

(a) where it is for the variation or revocation of an order under Article 4, 8, 9 or 20 for periodical payments, by either party to the marriage in question; and

(b) where it is for the variation of an order made under Article 4(1)(c), 8 or 9 for periodical payments to or in respect of a child, also by the child himself, if he has attained the age of 16.".

105. After Article 22A insert the following Article—

"Revival of orders for periodical payments

22B.—(1) Where an order made by the court under this Order for the making of periodical payments to or in respect of a child (other than an interim maintenance order) ceases to have effect—

(a) on the date on which the child attains the age of 16, or

(b) at any time after that date but before or on the date on which he attains the age of 18,

the child may apply to the court for an order for its revival.

SCH. 9

(2) If on such an application it appears to the court that—

(a) the child is, will be or (if an order were made under this paragraph) would be receiving instruction at an educational establishment or undergoing training for a trade, profession or vocation, whether or not while in gainful employment, or

(b) there are special circumstances which justify the making of an order under this paragraph,

the court shall have power by order to revive the order from such date as the court may specify, not being earlier than the date of the making of the application.

(3) Any order revived under this Article may be varied or revoked under Article 22 in the same way as it could have been varied or revoked had it continued in being.".

106. In Article 25(1) (supplementary provisions with respect to variation and revocation of orders)—

(a) for "16(3), 22 or 23" substitute "22";

(b) for "Article 22" substitute "that Article".

107.—(1) In Article 27 (effect on certain orders of parties living together), in paragraph (1), for ", 8 or 13(2)" substitute "or 8".

(2) In paragraph (2) of that Article—

(a) in sub-paragraph (a), for ", 8 or 13(2)" substitute "or 8";

(b) at the end of that sub-paragraph, add "or".

108. In Article 31(5) (appeals), for "Articles 16(3), 22 and 23" substitute "Article 22".

109. In Article 33 (procedure), for paragraph (1) substitute the following paragraph—

"(1) Article 165 of the Children (Northern Ireland) Order 1995 (provision which may be made by magistrates' courts rules, etc.) shall apply for the purpose of giving effect to this Order as it applies for the purpose of giving effect to that Order, except that in the application of that Article by virtue of this paragraph "relevant proceedings" means any application made, or proceedings brought, under this Order and any part of such proceedings.".

110. In Article 39 (provisions as to payments required to be made to a child, etc.)—

(a) in paragraph (2) for "22(10)" substitute "22B";

(b) in paragraph (5) for "in the care of the Department, the Department" substitute "looked after by an authority (within the meaning of the Children (Northern Ireland) Order 1995), that authority".

The Legal Aid, Advice and Assistance (Northern Ireland) Order 1981 (NI 8)

111. In Schedule 1 (proceedings for which legal aid may be given under Part II of that Order), in Part I, in paragraph 3 (proceedings in court of summary jurisdiction) for sub-paragraph (f) substitute the following sub-paragraph—

"(f) proceedings under sections 97, 143 and 144(1) of the Children and Young Persons Act (Northern Ireland) 1968 and the Children (Northern Ireland) Order 1995;".

The Magistrates' Courts (Northern Ireland) Order 1981 (NI 26)

112. In Article 85 (orders for periodical payment: means of payment), in paragraph (8)—

(a) in sub-paragraph (a), after "1980" insert "; or under, or having effect as if made under, Schedule 1 to the Children (Northern Ireland) Order 1995";

(b) in sub-paragraph (b), for "that Order" substitute "those Orders".

113. In Article 88 (nature of domestic proceedings), after paragraph (de) insert the following paragraph—

"(df) under the Children (Northern Ireland) Order 1995;".

114. In Article 98(11) (enforcement of orders for the periodical payment of money)—

(a) after sub-paragraph (f) insert the following sub-paragraph—

"(ff) orders registered in a court of summary jurisdiction under Part II of the Maintenance Orders (Reciprocal Enforcement) Act 1972;";

(b) after sub-paragraph (i) insert the following sub-paragraph—

"(j) contribution orders under Article 41(2) of the Children (Northern Ireland) Order 1995,";

(c) for "(a), (b) or (d)" substitute "(a), (b), (d) or (ff)".

115. In Article 101 (attachment of earnings order), in paragraph (2) after "be" insert "made".

The Civil Jurisdiction and Judgments Act 1982 (c. 27)

116. In section 5 (recognition and enforcement of maintenance orders), in subsection (6) for the words from "in the same manner" to "that court" substitute "as an order made by that court to which that Article applies".

117.—(1) In section 36 (registration of maintenance orders), in subsection (5) for "a complaint" in both places where it occurs and "the complaint" substitute "an application" and "the application" respectively.

(2) After subsection (5) insert the following subsection—

"(5A) Article 165 of the Children (Northern Ireland) Order 1995 (provision which may be made by magistrates' courts rules, etc.) shall apply for the purpose of giving effect to subsection (5) above as it applies for the purpose of giving effect to that Order, except that in the application of that Article by virtue of this subsection "relevant proceedings" means any application made, or proceedings brought, by virtue of that subsection and any part of such proceedings.".

The Fines and Penalties (Northern Ireland) Order 1984 (NI 3)

118. In Schedule 2 (provisions creating offences for which fine is not increased), in paragraph 5 for "Sections 111(4), 146(4) and 157(5)" substitute "Section 146(4)".

The Surrogacy Arrangements Act 1985 (c. 49)

119. In section 1(2)(b) (meaning of "surrogate mother", etc.), for "the parental rights being exercised" substitute "parental responsibility being met".

The Child Abduction (Northern Ireland) Order 1985 (NI 17)

120. In Article 2(2) (interpretation), at the end of sub-paragraph (c) add—

"and

(d) references to a child's parents and to a child whose parents were (or were not) married to each other at the time of his birth shall be construed in accordance with Article 155 of the Children (Northern Ireland) Order 1995 (which extends their meaning)".

121.—(1) Article 3 (offence of abduction of child by parent, etc.) shall be amended as follows.

(2) In paragraph (1), for "(3)" substitute "(2A) to (3A)".

(3) For paragraph (2) substitute the following paragraphs—

"(2) A person is connected with a child for the purposes of this Article if—

(a) he is a parent of the child; or

(b) in the case of a child whose parents were not married to each other at the time of his birth, there are reasonable grounds for believing that he is the father of the child; or

(c) he is a guardian of the child; or

(d) he is a person in whose favour a residence order is in force with respect to the child; or

(e) he has custody of the child.

(2A) A person does not commit an offence under this Article by taking or sending a child out of the United Kingdom without obtaining the appropriate consent if—

(a) he is a person in whose favour there is a residence order in force with respect to the child, and

(b) he takes or sends him out of the United Kingdom for a period of less than one month.

(2B) Paragraph (2A) does not apply if the person taking or sending the child out of the United Kingdom does so in breach of an order under Part III of the Children (Northern Ireland) Order 1995.".

(4) For the words in paragraph (3) from "but sub-paragraph (c)" to "1886" substitute the following paragraph—

"(3A) Paragraph (3)(c) does not apply if—

(a) the person who refused to consent is a person—

(i) in whose favour there is a residence order in force with respect to the child; or

(ii) who has custody of the child; or

(b) the person taking or sending the child out of the United Kingdom is, by so acting, in breach of an order made by a court in the United Kingdom.".

(5) For paragraphs (5) and (6) substitute the following paragraph—

"(5) In this Article—

"the appropriate consent", in relation to a child, means—

(a) the consent of each of the following—

(i) the child's mother;

226

(ii) the child's father, if he has parental responsibility for him;

(iii) any guardian of the child;

(iv) any person in whose favour a residence order is in force with respect to the child;

(v) any person who has custody of the child; or

(b) the leave of the court granted under any provision of Part III of the Children (Northern Ireland) Order 1995; or

(c) if any person has custody of the child, the leave of the court which awarded custody to him;

"guardian of a child", "residence order" and "parental responsibility" have the same meaning as in the Children (Northern Ireland) Order 1995;

and for the purposes of this Article a person shall be treated as having custody of a child if there is in force an order of a court in the United Kingdom awarding him (whether solely or jointly with another person) custody, legal custody or care and control of a child.".

(6) In paragraph (7), for "received into or committed to the care of the Department of Health and Social Services" substitute "in the care of an authority (within the meaning of the Children (Northern Ireland) Order 1995)".

122.—(1) Article 4 (offence of abduction of child by other persons) shall be amended as follows.

(2) In paragraph (1), for "paragraph (2), a person not falling within Article 3(2)(a) or (b)" substitute "paragraph (3), a person, other than one mentioned in paragraph (2),".

(3) For paragraph (2) substitute the following paragraphs—

"(2) The persons are—

(a) where the father and mother of the child in question were married to each other at the time of his birth, the child's father and mother;

(b) where the father and mother of the child in question were not married to each other at the time of his birth, the child's mother; and

(c) any other person mentioned in sub-paragraphs (c) to (e) of Article 3(2).

(3) In proceedings against any person for an offence under this Article, it shall be a defence for that person to prove—

(a) where the father and mother of the child in question were not married to each other at the time of his birth—

(i) that he is the child's father; or

(ii) that, at the time of the alleged offence, he believed, on reasonable grounds, that he was the child's father; or

(b) that, at the time of the alleged offence, he believed that the child had attained the age of 16.".

123.—(1) The Schedule (modifications of Article 3 for children in certain cases) shall be amended as follows.

(2) In the cross-heading immediately preceding paragraph 1, for the words from "received into" to "Social Services" substitute "in the care of an authority".

(3) In paragraph 1—

(a) in sub-paragraph (1), for the words from "received into" to "Social Services" substitute "in the care of an authority (within the meaning of the Children (Northern Ireland) Order 1995)";

(b) in sub-paragraph (2)(a), for "Department of Health and Social Services" substitute "authority";

(c) in sub-paragraph (2)(b), for "(3), (4) and (6)" substitute "(2A) to (4)".

(4) In paragraph 2(2)(b), for "(3), (4) and (6)" substitute "(2A) to (4)".

(5) In paragraph 3(2)—

(a) in head (a), for the words from "parental rights and duties" to "1987" substitute "order has been varied under Article 21 of the Adoption (Northern Ireland) Order 1987 so as to give parental responsibility to another agency";

(b) in head (b) for "(3), (4) and (6)" substitute "(2A) to (4)".

(6) In paragraph 4(2)(b), for "(3), (4) and (6)" substitute "(2A) to (4)".

The Family Law Act 1986 (c. 55)

124. For section 19 (jurisdiction in cases other than divorce, etc.) substitute the following sections—

"Jurisdiction: general.

19.—(1) A court in Northern Ireland shall not have jurisdiction to make a section 1(1)(c) order with respect to a child in or in connection with matrimonial proceedings in Northern Ireland unless the condition in section 19A of this Act is satisfied.

(2) A court in Northern Ireland shall not have jurisdiction to make a section 1(1)(c) order in a non-matrimonial case (that is to say, where the condition in section 19A is not satisfied) unless the condition in section 20 of this Act is satisfied.

(3) A court in Northern Ireland shall not have jurisdiction to make a section 1(1)(e) order unless—

(a) the condition in section 20 of this Act is satisfied, or

(b) the child concerned is present in Northern Ireland on the relevant date and the court considers that the immediate exercise of its powers is necessary for his protection.

Jurisdiction in or in connection with matrimonial proceedings.

19A.—(1) The condition referred to in section 19(1) of this Act is that the matrimonial proceedings are proceedings in respect of the marriage of the parents of the child concerned and—

(a) the proceedings—

(i) are proceedings for divorce or nullity of marriage, and

(ii) are continuing;

(b) the proceedings—

    (i) are proceedings for judicial separation,

    (ii) are continuing,

and the jurisdiction of the court is not excluded by subsection (2) below; or

(c) the proceedings have been dismissed after the beginning of the trial but—

    (i) the section 1(1)(c) order is being made forthwith, or

    (ii) the application for the order was made on or before the dismissal.

(2) For the purposes of subsection (1)(b) above, the jurisdiction of the court is excluded if, after the grant of a decree of judicial separation, on the relevant date, proceedings for divorce or nullity in respect of the marriage are continuing in England and Wales or Scotland.

(3) Subsection (2) above shall not apply if the court in which the other proceedings there referred to are continuing has made—

(a) an order under section 2A(4) or 13(6) of this Act (not being an order made by virtue of section 13(6)(a)(i)), or

(b) an order under section 5(2) or 14(2) of this Act which is recorded as being made for the purpose of enabling Part I proceedings to be taken in Northern Ireland with respect to the child concerned.

(4) Where a court—

(a) has jurisdiction to make a section 1(1)(c) order in or in connection with matrimonial proceedings, but

(b) considers that it would be more appropriate for Part I matters relating to the child to be determined outside Northern Ireland,

the court may by order direct that, while the order under this subsection is in force, no section 1(1)(c) order shall be made by any court in or in connection with those proceedings.".

125. In section 20 (habitual residence or presence of child concerned)—

(a) in subsection (1), for "section 19" substitute "section 19(2)";

(b) in subsection (2), for "proceedings for divorce, nullity or judicial separation" substitute "matrimonial proceedings".

126.—(1) Section 23 (duration and variation of Part I orders) shall be amended as follows.

(2) For subsection (3) substitute the following subsections—

"(3) A court in Northern Ireland shall not have jurisdiction to vary a Part I order if, on the relevant date, matrimonial proceedings are continuing in England and Wales or Scotland in respect of the marriage of the parents of the child concerned.

(3A) Subsection (3) above shall not apply if—

(*a*) the Part I order was made in or in connection with proceedings for divorce or nullity in Northern Ireland in respect of the marriage of the parents of the child concerned; and

(*b*) those proceedings are continuing.

(3B) Subsection (3) above shall not apply if—

(*a*) the Part I order was made in or in connection with proceedings for judicial separation in Northern Ireland;

(*b*) those proceedings are continuing; and

(*c*) the decree of judicial separation has not yet been granted.".

(3) In subsection (5), for the words from "variation of" to "if the ward" substitute "variation of a section 1(1)(*e*) order if the child concerned".

(4) For subsections (6) and (7) substitute the following subsections—

"(6) Subsection (7) below applies where a Part I order which is—

(*a*) a residence order (within the meaning of the Children (Northern Ireland) Order 1995) in favour of a person with respect to a child,

(*b*) an order made in the exercise of the High Court's inherent jurisdiction with respect to children by virtue of which a person has care of a child, or

(*c*) an order—

(i) of a kind mentioned in section 1(3)(*a*) of this Act,

(ii) under which a person is entitled to the actual possession of a child,

ceases to have effect in relation to that person by virtue of subsection (1) above.

(7) Where this subsection applies, any family assistance order made under Article 16 of the Children (Northern Ireland) Order 1995 with respect to the child shall also cease to have effect.

(8) For the purposes of subsection (7) above the reference to a family assistance order under Article 16 of the Children (Northern Ireland) Order 1995 shall be deemed to include a reference to an order for the supervision of a child made under—

(*a*) Article 47 of the Matrimonial Causes (Northern Ireland) Order 1978, or

(*b*) Article 11 of the Domestic Proceedings (Northern Ireland) Order 1980;

but this subsection shall cease to have effect once all such orders for the supervision of children have ceased to have effect in accordance with Schedule 8 to the Children (Northern Ireland) Order 1995.".

127. For section 24 (interpretation of Chapter IV) substitute the following section—

"Interpretation of Chapter IV.

24. In this Chapter—

(*a*) "child" means a person who has not attained the age of eighteen;

(*b*) "matrimonial proceedings" means proceedings for divorce, nullity of marriage or judicial separation;

(*c*) "the relevant date" means, in relation to the making or variation of an order—

(i) where an application is made for an order to be made or varied, the date of the application (or first application, if two or more are determined together), and

(ii) where no such application is made, the date on which the court is considering whether to make or, as the case may be, vary the order; and

(d) "section 1(1)(c) order" and "section 1(1)(e) order" mean orders falling within section 1(1)(c) and (e) of this Act respectively.".

The Education and Libraries (Northern Ireland) Order 1986 (NI 3)

128. In Article 2 (interpretation)—

(a) in paragraph (2), for the definition of "parent" substitute the following definition—

" "parent" shall be construed subject to paragraphs (2D) to (2F);";

(b) after paragraph (2C) insert the following paragraphs—

"(2D) In the Education Orders "parent", in relation to a child or young person, includes any person—

(a) who is not a parent of his but who has parental responsibility for him, or

(b) who has care of him,

except for the purposes of the provisions specified in paragraph (2E) where it only includes such a person if he is an individual.

(2E) The provisions referred to in paragraph (2D) are—

(a) Article 13 and Schedules 4 to 8;

(b) Articles 69, 70 and 126 of, and Schedule 5 to, the 1989 Order.

(2F) For the purposes of paragraph (2D)—

(a) "parental responsibility" has the same meaning as in the Children (Northern Ireland) Order 1995; and

(b) in determining whether an individual has care of a child or young person any absence of the child or young person at a hospital or boarding school and any other temporary absence shall be disregarded.".

129. In Article 39(1) (complaints), after sub-paragraph (d) insert the following sub-paragraph—

"(e) that there has been a failure, in relation to a child provided with accommodation by the school, to comply with the duty imposed by Article 176 of the Children (Northern Ireland) Order 1995 (welfare of children accommodated in schools);".

130. In paragraph 5 of Schedule 13—

(a) for sub-paragraph (1) (duty to institute proceedings under paragraph 4(1)) substitute the following sub-paragraph—

"(1) Before instituting proceedings against a parent for an offence under paragraph 4(1) a board shall consider whether it would be appropriate, instead of or as well as instituting the proceedings, to apply for an education supervision order with respect to the child.";

(*b*) in sub-paragraph (3) (power to bring child before juvenile court to secure efficient full-time education), for "bring the child before a juvenile court" substitute "apply for an education supervision order";

(*c*) after that sub-paragraph add the following sub-paragraph—

"(4) In this Schedule "education supervision order" means an education supervision order under the Children (Northern Ireland) Order 1995.".

131. For paragraph 6 of Schedule 13 substitute the following paragraph—

"6.—(1) The court before which a prosecution is brought for an offence under paragraph 4 may direct the board to apply for an education supervision order unless the board, having consulted the appropriate authority, decides that the child's welfare will be satisfactorily safeguarded even though no education supervision order is made.

(2) Where, following such a direction, the board decides not to apply for an education supervision order, the board shall inform the court of its reasons for the decision.

(3) Unless the court directs otherwise, the board shall so inform the court within eight weeks from the date on which the direction was given.

(4) Where—

(*a*) a board applies for an education supervision order with respect to a child who is the subject of a school attendance order; and

(*b*) the court decides that Article 55(2) of the Children (Northern Ireland) Order 1995 prevents it from making the order,

the court may direct that the school attendance order shall cease to have effect.

(5) In sub-paragraph (1) "the appropriate authority" means the appropriate authority within the meaning of paragraph 9 of Schedule 4 to the Children (Northern Ireland) Order 1995.".

The Mental Health (Northern Ireland) Order 1986 (NI 4)

132. In Article 32(2) (definition of "nearest relative"), for "his mother" substitute "—

(*a*) his mother, and

(*b*) if his father has parental responsibility for him within the meaning of the Children (Northern Ireland) Order 1995, his father".

133. For Article 33 (children and young persons in care of Department) substitute the following Article—

"Children and young persons in care

33. Where a patient who is a child or young person is in the care of a Board or HSS trust by virtue of a care order within the meaning of the Children (Northern Ireland) Order 1995, the Board or trust shall be deemed to be the nearest relative of the patient in preference to any person except the patient's husband or wife (if any).".

134. In Article 34 (nearest relative of minor under guardianship, etc.)—

(*a*) for paragraph (1) substitute the following paragraph—

"(1) Where—

232

(*a*) a guardian has been appointed for a person who has not attained the age of 18 years; or

(*b*) a residence order (as defined by Article 8 of the Children (Northern Ireland) Order 1995) is in force with respect to such a person,

the guardian (or guardians, where there is more than one) or the person named in the residence order shall, to the exclusion of any other person, be deemed to be his nearest relative.";

(*b*) for paragraph (3) substitute the following paragraph—

"(3) In this Article "guardian" does not include a guardian under this Part.".

135. In Article 86(8) (functions of the Mental Health Commission), for "section 126 of the Children and Young Persons Act (Northern Ireland) 1968" substitute "Article 74 of the Children (Northern Ireland) Order 1995".

136. In Article 122(1)(*e*) (protection of women suffering from severe mental handicap), for "the lawful care or charge of" substitute "parental responsibility for or care of".

137. In Article 127(2) (voluntary use of services by minor who is 16 or over), for "notwithstanding any right of custody or control vested by law in his parent or guardian" substitute "even though there are one or more persons who have parental responsibility for him (within the meaning of the Children (Northern Ireland) Order 1995)".

The Adoption (Northern Ireland) Order 1987 (NI 22)

138.—(1) Article 2(2) (interpretation) shall be amended in accordance with the following provisions of this paragraph.

(2) In the definition of "adoption agency" (which includes for the purposes of Articles 11 and 21 adoption agencies in England and Wales and Scotland), for the words "and 21" substitute ", 13, 17 to 22, 24 and 28 to 32".

(3) For the definition of "adoption order" substitute the following definition—

" "adoption order"—

(*a*) means an order under Article 12(1);

(*b*) in Articles 12(3) and (4), 17 to 20, 25(3), 28, 29 and 31 to 33 includes an order under section 12 of the Adoption Act 1976 or section 12 of the Adoption (Scotland) Act 1978 (adoption orders in England and Wales and Scotland);

(*c*) in Articles 28, 29 and 31 to 33 includes an order under Article 57, section 55 of the Adoption Act 1976 or section 49 of the Adoption (Scotland) Act 1978 (adoption by persons domiciled outside Northern Ireland or England and Wales or Scotland);".

(4) For the definition of "guardian" substitute the following definition—

" "guardian" has the same meaning as in the Children (Northern Ireland) Order 1995;".

(5) For the definition of "order freeing a child for adoption" substitute the following definition—

" "order freeing a child for adoption" means an order under Article 17(1) or 18(1) and in Articles 28(2) and 58A(1) includes an order under section 18 of the Adoption Act 1976 or section 18 of the

Adoption (Scotland) Act 1978;".

(6) For the definition of "the parental rights and duties" substitute the following definitions—

" "parent" means, in relation to a child, any parent who has parental responsibility for the child under the Children (Northern Ireland) Order 1995;

"parental responsibility" and "parental responsibility agreement" have the same meaning as in the Children (Northern Ireland) Order 1995;".

(7) For the definition of "prescribed" substitute the following definition—

" "prescribed" in Articles 4, 33 and 59 means prescribed by regulations made by the Department, in Articles 54 and 54A means prescribed by regulations made by the Department of Finance and Personnel and elsewhere means prescribed by adoption rules;".

(8) In the definition of "relative" omit ", where the child is illegitimate, the father of the child and" and for "the child were the legitimate child of his mother and father" substitute "Article 155. of the Children (Northern Ireland) Order 1995 applied to this definition".

(9) After the definition of "statutory provision" insert the following definition—

" "upbringing" has the same meaning as in the Children (Northern Ireland) Order 1995;".

139.—(1) In Article 2(3)—

(*a*) for "transferring the actual custody of a child to" substitute "placing a child with";

(*b*) in sub-paragraph (*b*) for "transfer of the child to the actual custody of" substitute "placing of the child with".

(2) After paragraph (3) add the following paragraphs—

"(4) In this Order, in determining with what person, or where, a child has his home, any absence of the child at a hospital or at a school providing accommodation for him and any other temporary absence shall be disregarded.

(5) In this Order references to a child who is in the care of or looked after by a Board or HSS trust have the same meaning as in the Children (Northern Ireland) Order 1995.".

140.—(1) In Article 12 (adoption orders), for paragraphs (1) to (3) substitute the following paragraphs—

"(1) An adoption order is an order giving parental responsibility for a child to the adopters, and such an order may be made by an authorised court on the application of the adopters.

(2) The order does not affect parental responsibility so far as it relates to any period before the making of the order.

(3) The making of an adoption order operates to extinguish—

(*a*) the parental responsibility which any person has for the child immediately before the making of the order;

(*b*) any order of a court under the Children (Northern Ireland) Order 1995;

(c) any duty arising by virtue of an agreement or the order of a court to make payments, so far as the payments are in respect of the child's maintenance or upbringing for any period after the making of the order.".

(2) In paragraph (4) for "(3)(*b*)" substitute "(3)(*c*)".

141. For Article 14 (adoption by married couple) substitute the following Article—

"Adoption by married couple

14.—(1) An adoption order shall not be made on the application of more than one person except in the circumstances specified in paragraphs (2) and (3).

(2) An adoption order may be made on the application of a married couple where both the husband and the wife have attained the age of 21 years.

(3) An adoption order may be made on the application of a married couple where—

(*a*) the husband or the wife—

(i) is the father or mother of the child; and

(ii) has attained the age of 18 years;

and

(*b*) his or her spouse has attained the age of 21 years.

(4) An adoption order shall not be made on the application of a married couple unless at least one of them is domiciled in a part of the United Kingdom, or in any of the Channel Islands or in the Isle of Man.".

142. In Article 16 (parental agreement)—

(*a*) in paragraph (2)(*c*), for "the parental duties in relation to" substitute "his parental responsibility for";

(*b*) in paragraph (5), for "the rights and powers of a parent of" and "the exercise of parental rights in respect of" substitute in each case "parental responsibility for".

143.—(1) In Article 17 (freeing child for adoption with parental agreement), for paragraph (1) substitute the following paragraph—

"(1) Subject to paragraph (2), where, on the joint application of the parents or guardian of the child and an adoption agency, an authorised court is satisfied in the case of each parent or guardian that he freely, and with full understanding of what is involved, agrees—

(*a*) generally, and

(*b*) either unconditionally or subject only to a condition with respect to the religious persuasion in which the child is to be brought up,

to the making of an adoption order, the court shall make an order declaring the child free for adoption.".

(2) For paragraph (3) (effect of order) substitute the following paragraph—

"(3) On the making of an order under paragraph (1), parental responsibility for the child is given to the adoption agency, and paragraphs (2) to (4) of Article 12 shall apply as if the order were an adoption order and the agency were the adopters.".

(3) For paragraph (6) substitute the following paragraphs—

"(6) Before making an adoption order or an order under paragraph (1) in the case of a child whose father does not have parental responsibility for him, the court shall satisfy itself in relation to any person claiming to be the father that—

(a) he has no intention of applying for—

(i) an order under Article 7(1) of the Children (Northern Ireland) Order 1995, or

(ii) a residence order under Article 10 of that Order, or

(b) if he did make any such application, it would be likely to be refused.

(7) Paragraphs (5) and (7) of Article 12 shall apply in relation to the making of an order under this Article as they apply in relation to the making of an order under Article 12.".

144.—(1) In Article 18 (freeing child for adoption without parental agreement), after paragraph (2) insert the following paragraph—

"(2A) For the purposes of paragraph (2) a child is in the care of an adoption agency if the adoption agency is a Board or HSS trust and he is in its care.".

(2) In paragraph (3) (application of provisions of Article 17), for "(5) and (6)" substitute "and (5) to (7)".

145. In Article 19(3) (progress reports to former parent), for "in which the parental rights and duties were vested" substitute "to which parental responsibility was given".

146.—(1) In Article 20 (revocation of order freeing child for adoption), in paragraph (1), for "the parental rights and duties" substitute "parental responsibility for the child".

(2) In paragraph (2), for "the parental rights and duties" substitute "parental responsibility".

(3) For paragraph (3) (effect of revocation) substitute the following paragraphs—

"(3) The revocation of an order under Article 17(1) or 18(1) ("a freeing order") operates—

(a) to extinguish the parental responsibility given to the adoption agency under the freeing order;

(b) to give parental responsibility for the child to—

(i) the child's mother; and

(ii) where the child's father and mother were married to each other at the time of his birth, the father; and

(c) to revive—

(i) any parental responsibility agreement,

(ii) any order under Article 7(1) of the Children (Northern Ireland) Order 1995, and

(iii) any appointment of a guardian in respect of the child (whether made by a court or otherwise),

extinguished by the making of the freeing order.

(3A) Subject to paragraph (3)(c), the revocation does not—

(*a*) operate to revive—

    (i) any order under the Children (Northern Ireland) Order 1995, or

    (ii) any duty referred to in Article 12(3)(*c*),

    extinguished by the making of the freeing order; or

(*b*) affect any person's parental responsibility so far as it relates to the period between the making of the freeing order and the date of revocation of that order.".

147. For Article 21 (transfer of parental rights and duties between adoption agencies) substitute the following Article—

"Variation of order under Article 17(1) or 18(1) so as to substitute one adoption agency for another

21.—(1) On an application to which this Article applies, an authorised court may vary an order under Article 17(1) or 18(1) so as to give parental responsibility for the child to another adoption agency ("the substitute agency") in place of the agency for the time being having parental responsibility for the child under the order ("the existing agency").

(2) This Article applies to any application made jointly by—

(*a*) the existing agency; and

(*b*) the would-be substitute agency.

(3) Where an order under Article 17(1) or 18(1) is varied under this Article, Article 19 shall apply as if the substitute agency had been given responsibility for the child on the making of the order.".

148.—(1) In Article 22 (notification to Board or HSS trust of adoption application, where child not placed by adoption agency), after paragraph (1) insert the following paragraphs—

"(1A) An application for such an adoption order shall not be made unless the person wishing to make the application has, within the period of two years preceding the making of the application, given notice as mentioned in paragraph (1).

(1B) In paragraphs (1) and (1A) the references to the area in which the applicant or person has his home are references to the area in which he has his home at the time of giving the notice.".

(2) In paragraphs (4) and (5) for "in the care of" substitute "looked after by".

149. In Article 25 (restrictions on making adoption orders), for paragraph (3) (definition of "British adoption order") substitute the following paragraph—

"(3) In this Article "British adoption order" means—

(*a*) an adoption order or an order under the Adoption Act (Northern Ireland) 1967; or

(*b*) an order under any provision for the adoption of a child effected under the law of any of the following countries, that is to say, the Channel Islands, the Isle of Man and a colony, which is a British territory for the purposes of section 24 of the Adoption Act 1976.".

150. In Article 26(1) (interim orders) for "vesting the legal custody of the

child in" substitute "giving parental responsibility for the child to".

151.—(1) In Article 28 (restrictions on removal where adoption agreed or application made under Article 17(1) or 18(1)), in paragraphs (1) and (2) for "actual custody" substitute "home".

(2) After paragraph (2) insert the following paragraph—

"(2A) For the purposes of paragraph (2) a child is in the care of an adoption agency if the adoption agency is a Board or HSS trust and he is in its care.".

152.—(1) In Article 29 (restrictions on removal where applicant has provided home for five years), in paragraphs (1) and (2) for "actual custody" substitute "home".

(2) After paragraph (2) there shall be inserted the following paragraph—

"(2A) In paragraphs (1) and (2) "any enactment" does not include Article 22(2) of the Children (Northern Ireland) Order 1995.".

(3) For paragraph (3) substitute the following paragraph—

"(3) In any case where paragraph (1) or (2) applies and—

(a) the child was being looked after by a Board or HSS trust before he began to have his home with the applicant or, as the case may be, the prospective adopter, and

(b) the child is still being looked after by the Board or HSS trust,

the Board or HSS trust shall not remove him from the home of the applicant or the prospective adopter except in accordance with Article 31 or 32 or with the leave of a court.".

(4) In paragraph (5) for "in the care of an another Board or of an HSS trust or a voluntary organisation" substitute "looked after by another Board or an HSS trust or to be provided with accommodation by a voluntary organisation".

(5) In paragraph (5A) for "in the care of another HSS trust or of a Board or voluntary organisation" substitute "looked after by another HSS trust or a Board or to be provided with accommodation by a voluntary organisation".

153. In Article 30 (return of child taken away in breach of Article 28 or 29), for paragraphs (1) and (2) substitute the following paragraphs—

"(1) An authorised court may, on the application of a person from whose home a child has been removed in breach of—

(a) Article 28 or 29;

(b) section 27 or 28 of the Adoption Act 1976; or

(c) section 27 or 28 of the Adoption (Scotland) Act 1978,

order the person who has so removed the child to return the child to the applicant.

(2) An authorised court may, on the application of a person who has reasonable grounds for believing that another person is intending to remove a child from his home in breach of—

(a) Article 28 or 29;

(b) section 27 or 28 of the Adoption Act 1976; or

(c) section 27 or 28 of the Adoption (Scotland) Act 1978,

by order direct that other person not to remove the child from the applicant's home in breach of any of those provisions.".

154.—(1) In Article 31 (return of children placed for adoption by adoption agencies), in paragraph (1)—

(*a*) for "delivered into the actual custody of" substitute "placed with";

(*b*) in sub-paragraph (*a*), for "retain the actual custody of the child" substitute "give the child a home";

(*c*) in sub-paragraph (*b*), for "actual custody" substitute "home".

(2) In paragraph (3), for "in his actual custody" substitute "with him".

155. For Article 32 (application of Article 31 where child not placed for adoption) substitute the following Article—

"Application of Article 31 where child not placed for adoption

32.—(1) Where a person serves a notice in pursuance of Article 22(1) on the Board or HSS trust within whose area he has his home of his intention to apply for an adoption order in respect of a child—

(*a*) who is (when the notice is given) being looked after by a Board or HSS trust; but

(*b*) who was placed with that person otherwise than in pursuance of such arrangements as are mentioned in Article 31(1),

Article 31 shall apply as if the child had been placed in pursuance of such arrangements, except that where the application is refused by the court or withdrawn the child need not be returned to the Board or HSS trust in whose care he is unless the Board or HSS trust so requires.

(2) Where notice of intention is served as described in paragraph (1) in respect of any child who is (when the notice is given) being looked after by a Board or HSS trust then, until the application for an adoption order has been made and disposed of, any right of the Board or HSS trust to require the child to be returned to it otherwise than in pursuance of Article 31 shall be suspended.

(3) While the child has his home with the person by whom the notice is served no contribution shall be payable (whether under a contribution order or otherwise) in respect of the child by any person liable under Articles 38 to 43 of the Children (Northern Ireland) Order 1995 to make contributions in respect of him (but without prejudice to the recovery of any sum due at the time the notice is served), unless 12 weeks have elapsed since the service of the notice without the application being made or the application has been refused by the court or withdrawn.

(4) Nothing in this Article affects the right of any person who has parental responsibility for a child to remove him under Article 22(2) of the Children (Northern Ireland) Order 1995.".

156.—(1) In Article 33 (meaning of "protected child"), after paragraph (1) insert the following paragraph—

"(1A) A child shall be deemed to be a protected child for the purposes of this Part if he is a protected child within the meaning of—

(*a*) section 32 of the Adoption Act 1976; or

(*b*) section 32 of the Adoption (Scotland) Act 1978.".

(2) In paragraph (2)(*a*), for heads (i) to (iii) substitute the following heads—

"(i) any school in which he is receiving full-time education;

(ii) any children's home or voluntary home;

(iii) any hospital;

(iv) any home or institution not specified in heads (i) to (iii) but provided by the Secretary of State, a government department or a prescribed public body; or".

(3) After paragraph (2) insert the following paragraph—

"(2A) Paragraph (2)(a) shall be construed in accordance with Article 2(2) of the Children (Northern Ireland) Order 1995 (interpretation).".

(4) For paragraph (3) substitute the following paragraphs—

"(3) A protected child ceases to be a protected child—

(a) on the grant or refusal of the application for an adoption order;

(b) on the notification to the Board or HSS trust for the area where the child has his home that the application for an adoption order has been withdrawn;

(c) in a case where no application is made for an adoption order, on the expiry of the period of two years from the giving of the notice;

(d) on the making of a residence order, a care order or a supervision order under the Children (Northern Ireland) Order 1995 in respect of the child;

(e) on the appointment of a guardian for him under that Order;

(f) on his attaining the age of 18 years; or

(g) on his marriage,

whichever first occurs.

(4) In paragraph (3)(d) the references to a care order and a supervision order do not include references to an interim care order or interim supervision order.".

157.—(1) In Article 36 (notices and information to be given to Boards or Health and Social Services trusts), in paragraph (1) for "who has a protected child in his actual custody" substitute "with whom a protected child has his home".

(2) In paragraph (2) for "in whose actual custody he was" substitute "with whom he had his home".

158.—(1) In Article 54 (disclosure of birth records of adopted children), in paragraph (1) for "paragraphs (4) to (6)" substitute "the provisions of this Article".

(2) For paragraphs (3) to (6) substitute the following paragraphs—

"(3) Before supplying any information to an applicant under paragraph (1), the Registrar General shall inform the applicant that counselling services are available to him—

(a) if he is in Northern Ireland—

(i) from the Board or HSS trust in whose area he is living;

(ii) where the adoption order relating to him was made in Northern Ireland, from the Board or HSS trust in whose area the court which made the order sat; or

(iii) from any other Board or HSS trust;

(b) if he is in England and Wales—

(i) at the General Register Office;

(ii) from the local authority in whose area he is living;

(iii) where the adoption order relating to him was made in England and Wales, from the local authority in whose area the court which made the order sat; or

(iv) from any other local authority;

(c) if he is in Scotland—

(i) from the regional or islands council in whose area he is living;

(ii) where the adoption order relating to him was made in Scotland, from the council in whose area the court which made the order sat; or

(iii) from any other regional or islands council;

(d) if he is in the United Kingdom and his adoption was arranged by an adoption society—

(i) registered under Article 4; or

(ii) approved under section 3 of the Adoption Act 1976; or

(iii) approved under section 3 of the Adoption (Scotland) Act 1978,

from that society.

(4) Where an adopted person who is in Northern Ireland—

(a) applies for information under—

(i) paragraph (1), or

(ii) section 51 of the Adoption Act 1976, or

(b) is supplied with information under section 45 of the Adoption (Scotland) Act 1978,

it shall be the duty of any body mentioned in paragraph (5) to provide counselling for him if asked by him to do so.

(5) The bodies are—

(a) any Board or HSS trust; and

(b) any adoption society falling within paragraph (3)(d) in so far as it is acting as an adoption society in Northern Ireland.

(6) If the applicant chooses to receive counselling from a body falling within paragraph (3), the Registrar General shall send to the body the information to which the applicant is entitled under paragraph (1).

(7) Where a person—

(a) was adopted before 18th December 1987, and

(b) applies for information under paragraph (1),

the Registrar General shall not supply the information to him unless he has attended an interview with a counsellor arranged by a body from whom counselling services are available as mentioned in paragraph (3).

(8) Where the Registrar General is prevented by paragraph (7) from supplying information to a person who is not living in the United Kingdom, he may supply the information to any body which—

(a) the Registrar General is satisfied is suitable to provide counselling to that person, and

(b) has notified the Registrar General that it is prepared to provide such counselling.".

159. After Article 54 insert the following Article—

"Adoption Contact Register

54A.—(1) The Registrar General shall maintain at the General Register Office a register to be called the Adoption Contact Register.

(2) The register shall be in two parts—

(*a*) Part I: Adopted Persons; and

(*b*) Part II: Relatives.

(3) The Registrar General shall, on payment of such fee as may be prescribed, enter in Part I of the register the name and address of any adopted person who fulfils the conditions in paragraph (4) and who gives notice that he wishes to contact any relative of his.

(4) The conditions are that—

(*a*) a record of the adopted person's birth is kept by the Registrar General; and

(*b*) the adopted person has attained the age of 18 years and—

(i) has been supplied by the Registrar General with information under Article 54; or

(ii) has satisfied the Registrar General that he has such information as is necessary to enable him to obtain a certified copy of the record of his birth.

(5) The Registrar General shall, on payment of such fee as may be prescribed, enter in Part II of the register the name and address of any person who fulfils the conditions in paragraph (6) and who gives notice that he wishes to contact an adopted person.

(6) The conditions are—

(*a*) that a record of the adopted person's birth is kept by the Registrar General; and

(*b*) that the person giving notice under paragraph (5) has attained the age of 18 years and has satisfied the Registrar General that—

(i) he is a relative of the adopted person; and

(ii) he has such information as is necessary to enable him to obtain a certified copy of the record of the adopted person's birth.

(7) The Registrar General shall, on receiving notice from any person named in an entry in the register that he wishes the entry to be cancelled, cancel the entry.

(8) Any notice given under this Article must be in such form as may be determined by the Registrar General.

(9) The Registrar General shall transmit to an adopted person whose name is entered in Part I of the register the name and address of any relative in respect of whom there is an entry in Part II of the register.

(10) Any entry cancelled under paragraph (7) ceases from the time of cancellation to be an entry for the purposes of paragraph (9).

(11) The register shall not be open to public inspection or search and the Registrar General shall not supply any person with information entered in the register (whether in an uncancelled or a cancelled entry) except in accordance with this Article.

(12) The register may be kept by means of a computer.

(13) In this Article—

(a) "relative" means any person (other than an adoptive relative) who is related to the adopted person by blood (including half-blood) or marriage; and

(b) "address" includes any address at or through which the person concerned may be contacted.".

160.—(1) In Article 57 (adoption by persons domiciled outside Northern Ireland), for paragraph (1) substitute the following paragraph—

"(1) Where on an application made in respect of a child by a person who is not domiciled in Northern Ireland or England and Wales or Scotland an authorised court is satisfied that he intends to adopt the child under the law of or within the country in which the applicant is domiciled, the court may, subject to the provisions of this Article, make an order giving him parental responsibility for the child.".

(2) In paragraph (2) for "14(2)" substitute "14(4)".

161. In Article 58(1) (restriction on removal of children for adoption outside Northern Ireland)—

(a) after "Article 57" insert ", section 55 of the Adoption Act 1976 or section 49 of the Adoption (Scotland) Act 1978";

(b) for "transferring the actual custody of a child to" substitute "placing a child with".

162. After Article 58 insert the following Article—

"Orders made in adoption proceedings outside Northern Ireland

58A.—(1) Paragraphs (2) to (4) of Article 12 shall apply in relation to an order freeing a child for adoption (other than an order under Article 17(1) or 18(1)) as if it were an adoption order; and, on the revocation in England and Wales or Scotland of an order freeing a child for adoption, paragraphs (3) and (3A) of Article 20 shall apply as if the order had been revoked under that Article.

(2) Articles 12(3) and (4) and 49 shall apply in relation to a child who is the subject of an order which is similar to an order under Article 57 and is made in any part of Great Britain or the Channel Islands or in the Isle of Man, as they apply in relation to a child who is the subject of an adoption order.".

163.—(1) In Article 59 (prohibition on certain payments), in paragraph (1), after "this Article" insert "and Article 59A".

(2) In paragraph (2)(d) for "in the actual custody of" substitute "with".

164. After Article 59 insert the following Article—

"Permitted allowances

59A.—(1) The Department may make regulations for the purpose of enabling adoption agencies to pay allowances to persons who have adopted, or intend to adopt, children in pursuance of arrangements made by the agencies.

(2) Article 59(1) shall not apply to any payment made by an adoption agency in accordance with the regulations.

(3) The regulations may, in particular, make provision as to—

(a) the procedure to be followed by any agency in determining whether a person should be paid an allowance;

(b) the circumstances in which an allowance may be paid;

(c) the factors to be taken into account in determining the amount of an allowance;

(d) the procedure for review, variation and termination of allowances; and

(e) the information about allowances to be supplied by any agency to any person who is intending to adopt a child.

(4) Any scheme approved under Article 59(4) shall be revoked as from the commencement of this Article.

(5) Article 59(1) shall not apply in relation to any payment made—

(a) in accordance with a scheme revoked under paragraph (4) or Article 59(5)(b); and

(b) to a person to whom such payments were made before the revocation of the scheme.

(6) Paragraph (5) shall not apply where any person to whom any payments may lawfully be made by virtue of paragraph (5) agrees to receive (instead of such payments) payments complying with regulations made under this Article.".

165. In Article 64(3) (appeal from county court), for "paragraphs (2) and (4)" substitute "paragraph (2)".

166. For Article 66 (guardians ad litem) substitute the following Articles—

"Guardians ad litem

66.—(1) For the purpose of any application for an adoption order or an order freeing a child for adoption or an order under Article 20 or 57, an authorised court shall appoint a guardian ad litem for the child concerned.

(2) The guardian ad litem—

(a) shall be appointed in accordance with adoption rules; and

(b) shall be under a duty to safeguard the interests of the child in the prescribed manner.

Panels for selection of guardians ad litem

66A.—(1) The Department may by regulations provide for the establishment of panels of persons from whom guardians ad litem appointed under Article 66 must be selected.

(2) The regulations may, in particular, make provision—

(a) for the constitution, administration and procedures of panels and for the appointment of panel managers;

(b) for the defrayment of expenses and for the payment of fees and allowances;

(c) as to the qualifications for appointment as a guardian ad litem;

(d) as to the training to be given to guardians ad litem or to persons with a view to their appointment as guardians ad litem; and

(e) for monitoring the work of guardians ad litem.

(3) Adoption rules may make provision as to the assistance which any guardian ad litem may be required by the court to give to it.

(4) The Department may, with the approval of the Department of Finance and Personnel, make such grants as the Department considers appropriate with respect to expenditure incurred under regulations made under this Article.".

167. In paragraph 1 of Schedule 1 (membership of Appeal Tribunals)—

(a) after "barrister-at-law" insert "or solicitor";

(b) for "Lord Chief Justice" substitute "Lord Chancellor".

The Disabled Persons (Northern Ireland) Act 1989 (c. 10)

168. In section 1(3)(b) (circumstances in which regulations may provide for the appointment of authorised representatives of disabled persons), for "in the care of the Department to be made by a" substitute "looked after by a relevant authority to be made by the".

169. In section 2(5) (places where authorised representative may visit disabled person if he is residing there), for paragraph (e) substitute the following paragraph—

"(e) in accommodation provided by or on behalf of a relevant authority under Part IV of the Children (Northern Ireland) Order 1995 or by a voluntary organisation or other person in accordance with arrangements made by a relevant authority under Article 18 of that Order, or".

170.—(1) In section 11(1) (interpretation)—

(a) in the definition of "parent", for the words from "includes" to "child" substitute "in relation to a disabled person under the age of 16, includes a person who is not a parent of his but who has parental responsibility for him (within the meaning of the Children (Northern Ireland) Order 1995)";

(b) in the definition of "personal social services", after the words "1978 Act" add "or under Part IV of the Children (Northern Ireland) Order 1995".

(2) After that subsection insert the following subsection—

"(1A) In this Act any reference to a child who is looked after by a relevant authority has the same meaning as in the Children (Northern Ireland) Order 1995.".

The Matrimonial and Family Proceedings (Northern Ireland) Order 1989 (NI 4)

171. For Article 32 (declarations of legitimacy or legitimation) substitute the following Article—

"Declaration of parentage, legitimacy or legitimation

32.—(1) Any person may apply to the court for a declaration—

(a) that a person named in the application is or was his parent; or

(b) that he is the legitimate child of his parents.

(2) Any person may apply to the court for one (or for one or, in the alternative, the other) of the following declarations, that is to say—

(a) a declaration that he has become a legitimated person;

(b) a declaration that he has not become a legitimated person.

(3) A court shall have jurisdiction to entertain an application under this

Article if (and only if) the applicant—

(a) is domiciled in Northern Ireland on the date of the application; or

(b) has been habitually resident in Northern Ireland throughout the period of one year ending with that date.

(4) Where a declaration is made on an application under paragraph (1), the prescribed officer of the court shall notify the Registrar General, in such a manner and within such period as may be prescribed, of the making of that declaration.

(5) In this Article—

"legitimated person" means a person legitimated or recognised as legitimated—

(a) under section 1 or 8 of the Legitimacy Act (Northern Ireland) 1928; or

(b) by a legitimation (whether or not by virtue of the subsequent marriage of his parents) recognised by the law of Northern Ireland and effected under the law of another country;

"prescribed" means prescribed by rules of court;

"Registrar General" has the same meaning as in the Births and Deaths Registration (Northern Ireland) Order 1976;

"rules of court" has the same meaning as that given in Article 36(5).".

172. In Article 36 (supplementary provisions as to declarations), in paragraph (2), at the end of sub-paragraph (c) add "and on persons who may be affected by any declaration applied for".

The Police and Criminal Evidence (Northern Ireland) Order 1989 (NI 12)

173. In Article 2(2) (interpretation), in the definition of "parent or guardian", in paragraph (b) after "Board" in both places where it occurs insert "or Health and Social Services trust".

174. In Article 38(13)(a) (duties of custody officer before charge), after "1968" insert "or Article 49(1) of the Children (Northern Ireland) Order 1995".

The Insolvency (Northern Ireland) Order 1989 (NI 19)

175. In Article 255(8) (effect of discharge of bankrupt), for the definition of "family proceedings" substitute the following definition—

" "family proceedings" has the meaning given by Article 12(5) of the Family Law (Northern Ireland) Order 1993;".

The Horses (Protective Headgear for Young Riders)
(Northern Ireland) Order 1990 (NI 16)

176. In Article 3(2)(a) (causing or permitting child under 14 to ride on road without protective headgear), for "custody, charge or care of" substitute "responsibility for".

The Access to Personal Files and Medical Reports
(Northern Ireland) Order 1991 (NI 14)

177. In the Schedule (accessible personal information), in paragraph 1, after paragraph (e) of the entry relating to a Health and Social Services Board add the following—

"(*f*) the Children (Northern Ireland) Order 1995".

The Child Support (Northern Ireland) Order 1991 (NI 23)

178. In Article 2(2) (interpretation), in the definition of "parental responsibility", for the words from ", as respects" to the end substitute "has the same meaning as in the Children (Northern Ireland) Order 1995".

179. In Article 4(4)(*c*) (meaning of certain other terms), for the words from "having" to "court" substitute "in whose favour residence orders under Article 8 of the Children (Northern Ireland) Order 1995 are in force".

180. In Article 10(11) (definition of "maintenance order"), after sub-paragraph (*d*) insert the following sub-paragraph—

"(*dd*) Schedule 1 to the Children (Northern Ireland) Order 1995; or".

181. In Article 27(2) (disputes about parentage)—

(*a*) in Case C, in paragraph (*a*)(i) after "under" insert "Article 32 of the Matrimonial and Family Proceedings (Northern Ireland) Order 1989 or";

(*b*) in Case E—

(i) after "England and Wales" insert "or Northern Ireland";

(ii) after "1968" insert "or section 8 of the Civil Evidence Act (Northern Ireland) 1971".

182. In Article 28 (reference to court for declaration of parentage)—

(*a*) in paragraph (1) for "a court of summary jurisdiction" substitute "the court";

(*b*) after paragraph (3) add the following paragraph—

"(4) In this Article "the court" means, subject to any provision made under Schedule 7 to the Children (Northern Ireland) Order 1995, the High Court, a county court or a court of summary jurisdiction.".

183. In Article 42(2) (jurisdiction of courts in certain proceedings), after "means" insert ", subject to any provision made under Schedule 7 to the Children (Northern Ireland) Order 1995,".

*The Children and Young Persons (Protection from Tobacco)
(Northern Ireland) Order 1991 (NI 25)*

184. In Article 6(1)(*a*) (enforcement action by district councils), after "4" insert "and 5".

*The Social Security Contributions and Benefits
(Northern Ireland) Act 1992 (c. 7)*

185. In section 139 (meaning of "person responsible for child"), in subsection (3)(*c*) after "1972" add "or under the Children (Northern Ireland) Order 1995".

The Social Security Administration (Northern Ireland) Act 1992 (c. 8)

186. In section 74 (recovery of social fund awards), for subsection (7) substitute the following subsection—

"(7) Any reference in subsection (6) to children of whom the man or the woman is the father or the mother shall be construed in accordance with Article 155 of the Children (Northern Ireland) Order 1995.".

The Housing (Northern Ireland) Order 1992 (NI 15)

187. In Article 52(6) (definition of "disabled person"), at the end of sub-paragraph (*b*) add—

"and

(*c*) any person who for the purposes of Part IV of the Children (Northern Ireland) Order 1995 is a child in need by virtue of Article 17(*c*) of that Order (disabled children)".

The Registered Homes (Northern Ireland) Order 1992 (NI 20)

188. In Article 3(2) (exclusions from definition of "residential care home"), for sub-paragraph (*d*) substitute the following sub-paragraph—

"(*d*) any voluntary or children's home within the meaning of the Children (Northern Ireland) Order 1995 or any home provided under Part VII of that Order;".

189. In Article 16(2) (exclusions from definition of "nursing home"), for sub-paragraph (*d*) substitute the following sub-paragraph—

"(*d*) any voluntary or children's home within the meaning of the Children (Northern Ireland) Order 1995 or any home provided under Part VII of that Order;".

190. In Article 30(1) (constitution of Registered Homes Tribunals), after "27" insert "or under Part VIII or IX of the Children (Northern Ireland) Order 1995".

The Access to Health Records (Northern Ireland) Order 1993 (NI 4)

191. In Article 2(2) (interpretation), in the definition of "parental responsibility" for "Child Support (Northern Ireland) Order 1991" substitute "Children (Northern Ireland) Order 1995".

SCHEDULE 10

REPEALS

Chapter or Number	Short Title	Extent of Repeal
1662 c. 19 (Ir.).	The Tenures Abolition Act (Ireland) 1662.	Sections 6, 7, 15 and 16.
1873 c. 12.	The Custody of Infants Act 1873.	The whole Act.
1885 c. 69.	The Criminal Law Amendment Act 1885.	In section 10, in the proviso the words ", or guardian". Section 12.
1886 c. 27.	The Guardianship of Infants Act 1886.	The whole Act.
1891 c. 3.	The Custody of Children Act 1891.	The whole Act.
1908 c. 45.	The Punishment of Incest Act 1908.	Section 1(4).
1920 c. 33.	The Maintenance Orders (Facilities for Enforcement) Act 1920.	Section 4A(5)(a) and (b). Section 11(d).
1924 c. 27 (N.I.).	The Illegitimate Children (Affiliation Orders) Act (Northern Ireland) 1924.	The whole Act.
1950 c. 5 (N.I.).	The Children and Young Persons Act (Northern Ireland) 1950.	In section 13(3) the words from "and in section twelve" to "circumstances)". In Schedule 6, the entry relating to the Illegitimate Children (Affiliation Orders) Act (Northern Ireland) 1924.
1951 c. 25 (N.I.).	The Age of Marriage Act (Northern Ireland) 1951.	Section 2.
1954 c. 21 (N.I.).	The Marriages Act (Northern Ireland) 1954.	In section 6(1), the definition of "minor". The Schedule.
1955 c. 18.	The Army Act 1955.	In section 150(5), the words from "references to a sum" to the end. Section 215(6).
1955 c. 19.	The Air Force Act 1955.	In section 150(5), the words from "references

Chapter or Number	Short Title	Extent of Repeal
		to a sum" to the end. Section 213(6).
1957 c. 53.	The Naval Discipline Act 1957.	In section 101(5), the words from "and includes" to the end. Section 124(5).
1966 c. 35 (N.I.).	The Maintenance and Affiliation Orders Act (Northern Ireland) 1966.	Sections 1, 3 to 5, 20, 21, 23 and the Schedule.
1968 c. 34 (N.I.).	The Children and Young Persons Act (Northern Ireland) 1968.	Part I.
		Sections 27 and 28.
		Section 32.
		Part III.
		In section 50(2) the words from "so however that" to the end.
		In section 51—
		(a) in subsection (1) paragraph (b) and the immediately preceding "or", in paragraph (i) the words "or (b)" and paragraph (ii) and the immediately preceding "and";
		(b) in subsection (2) the words "or (b)".
		Section 52(8)(a).
		In section 66(3) the word "108".
		Section 85(4).
		Section 92.
		Sections 93 to 95.
		Section 96(2) and (3).
		In section 97(2) the words from ", and upon such revocation" to the end.
		Section 98.

Chapter or Number	Short Title	Extent of Repeal
		In section 99 the words from "any child or young person in respect of whom" to "committed, or", the words "94, 96 or" and the words ", and any child or young person who has taken refuge in a place of safety,".
		In section 100—
		(a) in subsection (1) paragraphs (a) and (b), paragraph (d) and the immediately preceding "or", the words "removed or" in both places where they occur and the words from "or received" to the end;
		(b) subsections (3) and (4);
		(c) in subsection (5) the words "or justice of the peace is under the age of five or" and the words "or justice" in the second and third places where they occur.
		In section 101—
		(a) in subsection (1) the words "or a justice of the peace", the words "or (3)", the words "or justice of the peace", the words "or justice" in the second place where they occur, the words "95 or", and the words ", or

Chapter or Number	Short Title	Extent of Repeal
		the justice,''; (*b*) in subsection (3) the words from ''or any other justice'' to ''absence of the child''; (*c*) in subsection (4) the words ''or has taken refuge in a place of safety'' and the words ''or (3)''.
		In section 102(1) the words ''or justice of the peace'' and the words ''or justice'' in the second and third places where they occur.
		Parts VI to VIII.
		Section 132(6).
		Section 133(4).
		Section 149(3).
		In section 151(1) the words '', or of the Adoption (Northern Ireland) Order 1987,''.
		Section 152.
		Sections 154 to 160.
		Section 162.
		Sections 164 and 165.
		Section 169.
		In section 170(2) the words ''105(8) or (9)''.
		Section 172(1).
		In section 173, in subsection (1) paragraphs (*b*) and (*c*), and subsections (2), (5) and (6).
		Section 175.
		In section 177(1) paragraphs (*e*) to (*g*).

Chapter or Number	Short Title	Extent of Repeal
		In section 180(1) the definitions of "broadcast" and "in need of care, protection and control", in the definition of "place of safety" the words from "any home" to "Part VII", and the definition of "special reception centre".
		In Schedule 3 paragraph 2A.
		In Schedule 6 paragraphs 3, 4 and 6.
		In Schedule 7 paragraphs 4, 10, 38, 40 and 41.
1969 c. 22 (N.I.).	The Adoption (Hague Convention) Act (Northern Ireland) 1969.	In section 12, in the definition of "specified order" the words "Great Britain or".
1969 c. 28 (N.I.).	The Age of Majority Act (Northern Ireland) 1969.	In Part I of Schedule 1 the entries relating to the Tenures Abolition Act (Ireland) 1662, the Criminal Law Amendment Act 1885, the Punishment of Incest Act 1908, the Illegitimate Children (Affiliation Orders) Act (Northern Ireland) 1924 and the Marriages Act (Northern Ireland) 1954.
1972 c. 18.	The Maintenance Orders (Reciprocal Enforcement) Act 1972.	Section 3(3).
		Section 7(8).
		Section 17(5) and (7A).
		Section 30(3), (4) and (5).
		Section 38A(3)(b).
1972 c. 49.	The Affiliation Proceedings (Amendment) Act 1972.	Section 2(2).
		In section 4(2) the words from ", except" to "1972,".

Chapter or Number	Short Title	Extent of Repeal
1972 NI 14.	The Health and Personal Social Services (Northern Ireland) Order 1972.	Article 17(1)(c) and (cc). Articles 72 and 73. In Article 87(1) the words from "other than" to "paragraph (2)". Article 102. In Schedule 16, Part I. In Schedule 17, paragraph 9.
1977 NI 17.	The Family Law Reform (Northern Ireland) Order 1977.	Articles 3 and 4. Article 6. Article 15.
1978 c. 23.	The Judicature (Northern Ireland) Act 1978.	Section 27. In Part II of Schedule 5, in the entries relating to the Children and Young Persons Act (Northern Ireland) 1968, in the entry relating to sections 67(b) and 101(3) the words "and 101(3)" and the entry relating to section 156(7).
1978 NI 15.	The Matrimonial Causes (Northern Ireland) Order 1978.	In Article 2(2), the definition of "custody". Article 43(1)(ii), (2) and (3). Articles 45 to 47. In Schedule 1, in paragraph 11, in sub-paragraph (1), the definitions of "custody" and "education" and in sub-paragraph (3) the word "four".
1980 c. 25.	The Insurance Companies Act 1980.	In Schedule 3 paragraph 4.
1980 NI 5.	The Domestic Proceedings (Northern Ireland) Order 1980.	In Article 2— (a) in paragraph (2), the definition of "actual custody";

Chapter or Number	Short Title	Extent of Repeal
		(b) paragraph (3).
		Articles 11 to 17.
		In Article 20—
		(a) in paragraph (1), the words "the following powers, that is to say" and sub-paragraph (ii);
		(b) paragraphs (2) and (4);
		(c) in paragraph (7), the words "and one interim custody order";
		(d) in paragraph (8), the words "or 23".
		In Article 22—
		(a) paragraph (4);
		(b) in paragraph (9), the words ", subject to the provisions of Article 13(8),";
		(c) paragraphs (10) and (13).
		Article 23.
		Articles 25(1) and 26.
		In Article 27—
		(a) in paragraph (1), sub-paragraph (b) and the immediately preceding "or";
		(b) in paragraph (2), sub-paragraphs (c) and (d).
		In Article 31(1), the words "or interim custody order".
		Articles 32(2) and (3).
		Article 33(2).
		Articles 37 and 38.
		In Article 39(5), the

Chapter or Number	Short Title	Extent of Repeal
		words "Notwithstanding Article 2(3),".
		In Schedule 2—
		(a) paragraph 1;
		(b) in paragraph 2, sub-paragraphs (c) and (d);
		(c) paragraphs 4 and 6.
		In Schedule 3, paragraphs 9, 11 and 15.
1981 NI 8.	The Legal Aid, Advice and Assistance (Northern Ireland) Order 1981.	In Part I of Schedule 1, in paragraph 3, sub-paragraph (a) and in sub-paragraph (d) the words "(a) or".
1981 NI 26.	The Magistrates' Courts (Northern Ireland) Order 1981.	Article 85(8)(a)(i).
		In Article 100(2), the definition of "prescribed person".
		Article 101(3)(b)(ii).
		In Article 108(6) the words ", the prescribed person".
		In Schedule 6 paragraphs 76, 88 to 91, 94, 95, 103, 104, 106, 107, 110 to 112, 152 and 162.
1982 c. 50.	The Insurance Companies Act 1982.	In Schedule 5 paragraph 7.
1984 c. 42.	The Matrimonial and Family Proceedings Act 1984.	Section 45.
		In section 48(2), the words from "and section 45" to the end.
1984 c. 46.	The Cable and Broadcasting Act 1984.	In Schedule 5 paragraph 24.
1984 NI 3.	The Fines and Penalties (Northern Ireland) Order 1984.	In Schedule 2, paragraph 13.
1985 NI 17.	The Child Abduction (Northern Ireland) Order 1985.	In Article 2(2), the word "and" immediately preceding sub-paragraph (c).

Chapter or Number	Short Title	Extent of Repeal
		In the Schedule, in paragraph 2(1)— (*a*) head (*a*); (*b*) in head (*b*) the words from "8(1)" to "32(1),"; (*c*) head (*c*).
1986 c. 55.	The Family Law Act 1986.	In section 20, subsections (4) to (6).
		Section 21.
		In section 35, subsection (2).
		Section 66.
		In section 69(7) the words "section 66;".
		In Schedule 1, paragraphs 2, 32 and 33.
1986 NI 3.	The Education and Libraries (Northern Ireland) Order 1986.	In Schedule 13— (*a*) in paragraph 4(2) the words from "or to imprisonment" to the end; (*b*) paragraph 5, sub-paragraph (2) and in sub-paragraph (3) the words from the beginning to "1968,"; (*c*) paragraphs 7 and 9; (*d*) in paragraph 10(2), in head (*a*) the words "(2) or" and in head (*b*) the words from "and conduct" to "juvenile court".
		In Schedule 18 the amendments of sections 27(1), 37(1)(*a*) and (4)(*a*)(i), 40(6), 85(4), 149 and 173(1)(*b*) of the Children and

Chapter or Number	Short Title	Extent of Repeal
		Young Persons Act (Northern Ireland) 1968 and of the Legal Aid, Advice and Assistance (Northern Ireland) Order 1981.
1986 NI 4.	The Mental Health (Northern Ireland) Order 1986.	In Article 32(4) sub-paragraph (*d*) and the immediately preceding word "or".
		Article 34(4).
		In Part II of Schedule 5, the amendments of the Marriages Act (Northern Ireland) 1954 and the amendments of sections 95, 110 and 126 of the Children and Young Persons Act (Northern Ireland) 1968.
1986 NI 18.	The Social Security (Northern Ireland) Order 1986.	Article 26. In Schedule 9, paragraph 66.
1987 NI 22.	The Adoption (Northern Ireland) Order 1987.	In Article 2(2)— (*a*) the definition of "actual custody"; (*b*) the definition of "place of safety".
		Article 11(5).
		Article 15(4).
		Article 16(5)(*b*).
		Article 27.
		Article 35.
		Article 37(1)(*c*).
		Article 38(1) and (3).
		Article 57(4).
		In Article 59— (*a*) in paragraph (3) the words from "and the court" to the end;

Chapter or Number	Short Title	Extent of Repeal
		(b) paragraphs (4) to (11).
		In Article 64—
		(a) in paragraph (1) the words "Subject to paragraph (4),";
		(b) in paragraph (2) the words "Subject to paragraph (4),";
		(c) paragraph (4).
		In Schedule 3, paragraph 2(1).
		In Schedule 4 paragraphs 2 to 5, 11, 12 and 15.
1989 c. 10.	The Disabled Persons (Northern Ireland) Act 1989.	In section 11(1), the definition of "guardian".
1989 c. 41.	The Children Act 1989.	In Schedule 13, paragraph 69(a).
1989 NI 4.	The Matrimonial and Family Proceedings (Northern Ireland) Order 1989.	In Schedule 2, paragraphs 11 and 21.
1989 NI 12.	The Police and Criminal Evidence (Northern Ireland) Order 1989.	In Article 2(2), in the definition of "parent or guardian" paragraph (a).
		In Schedule 2 the entry relating to section 16 of the Child Care Act 1980.
		In Schedule 6 paragraph 6(1).
1990 NI 2.	The Employment (Miscellaneous Provisions) (Northern Ireland) Order 1990.	In Parts II and III of Schedule 3 the entries relating to the Children and Young Persons Act (Northern Ireland) 1968.
1990 c. 42.	The Broadcasting Act 1990.	In Schedule 20 paragraph 15(1) and (2).
		In Schedule 22, in paragraph 4 the word "24,".
1991 NI 1.	The Health and Personal Social Services (Northern	In Part II of Schedule 5 the amendments of the

SCH. 10

Chapter or Number	Short Title	Extent of Repeal
	Ireland) Order 1991.	Children and Young Persons Act (Northern Ireland) 1968.
1991 NI 23.	The Child Support (Northern Ireland) Order 1991.	In Article 10(11) sub-paragraph (*a*) and in sub-paragraph (*d*) the word "or".
1991 NI 25.	The Children and Young Persons (Protection from Tobacco) (Northern Ireland) Order 1991.	In Article 6(1)(*a*) the words "3 and".
1992 c. 8.	The Social Security Administration (Northern Ireland) Act 1992.	Section 101(2) and (3).
1992 c. 9.	The Social Security (Consequential Provisions) (Northern Ireland) Act 1992.	In Schedule 2, paragraph 32(5) and (6).
1992 c. 56.	The Maintenance Orders (Reciprocal Enforcement) Act 1992.	In Schedule 1, paragraph 14. In Schedule 2, paragraph 2.
1992 NI 15.	The Housing (Northern Ireland) Order 1992.	In Article 52(6), the word "or" immediately preceding sub-paragraph (*b*).
1993 NI 6.	The Family Law (Northern Ireland) Order 1993.	In Schedule 1, paragraphs 10 to 12 and 15. In Schedule 5 the entry relating to section 27(9) of the Maintenance Orders (Reciprocal Enforcement) Act 1972.
1994 NI 2.	The Health and Personal Social Services (Northern Ireland) Order 1994.	In Schedule 1 the entry relating to Article 52(2) of the Health and Personal Social Services (Northern Ireland) Order 1972 and the entries relating to Article 27 and Article 35 of the Adoption (Northern Ireland) Order 1987.

EXPLANATORY NOTE

(This note is not part of the Order)

This Order replaces the provisions of the Children and Young Persons Act (Northern Ireland) 1968 which are the responsibility of the Department of Health and Social Services and also amends the law relating to illegitimacy and guardianship.

Part II makes the welfare of a child the court's paramount consideration in certain proceedings (Article 3) and defines the concept of parental responsibility for the purposes of the Order (Article 6). Part III provides for various orders with respect to children in family proceedings.

Part IV imposes general and specific duties on Health and Social Services Boards and Health and Social Services trusts towards children in need and their families and towards children looked after by Boards or trusts. Part V provides for care and supervision orders and Part VI provides for child assessment orders and orders for the emergency protection of children. Parts VII to IX regulate homes provided for children by Health and Social Services Boards, Health and Social Services trusts, voluntary organisations and others. Parts X and XI make provision relating to private arrangements for fostering children and child minding and day care for children under twelve. Part XII imposes restrictions on the employment of children and on performances involving children.

Part XIII contains general provisions relating to the Department of Health and Social Services' supervisory functions and responsibilities.

Part XIV provides for parents not being married to each other to have no effect in law on relationships deduced through parents. Part XV provides for the appointment of guardians. Part XVI contains provisions relating to jurisdiction and procedure and Part XVII contains miscellaneous and general provisions.

STATUTORY INSTRUMENTS

1995 No. 755 (N.I. 2)

NORTHERN IRELAND

The Children (Northern Ireland) Order 1995

£18.50

Reprinted 1996

Printed in the United Kingdom for HMSO
WO 1398 C10 9/96 22.0.0 47228 ON 361599